The Making of Modern Lebanon

Preface

I lived in Lebanon from 1974 to 1981. Those were exciting, invigorating and – yes – sometimes terrifying years. After a few months studying Arabic, I worked as a journalist, covering Lebanese and Middle Eastern developments in some detail for the London *Sunday Times*, the *Christian Science Monitor*, and other publications.

This immersion in detail was extremely valuable from one point of view. I came to meet most of the protagonists in the Lebanese drama in person; and was able, through my constant travels around the country and my many lines into the country's ever-active political gossip network, to work out my own rough and ready way of assessing their actions. Still, many things about the country continued to puzzle me: what I was seeing and living through was very different indeed from the rosy picture portrayed in much recent Western writing on the subject.

After I left Lebanon, I continued to follow the country's affairs closely. So when Roger Owen, Director of the Middle East Centre at St Antony's College, Oxford, and Mark Cohen of Hutchinson's proposed that I write a country study of Lebanon for their new series, I jumped at the opportunity. I knew, even at that point, that in order to make sense of such a study, I would have to start learning rapidly about the historical antecedents of Lebanon's present woes; and I relished the idea of locking myself into a library with that in mind. I am grateful to the Center for Contemporary Arab Studies (CCAS) at Georgetown University for giving me an honorary position there for the year 1983–4, which came with full library privileges.

Luckily, in the course of this historical reading, I found answers to many of the specific questions which had been nagging me about Lebanon, and a general perspective within which I could slowly start making sense of the experiences I had lived through in the country. In the process, I became humbly appreciative of the insight shown by such distinguished historians as Albert Hourani of Oxford, and Kamal Salibi of the American University of Beirut.

Contents

First published in 1985 by Hutchinson, London

Published in 1985 in the United States of America by
  WESTVIEW PRESS
  Frederick A. Praeger, Publisher
  5500 Central Avenue
  Boulder, Colorado 80301

Library of Congress Catalog Card Number 85-51254

ISBN 0-8133-0307-9

Printed and bound in Great Britain

The Making of
Modern Lebanon

Helena Cobban

Westview Press
Boulder, Colorado

In the summer of 1983, I spent a month pursuing my researches in Beirut, During that time, I enjoyed the generous hospitality of Malik Khoury, to whom I am very grateful. In his family's gracious old Beirut residence, I appreciated both the sense that I was in town at a time when new developments were starting to stir, and the more arcane historical pleasure of living in the country's former presidential palace – with the first hand-painted example of the cedar-tree flag of the Republic of Lebanon mouldering (slightly) in its frame out in the hallway. What echoes those marble floors still preserved!

Many of my Lebanese friends and acquaintances gave me a considerable amount of their time during that month. Among them, let me give particular thanks to fellow journalists Michel Abu Jawdeh, of 'An-Nahar', Joseph Abu Khalil of 'Al-Amal', Sijaan Azzi of 'Voice of Free Lebanon', and Elias Khoury of 'Al-Safir'; researchers Ahmad Beydoun of the Lebanese University, Salim Nasr of CERMOC, and Ghassan Salamé of the Université St Joseph and the American University of Beirut; former Premier Selim al-Hoss, and veteran commentator Munah Solh.

After returning to Washington, DC my connection with the CCAS gave me continued access to the wisdom many of its staff members have accumulated on Lebanese political affairs. In particular, I profited from comments made by CCAS Director Michael C. Hudson and Visiting Professor Marius Deeb. In April 1984, the CCAS organized a symposium on Lebanon, which gave me a valuable opportunity to bounce some of my evolving ideas off (among many others) key-note speaker Albert Hourani, and Fuad I. Khuri and Kamal Salibi, both of the American University of Beirut.

Hourani, and Roger Owen, both worked diligently through portions of my original manuscript, making many useful suggestions. I am very grateful indeed for their help and support in this project. I am also grateful to my friend and 'general reader' Jean Van Wagenen, who tried to keep my prose style clear.

Finally, and above all, I want to record the role played by my husband William B. Quandt, who supported me in every way possible, even to the point of living closely with the Lebanon question himself throughout the year that I was writing the book. To him, and in the hopeful spirit of new beginnings, the book is therefore dedicated.

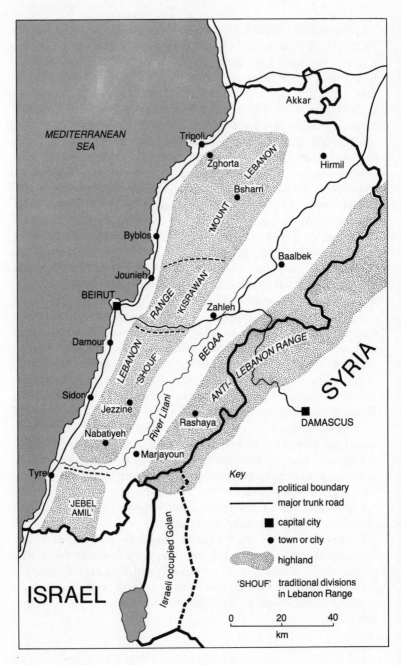

Map 1 The Lebanon

1   Introduction

Lebanon: the name means 'milky-white' – apparently in reference to the snowy caps which grace the country's mountain peaks for more than half the year.

How apt that the country should take its name from an attribute of these peaks! For it is the steeply soaring uplands of Lebanon which have, throughout history, provided that refuge for the heterodox which is the very basis of 'Lebanon'.

History is important in Lebanon, and doubly so in sorting out the apparent paradoxes of the recent period of troubles. For example: between 1975 and 1983 something like 2 per cent of the entire Lebanese population was killed by their fellow Lebanese citizens – to say nothing of the many thousands more who died at the hands of the Israelis, the Syrians, Palestinians or other outsiders. It was a period of chronic personal trauma for most Lebanese, of deep social and political upheaval, as well as mass violence.

Yet throughout that same period there was never any serious challenge to the bedrock of the country's political system.

Certainly, separate groups within Lebanon did indeed, in recent years, welcome the interventions of Israel or Syria in their country's affairs. But no significant Lebanese group called, during that whole period, for the integration of their country into the political system of either of these larger and more powerful neighbours.

There were political killings aplenty, and the national army disintegrated completely twice during that period. But the only coup attempt which took place, in early 1976, was at best a half-hearted affair, intended more as a theatrical adjunct to the civilian political process than as a serious attempt to bring the military to power.

More surprising than all this: not only were there no serious challenges in this whole period to the liberal democratic constitution under which Lebanon has been governed since 1926, but in 1976 and then twice in 1982 the Lebanese Parliament was able to hold presidential elections in full accordance with this constitution. True, the Parliament's own claim to legitimacy was becoming increasingly tenuous, since it had been prolonging its own term yearly since the original date of expiry in 1976. And true, in 1976 it had been able to meet only under the barrels of Syrian guns, and in 1982 under Israeli guns.

But despite all these well-understood weaknesses in the electoral process, none of those three presidential elections had its basic legitimacy seriously challenged even in the midst of the political mayhem which continued unblunted after the votes had been cast.

Thus, despite all the years of violence after 1975, a very deep political consensus still persisted in Lebanon. It reflected broad agreement not only on the basic question of the separateness of the country from its neighbours, but also on the maintenance of some kind of unitary political system which should be liberal, republican and in some way democratic. Lebanon was clearly no mere artificial 'banana republic'.

The paradox of how these elements of consensus were maintained amidst the continuing violence can be resolved, like all the other paradoxes which greet the eye of the observer in Lebanon, only through reference to Lebanon's long history. As an example, another seeming riddle: how could a young man not yet thirty be catapulted overnight into the leadership of Lebanon's most socially conservative sect – despite the fact that he had shocked all the sect's elders with the scandals of his marriage and his subsequent divorce?

The answer, in 1977, lay in the young man's family name. He was Walid Jumblatt, heir to a name endowed with some 300 years in the leadership of the Druze sect.

The continuity apparent in the Druze sect, as exemplified in the above conundrum, is paralleled by important elements of continuity in the country's other major sects. And it is these deep currents of continuity *at the level of the sect* which have historically provided the underpinning for the continuity of the system of sectarian coexistence which is the essence of the Lebanese system.

For about a millennium now, the major present-day sects have been living in the Lebanese Mountain, each with its own quite rich and varied inner life. The idea of the *interaction* of a number of these sects, which lies at the heart of the concept of 'Lebanon', persisted from the late sixteenth century down to the 1980s.

Even after the emergence of a 'Lebanese' polity, however, the sects continued to live out their own inner lives. And right down to the middle years of the present century many of the apparent manifestations of Western-style 'democracy' which made their appearance in Lebanon were themselves still built on basically sectarian foundations. The stresses and strains of the years following 1975 forced most of the political parties to drop what remained of their 'ideological' masks, revealing the solidly sectarian structures remaining underneath.

Ideological 'parties', an active and sometimes scurrilous press, and all the other paraphernalia of Western democracies – even the appearance of democracy itself – might come and go in Lebanon, and indeed frequently did. Only the sects, and the politics of the sects, seemed to live on for ever.

If history is crucial to understanding present-day Lebanon, then some grasp of the country's basic geographical dilemma is also important. Mount Lebanon has always had a tantalizing and difficult relationship with the world around it. True, its fastnesses have always offered a haven to the heterodox: but this haven has also been continually plagued by the fact that it is located right at the East Mediterranean intersection of some of the world's most strategic and jealously fought-over trade-routes.

The sensitive location of Mount Lebanon has ensured that none of the successive empires which contended for power around the Mountain was ever able to ignore what was going on inside it. The Muslim rulers who dominated the region from the seventh century onwards quickly found a way of dealing with the Mountain which caused the least damage to their own interests. Jealously guarding the coastal cities and the major inland trade-routes, they left the Mountain interior largely to its own devices, keeping the mountaineers on their toes by periodically inciting one clan or faction to go and fight another.

When the Ottoman Turks came to the area in AD 1516 they further refined this method of dealing with the Mountain, by recognizing the primacy of a single leader within it. Backed by his own local system of feudal control, this leader then became the 'Prince' of the Mountain.

The Prince was supposed to act as a kind of free-wheeling tax-farmer for the Ottomans inside the Mountain, while still recognizing the Ottomans' overall suzerainty. However, his bargaining power in this relationship was vastly increased by the ease with which the Mountain could defy any attempt by the Empire to subdue it. This meant that the Ottomans generally allowed the Prince of Mount

Lebanon much more latitude in the way he ruled than they did their many other tax farmers.

If the imperial armies, from Damascus, Baghdad, Jerusalem, Istanbul or Cairo, had ever been able easily to subdue the Lebanese Mountain, then 'Lebanon' would never have come into existence. But the tortuous mountain terrain eventually defied even the greatest of imperial generals. (Indeed, the Ottomans never thought it worthwhile to try to exercise direct control in the Mountain.)

Woe to any ambitious outside power which ventured where the Ottomans feared to tread, and hoped directly to mould the Lebanese system to its own plan! Rapidly would it find itself tied up in the persisting clan rivalries of a Lebanese system as tortuous and tangled at the political level as its terrain was for the military.

In turn, each of these ambitious outsiders would be forced to back off from the plans they started out with in Lebanon. In the 1830s, it took Egypt's Muhammed Ali just eight years to jettison his ambitions in Lebanon. A century later, it took the French twenty-three years and the internal crisis of the Vichy regime to back out of Lebanon. In more recent years, the Syrians, the Israelis and the Americans were each forced to implement a drastic scaling-down of ambitions entertained in and for Lebanon.

Between and after each of those earlier periods of foreign intervention in the country, some regime specifically local-Lebanese in its origins would prevail in the country. These regimes, moreover, showed a remarkable degree of historical continuity, with the only major change in the system occurring with the overthrow of the Shihab dynasty in 1842. (Even after 1842, Shihab family members continued to play an important role in Lebanese public life. From 1943 onwards, General Fuad Shihab was an important architect of independent Lebanon. In 1958 he became president; and his disciples continued to wield strong influence within the administration through to the early 1980s. Certainly, most of the achievements of this modern Shihab could be credited to the breadth of his own personal vision. But his entry into the ruling circles, and at least some of his popular appeal thereafter, both stemmed directly from the associations of his family name.)

Throughout the centuries of Lebanon's emergence, the local Lebanese regimes would generally tip a formal knee in the direction of imperial reality by paying some form of titular tribute to the outside imperial power, or powers. But their defence, in bad times, like their *raison d'être* at all times, continued to be provided by the refuge of Mount Lebanon.

The limestone bulk of the Mount Lebanon range rises steeply out of the Mediterranean, leaving only a thin, intermittent band of fertile alluvial plain along the coast. At its northern end, the range rises out of the Akkar plain, which historically formed a choice invasion route from the coast towards the Syrian interior.

Immediately south of the Akkar, the Mount Lebanon range quickly soars to its highest peak, at a height of 3556 metres (11,025 feet), right above the present-day 'Cedars' tourist resort. It then continues southwards for a total of 140 kms (88 miles), in a series of slightly lower peaks whose summits are never more than 25 kms (15 miles) from the Mediterranean coast. South of the road linking Beirut with Damascus, this same range then becomes known as the Shouf Mountains; and in south Lebanon, it becomes known as Jebel Amil. (It then continues south into present-day Israel as the Upper Galilee region.)

Rain clouds travelling in over Lebanon from the Mediterranean hit the mountain range with some force. The mean annual precipitation recorded in some mountain resorts comes to well over 1400 millimetres (55 inches). Much of this precipitation occurs as snowfall in winter. Then, each spring, as the snow melts, torrents of water race down the two sides of the mountain range. Over the millennia these spring melts have carved out stupendously steep and winding valleys in their rush westward, to the sea, and eastward into the Beqaa Valley.

These torrents were renowned in the ancient lore of the region. The Phoenician and Hellenic occupants of the Byblos area considered that the rich red hue assumed by one local stream in the spring represented the blood of the dying hunter Adonis. Throughout history, the valleys scoured out by the torrents have also helped greatly in making the Mountain's upper reaches unassailable.

For example, from the mountain village of Ras al-Metn one can signal easily to friends (or foes!) in Baalshmay, 3 kilometres away. But to travel between the two, one must take the road which winds a total of nearly 20 kilometres, first eastward into the fold of the valley, then doubling back upward and westward again. The entire length of that road is studded with ideal sites for a guerrilla ambush. This same picture is repeated over and over along the scores of valleys which twist and fork into each other crazily along the range's length. Small wonder that outside invaders often become hopelessly dependent on their local guides!

The Akkar plain, which abuts the Mount Lebanon range to the north, also lies within the present-day boundary of Lebanon. But it remains one of the country's least developed regions. Never more than 1000 metres above sea-level, the Akkar is still regularly traversed by clans of semi-nomads. The villages which dot it are small; in the early 1970s, one dozen of them remained the only villages in the whole country not tied into the national road system.

On its eastern side, the Lebanon range plunges steeply down to the Beqaa Valley. The Beqaa is a flat and fertile plain some 1000 metres (3000 feet) above sea-level, which apparently forms an extended northern branch of East Africa's Great Rift Valley.

Just north of Baalbek, a scarcely perceptible watershed divides the Beqaa. The waters to its south drain slowly southwards, gathering force until, as the River Litani, they burst eastwards through a steep rift in the Lebanon range in their rush toward the sea.

The northern reaches of the Beqaa are, because of their greater distance from the coast, among the driest parts of the country. Rainfall there averages only about 240 millimetres (less than 10 inches) each year. But the northern Beqaa also receives some of the spring melt from the mountains: north of the watershed, this water then drains northward, passing into Syria as the historic Orontes River.

The Beqaa's average east–west width is about 15 kms (10 miles), though it widens gradually towards the north. At its eastern edge rises the Anti-Lebanon mountain range, along whose ridge much of Lebanon's present eastern border with Syria has been drawn.

At the southern end of the Anti-Lebanon range rise the peaks of Jebel al-Sheikh (Mount Hermon), where the current international frontiers between Lebanon, Syria and Israel intersect. The Lebanese foothills of Jebel al-Sheikh are known as Wadi al-Taym: this region's waters flow, as the Hasbani and Wazzani Rivers, into Israel's northern finger.

So who were they and where did they come from, these people who first made of the inhospitable Mountain a home, and then used its very intractability to defend themselves as they created their own, very particular form of political entity?

The answers to this question are as many as the political viewpoints which criss-cross the country today. For the question of determining group or family origins is an essential part of political myth-making.

'The Phoenicians', many Lebanese will reply, when asked about their ancestors; or, in other cases, 'The Greeks'. Both these replies tend to stress the westward-looking, Mediterranean perspective of the interviewee. 'The Arabs' is a reply popular among most Lebanese Muslims, many of whom claim to be able to trace their *own family's lineage* directly back to the great tribes of the Arabian Peninsula. 'The Yemenis' is a more specific and more exalted version of 'The Arabs', which is used by many Christians as well as Muslims in Lebanon.

In fact, the noted Lebanese historian Kamal Salibi has argued quite convincingly that *all* the major indigenous groups still found in Lebanon today can be traced back to the successive waves of tribes from the Arabian Peninsula who settled the region *between the fifth and the eleventh centuries AD.*[1]* Certainly, the vast majority of Lebanese still share with the people of the Arabian/Syrian interior not only the basic structure of their language but also many of their most intimate and enduring social traditions.

Many of the divisions between the different religious groups which continue to plague Lebanese politics to the present can also, in Salibi's view, be traced back to that same period of large-scale Arab settlement in the country.

Professor Salibi's colleague at the American University of Beirut, the anthropologist Fuad Khuri, has made a useful distinction, in discussing these different religious groups in Lebanon, between the concept of a 'sect' and that of a 'minority'. His definition of a 'sect' is that it is a geographically compact group, which generally maintains the necessary instruments of social control outside the sphere of influence of the central authority. A 'minority' in Middle Eastern society is a group which is much more broadly geographically dispersed. Like other classic minorities in European societies, these Middle Eastern 'minorities' are much more vulnerable to the whims of the central authority than are the compact and generally well-defended 'sects'. The prime political concern of leaders of a 'minority' group is thus with the affairs of the state as such; while the leaders of a 'sect' are concerned primarily with maximizing the prerogatives of the *sect* as such, even where these conflict with the interests of the state.

The various 'sects' which dot the Arab East have each developed a strong geographic centre, in which more than 70 per cent of the sect's members generally continue to live. That centre has become over time the prime haven for the sect, with many of its locations becoming

---

* Superior figures refer to the Notes at the end of each chapter.

revered for their religious or historical associations, and thus serving as the destinations of pilgrimage by sect members.

According to this definition, Lebanese society contains three of the Middle East's dozen or so identifiable 'sects': the Maronites, the Shi-ites and the Druze.

The Sunni Muslims and all the other major religious groupings found in Lebanon would qualify, according to Khuri's theory, as 'minorities' rather than sects. (The Sunnis are a numerical majority, at the level of the whole region. But within Lebanon neither they nor any other religious group can make this claim. See Table 1.)

Here, then, is a brief introduction to each of these major groups.

Table 1   *Estimated evolution of sectarian composition of the Lebanese population (per cent)*

	1932 Government census	1968 Estimate by German contractors	1975 Estimate by Youssef Courbage	1983 Rough estimate by Lebanese demographers
Christians:				
Maronites	28.8	n.a.	23	n.a.
Greek Orthodox	9.8	n.a.	7	n.a.
Greek Catholic	5.9	n.a.	5	n.a.
Other Christians	6.8	n.a.	5	n.a.
Total Christians	51.3	46.22	40	33
Muslims:				
Sunnis	22.4	n.a.	26	n.a.
Shi-ites	19.6	n.a.	27	33
Druze	6.8	n.a.	7	n.a.
Total Muslims	48.8	52.87	60	66
Total population in millions	0.786*	2001*	2550	n.a.

* These totals include a small proportion (less than 1 per cent) of Jews.

Source: The figures for 1932, 1968 and 1975 are those published by *Fiches du monde arabe* (Beirut, Lebanon and Nicosia, Cyprus), on their card number 1699 (24 September 1980). The rough estimates for 1983 were those mentioned to me by several Lebanese social scientists that year.

The Maronites

The Maronite population of Lebanon currently stands at somewhere under 800,000 – or just under one-quarter of the total.[2]

The Maronite sect originally emerged in the sixth or seventh century AD, among some of the Christianized Arab tribes who had made their way to the northern parts of present-day Syria. Soon, these early Christian groups were to find themselves in conflict not only with the Muslim armies who swept into the region in AD 635 but also with the religious orthodoxy of the Byzantine empire which tried in vain to resist the Muslim advance into the region.

Pressed on all sides, the 'Maronites', as they became known in honour of one of their early leaders, made their way to the northern reaches of Mount Lebanon. There, they settled, hacking out vast expanses of terraces along the steep slopes of the mountain to create an agricultural base which made them largely self-supporting. The stunning tracery of those terraces – sometimes many scores of terraces high from the foot of a slope up to the tree line – is still visible in the northern parts of the Mountain today. These days, many of them bear serried rows of fruit-trees, though others are now left untended.

The Maronite cultivators' houses, traditionally square-built stone with metre-thick earth roofs, were nestled closely together in strategically-located villages, each with its own church or sometimes monastery. In those harsh early days the arts of war were certainly needed to ensure the survival of the community against awesome outside odds: but these same arts were often also turned inwards, in generations-long feuds between the various Maronite clans.

First allegiance of the hardy Maronite mountaineer was to his immediate family, then spreading out in widening circles to the various branches of his extended family. Within a village, members of between three and a dozen different clans might live together. The clans could maintain protracted disputes between themselves – over questions of family honour, or access to scarce resources – but the minute the village became exposed to a threat from outside, its members would stand together to resist it.

As the Maronite community of northern Lebanon became established, its growing population began to require new outlets. Groups from individual villages would then set out to form new Maronite communities outside the original area of settlement, to the north, east or – more usually – south. As they struck south along the Lebanon range, however, the new Maronite settlers encountered many existing settlements, first of Shi-ite Muslims, and then, as they penetrated even further southwards, areas where the Druze predominated. Still, the Maronite villagers' *drang nach suden* continued over the centuries, jumping along the easily-defended uplands of the Mount Lebanon range until its momentum finally petered out with a handful of Maronite villages in northern Galilee.

From the mid nineteenth century onwards, two new forces increasingly started to affect the distribution of the Maronite community. The first was the magnetic pull of urban development, which brought Maronite traders and professional people into all the towns of the area. The second was the lure of more distant opportunities, which sent a stream of Maronite migrants to Egypt, and increasingly, to both halves of the New World.

Throughout the present century, however, the rush towards the single urban centre of Beirut came to overshadow all other movements of the Maronite population. By 1983, it was estimated that more than 300,000 Maronites resided in Beirut and its ring of suburb-slums – despite the violence which still plagued the city.

The pressures of urbanization nurtured new kinds of political forces within the Maronite community. From the mid 1970s onwards, these new forces often appeared to be in competition with the older clan leaderships which still remained deeply rooted in the home villages.

However, these new internal rivalries at the political level seemed, even in the mid 1980s, to have had little detrimental effect on two of the community's most enduring traditional institutions. These were the two parallel hierarchies of the Maronite church itself: its Patriarch with the priestly structure under his control on the one hand; and on the other, the network of Maronite monasteries, which today is headed by the Abbot of the Order of Maronite Monks.

Throughout the centuries, the church hierarchies played a crucial role in transmitting the Maronites' sense of sect identity. They also played a role in the arena of temporal politics, whose effectiveness has continued little dented down to modern times.

In the twelfth century, it was with the Maronite *Patriarch* that Catholic France entered into relations. Relations with Catholic Europe were later strengthened when the Vatican itself granted open recognition of the sect's doctrinal 'orthodoxy', and established lasting institutional links with the Maronite church hierarchies. To the Maronites' continuing sense of their early Arabian roots was now added a long-term orientation towards Western Europe.

In recent times, the church hierarchies have continued to exert a strong influence on political developments inside the community. In the civil war of 1958, the Patriarch maintained a careful distance from the incumbent Maronite President of the Republic, Camille Chamoun: his attitude helped to tip the balance of Maronite opinion against Chamoun's bid to renew his presidential term, and to ensure the smooth succession of Fuad Shihab.

In the late 1970s, while the Maronite Patriarch maintained a less visible pose, the Abbot of the Maronite Monks played a correspondingly stronger role. Two successive holders of this post played crucial political roles throughout those years: the net effect of their intervention was to increase the strength of the sect's most combative politico-military forces.

The Shi-ites

If the clerical structures of Lebanon's Maronite sect appeared undented (or even strengthened?) by the turmoil of the late 1970s, then the same was certainly also true of the country's Shi-ite population.

By the early 1980s, the Lebanese Shi-ites were thought to number about 1 million, or around one-third of the country's population. By then, they were roughly evenly distributed between three major areas of settlement: the southern area including Jebel Amil and the ancient port of Tyre; the northern parts of the Beqaa, including Baalbek and Hirmil; and the sprawling southern suburbs of Beirut.

The origins of Shi-ite settlement in Lebanon were broadly contemporary with that of the Maronites. Shi-ism in Lebanon dates back to the earliest days of the great schism which divided the world Muslim community into Sunnis and Shi-ites in the middle of the seventh century AD.

From 660 until the middle of the tenth century, the East Mediterranean region was dominated by Sunni dynasties: the central and southern parts of Mount Lebanon then became vital points of refuge for those on the Shi-ite side of the divide. Between 969 and 1099, however, the Shi-ites were able to come out of the shadows throughout the region, as a strong Shi-ite dynasty was then flourishing over the water in Egypt. That period saw the high point of Shi-ism in Lebanon, with three local Shi-ite dynasties, based respectively in Sidon, Tripoli and Tyre, each enjoying a brief period in the limelight.

That flowering of Shi-ism in Lebanon was cut short by the arrival of the West European crusaders in 1099. And when the crusaders were finally ousted 200 years later it was Sunni armies, rather than Shi-ites, who were able to achieve this.

From the dawn of the fourteenth century down to the mid 1980s, Sunnism remained the dominant Muslim force in the East Mediterranean. Shi-ites survived in the region only as small communities in mountain redoubts ('sects', in Khuri's usage). Two of those communities survived within the boundaries of modern Lebanon. One was the community in Jebel Amil; the other, that in the northern Beqaa.

Both those communities followed the '12-imam' branch of Shi-ite belief. But though there were some links between the two groups over the centuries, each developed very specific social characteristics. Indeed, many observers consider that Shi-ite society in the Beqaa was more similar to the society of their northern Maronite neighbours than it was to that of their co-believers in Jebel Amil.

The Beqaa Shi-ites retained a vigorous tribal structure; and many of them continued living as semi-nomadic goat-herds down to modern times. (In past centuries, the coming of every spring would see 'goat wars' fought between the Maronites and the Beqaa Shi-ites, as goat-herds from both communities competed to lay first claim to the newly melted higher mountain pastures.) The life of the Beqaa Shi-ites was tough. They developed a free-wheeling hardiness to deal with the hostile outside environment, while inside the community a rigorous code of personal honour was enforced.

The Shi-ites of Jebel Amil traditionally led a more settled and stable life. Large, feudal-style landowners there exercised a powerful sway over the residents of whole villages. However, the rule of the landowners was also tempered by the existence of a parallel structure of Shi-ite clerics, imbued with their faith's heavy emphasis on social justice and correct living.

The Jebel Amil Shi-ites never established the kinds of large theological colleges which grew up in the cradle of '12-imam' Shi-ism, in southern Iraq. But throughout the centuries, Jebel Amil families struggled to send their sons to the Iraqi colleges so that they could come back as «*ulama* ('learned men' – the singular is «alim). Through the contacts made in Iraq, the Shi-ite «*ulama* of Jebel Amil thus kept in touch with their counterparts there and throughout the Shi-ite world.

The standard of learning of the Jebel Amil «ulama was often highly respected. In the early sixteenth century, for example, a new ruler in far-off Persia proclaimed that Shi-ism should be his country's new state religion. However, most of the Persians were still Sunnis. In order to explain the advantages and intricacies of the new faith to them, the ruler brought in many respected religious teachers – from Jebel Amil. Even down to present times, many Persian Shi-ites have continued to remember the wisdom of those early 'Amili' teachers.

The two Shi-ite areas of Jebel Amil and the Beqaa were not brought into the Lebanese political system until the French redrew the boundaries of Lebanon in 1920. Over the decades which followed they too became caught up in the process of urbanization which was already starting to change the shape of the Maronite community.

Then, in the 1960s, the steady trickle of Shi-ites into the Lebanese towns broadened suddenly into a flood, with the destination of most of the migrants now clearly identified as Beirut. There, the Shi-ite newcomers jostled for living space and jobs with the Maronites whom they often found had arrived just before them. Three particular areas near Beirut quickly became transformed into vast, Shi-ite-dominated suburb-slums.

As in the case of the Maronites, the rapid urbanization of many Shi-ites brought new politicial forces into play. But it also forged new bonds of communal identity between what had previously been two nearly separate groups of Shi-ites in the two 'home areas'.

It was then the clerical hierarchy of Jebel Amil which spawned a new political movement, called *Amal* ('hope'). This movement then tried to mobilize all the disparate strands of the Lebanese Shi-ite community together behind a single political leadership. The rise to power of the Shi-ite clerics in distant Iran (Persia) in 1979 certainly helped to fuel *Amal*'s rise in Lebanon. But the major causes of the movement's growth remained rooted deep in the long tradition of Shi-ism in the Mount Lebanon area itself.

The Druze

The Druze community in Lebanon numbered only about 250,000 in the late 1970s, or around 8 per cent of the national total. The Druze were thus by far the smallest of the country's three major sects. Nevertheless, they had played a key historical role in the emergence of the Lebanese system.

The Druze were, by origin, a near-mystic offshoot of Shi-ism which first came into existence in Cairo in AD 1017. Unlike more orthodox Muslims, Sunni or Shi-ite, the Druze developed a strong belief in re-incarnation. In this and other senses it appeared as a synthesis between Muslim teaching, the doctrine of more eastern religions, and some Hellenic and other pre-Islamic beliefs.

In the early years of the new sect, its followers proselytized widely. Their 'Divine Call' met with its most enthusiastic response among the Shi-ites who dominated the central parts of Mount Lebanon at that time. Then, in 1043, as a defence against the mounting attacks of the mainstream Shi-ites, the sect closed its doors to further conversion. Since then, in theory, no conversion has been condoned, either into or out of the sect. (The most notable exception to this rule was, ironically, that of the Jumblatts.) Over the years which followed the closing of the 'Divine Call', the Druze communities which had made brief appearances in Egypt, Northern India and other parts of the Shi-ite world disappeared from view. Only the Druze community centred in Lebanon remained. In addition to its largest base in the central part of Mount Lebanon, this community had an important settlement in Wadi al-Taym (which housed many of the 'shrines' of the sect), as well as satellite communities in northern Galilee and in the Hawran in southern Syria.

As had happened with the Maronites before them, the embattled position of the Mount Lebanon Druze forced them to develop both their martial skills and their sense of internal solidarity. In fact, the skill of the Druze warlords became renowned throughout the region in later centuries.

In the early sixteenth century, the Druze lords helped the (Sunni Muslim) Ottoman Turks to seize control of the region from the Egyptian Mamlukes (who were also Sunnis). In grateful recognition of the part the lords had played, the Ottomans, in 1516, appointed one of their number as 'Prince of Mount Lebanon'. That appointment, and the remarkable ability of the Druze-dominated confederation of warlords to maintain a stable regime in the mountain, nurtured the emergence of an inter-sectarian Lebanon.

Many thousands of Druze farmers toiled in villages in both Mount Lebanon and the Wadi al-Taym area. Nevertheless, the village organization of the Druze generally remained subordinate to the sect's strong family ties. Traditionally, the families were bound into a pyramid-like structure of clans and clan-based factions, each dominated by one of the great warlord families. These great families also enjoyed considerable feudal privileges. They acted as tax farmers over whole groups of villages which often contained cultivators from the Maronite and other Christian groups, as well as Druze.

Despite the continuity at the level of the Princedom, the politics of the great Druze leaders was still riven with a succession of long-lasting bi-polar factional rivalries. From the early eighteenth century right down to recent times the principal tribal division within Druze society was that between the 'Yazbeki' and the 'Jumblatti' factions.

The Druze have retained a vivid sense of the importance of family, and of the intricacies of their socio-political traditions. As recently as 1980, two social researchers were able to produce a list of all of the 333 family names currently used by the Druze, of which twenty-nine were still clearly identified as denoting 'aristocratic' families. More remarkable still, the researchers' Druze interviewees were clearly able to agree on the affiliation of each of the 333 families to either the Yazbeki or Jumblatti party. Only sixteen of the 333 were described as having split affiliations![3]

Alongside the persisting family/feudal structures, the sect has a religious hierarchy made up of various degrees of initiates into the esoteric secrets of its faith. The majority of Druze, while remaining loyal to the sect and observing most of its teachings about the integrity of personal conduct, never become initiated. However, any right-living Druze, male or female, may seek initiation into ever higher levels of the hierarchy. But their acceptance is tightly controlled by the existing hierarchy of initiates – at whose apex sits the sect's highest religious leader, the *sheikh al-«aql*.

This sheikh and the whole body of religious initiates wield important influence inside the sect. It was partly due to the continuing social conservatism of their teachings that the Druze of the Mountain never got caught up in the rush to urbanize to the same degree as the Maronites or Shi-ites. The Druze quarters dotted throughout West Beirut in the mid-1980s were still identifiable as swollen versions of Druze villages established there long before the growth of the city, rather than constituting wholly new communities of villagers uprooted *en masse* from elsewhere.

In the mid-1980s, the Druze religious hierarchy continued both to wield wide influence through its teachings, and to attract a stream of aspiring new initiates. But at times of particular stress, the sect still laid its highest premium on the value of military *action* rather than on anybody's *words*. For this reason, the sect's strongest concern at the political level has been to try to maximize its control within the country's armed forces, rather than in any other part of state apparatus. The sect's enduring stress on military values also ensured the continuing primacy of the feudal-style leaders, who until modern times remained the community members best placed to mobilize *the whole sect* around a military effort, when needed.

The Sunnis

The Sunnis of Lebanon are the largest and most powerful of the country's many 'minorities', as opposed to the three 'sects' described above. In the late 1970s, they numbered around 600,000, or just under 20 per cent of the national population.

The Sunnis' greatest numbers in Lebanon have for centuries been concentrated in and around the three coastal cities of Beirut, Tripoli and Sidon. The great Sunni merchant families of these cities are the true functional heirs of the Phoenicians, who in earlier times fanned out from their home-base in Lebanon to sell their wares throughout the Mediteranean.

Other Sunnis continue to live farmers' lives in villages in the northern Akkar plain, in the central parts of the Beqaa, in the hinterland of Sidon, and elsewhere. And a limited number of semi-nomadic Sunni pastoralists still herd their flocks across the country, some of them regularly criss-crossing its long border with Syria.

Sunnism in Lebanon dates back through an unbroken history to the first arrival of the early Muslim armies in the region, in AD 635 – two years after the death of the Prophet Muhammed. The two top generals commanding those armies were Yazid ibn Abi-Sufyan, and his brother, Mu«awiyah (when the Muslim community split into Shi-ite and Sunni factions twenty-five years later, Mu«awiyah was the first leader of the Sunnis).

Over the centuries which followed, Sunni predominance in the East Mediterranean (including Lebanon) made way first for the Shi-ite era, and then for the coming of the Crusaders. But from the beginning of the fourteenth century down to modern times, Sunnism remained the dominant force in the region.

Throughout the five centuries when Sunni empires ruled the region, the Sunni Lebanese merchants did business with, and inter-married with, their peers from throughout the empire. Even the humblest Sunni artisan or peasant could take comfort from the fact that his group represented the ruling orthodoxy in both religious and the temporal spheres. The Sunnis of Lebanon felt themselves part and parcel of the group in whose interest the empire exisited. They thus continued to relate primarily to the politics of that broader group, even after the Druze and Maronites of the Mount Lebanon interior had progressed quite far towards creating a new, local form of polity there.

During the First World War, the Ottoman empire, which was the last great Sunni empire of the region, collapsed. Dominance over Lebanon passed into the hands of the Catholic French. The cities of Beirut, Tripoli and Sidon, the Akkar plain and the Beqaa were then among the regions which the French joined to the local system which had already evolved in the Mountain.

The Sunnis of Lebanon never went through the traumas of accelerated urbanization experienced by the country's Maronites and Shi-ites. They never had to: their community had for many centuries before the present one been dominated by strong urban traditions. These traditions were very different from the clan-bound traditions of the three Lebanese sects. Family ties certainly remained important for the Lebanese Sunnis. But beyond the ties of the immediate family, several different types of other affiliation competed with the broader clan ties (which still stood generally unchallenged in the case of the sects). These additional ties included the professional ties of the Sunni craftsmen and traders in the cities; and the overtly ideological ties forged as different groups of Sunnis sought to influence (as members of the sects knew they never could) the broader political life of the empire.

Leaders in the Sunni community always knew they would have to compete for influence in a generally receptive market-place of *ideas*. They knew they could not rely – as their counterparts in the sects generally could – solely on family and clan pressures to ensure support when they needed it. This, and other historical factors, meant that Sunni society in Lebanon remained generally more loosely organized and more tolerant, at the political level, than were the three great Lebanese sects.

The Sunnis of Lebanon retained their local religious hierarchy. Under the French, the Mufti of Beirut was redesignated a Grand Mufti, and was put in overall charge of the Muftis in Tripoli and Sidon. The Muftis' major continuing task was to provide guide lines for the sermons given in all Sunni mosques on Fridays. A parallel structure of Sunni jurists under the control of the Muftis meanwhile concerned itself with details of inheritance and marriage settlements. But in general, the role of the clerical hierarchy remained much more limited in Sunni society than it was in the case of the Maronites or Shi-ites.

The lack of any developed clerical infrastructure also forced the

Muftis, if they wanted to exert public influence, to compete in the same 'market-place of ideas' in which the secular Sunni politicians competed. The political function the Sunni clerical institutions performed was thus much more limited than that performed by their counterparts in the three Lebanese 'sects'. The ever-shifting trends of urban public opinion had evolved a correspondingly much more powerful role inside Sunni society than in the sects.

The other minorities

Any straightforward listing of the thirteen other religious groups recognized in Lebanon would be dominated by the names of a panoply of Christian churches. Only two of the thirteen are not Christian. These are the country's indigenous *Jewish* community, which during the upheavals of the 1970s shrank from around 2,000 members to near extinction; and the «*Alawi* group of Shi-ites, which has a few hundred members in northern parts of Lebanon, not far from the Alawi-dominated area in Syria.

The names of the Christian 'other minorities' might evoke, for many Western readers, memories of their earliest readings about the schisms of the early church. There are Nestorians and Jacobites; two or three kinds of Armenians; Assyrians, Chaldeans and Greeks. The 'Greek' Christians pre-date the Maronites in their earliest settlement in Lebanon (see below). Most members of the other churches, by contrast, came to the country only during the past century. They sought refuge in its Maronite-dominated culture from persecution elsewhere throughout the Middle East.

Many of these Christian minorities now have their clerical institutions firmly based in Lebanon. I remember, in the early 1970s, travelling to the Maronites' shady hillside patriarchate for a 'summit' of the patriarchs of all the different Lebanese Christian groups: there were nine or ten of them in all! Lebanon must be the only country in the world which has a collective noun relating especially to a plenitude of patriarchs!

Largest and most important of these Christian groups are the *Greek Orthodox*. Numbering around 300,000 in the late 1970s, this group (like the Sunnis) clearly outnumbered the Druze. Yet – like the Sunnis again – it was widely dispersed geographically. It thus counted as a classic 'minority' within Professor Khuri's definition.

The Greek Orthodox are like the Sunnis in several other ways too. Predominantly town and city folk, there is only one area in Lebanon where substantial numbers of Orthodox farmers still cultivate the land. This is in the Koura plateau, which lies just south of Tripoli, between the Abu Ali River and the coast.

Members of this church are found throughout the other East Mediterranean countries, as well as in Lebanon. Despite its name, the church is not really Greek in any meaningful way today. But it certainly is Orthodox! Its congregations in the region are the direct descendants of some of Jesus' and Saint Paul's first converts to the Christian faith. Theirs was the Church and Empire of the Emperor Constantine, the first Roman Emperor to adopt Christianity as his state's orthodoxy. (This Roman connection is still recognized today in the group's description of itself as 'Roum Orthodox'.) Theirs, too, was the orthodoxy of Byzantium, when that became the Roman Empire's new capital. And in the centuries when Byzantium reigned supreme over the East Mediterranean, the half-Hellenized Orthodox communities of the region became further invigorated when many of the Arabian tribes who settled in the region also joined their church.

In 635, Byzantium lost the area of Syria and Lebanon to the Muslims. Later, Byzantium itself was taken by the Muslims; but the orthodoxy it had nurtured lived on in Greece, Russia and much of the rest of Eastern Europe. And in Western Asia, it lived on among the 'Greek Orthodox', who relatively quickly managed to adapt themselves to the new facts of Muslim domination.

So strongly did these 'Greek Orthodox' believers come to identify with their Arab environment that most of them opposed the efforts Catholic Europe launched during the Crusades, to 'save' Christianity in the region from the domination of the 'infidel' Muslims. Their basic loyalty to the Muslim powers was recognized by successive Muslim rulers, who entrusted them with many high administrative positions. (The Orthodox also had important skills in book-keeping and other administrative arts, which were sorely needed by the Muslims.)

The Greek Orthodox thus became largely symbiotic at the political level with a region-wide Muslim orthodoxy which, for the past five centuries, has been overwhelmingly Sunni. And throughout that relationship, they had a prolonged opportunity, which the Sunnis did not, to learn the delicate skills of survival as a classic minority. The wisdom the Orthodox accumulated in these skills certainly contributed to the stability of the Lebanese system at many dangerous turning-points in its history.

Always seeking opportunities for negotiation and compromise in their dealings with other groups, the Orthodox nevertheless retained a vigorous sense of their own identity and internal church life. Elections or appointments of new Orthodox bishops are still followed closely throughout the community: here are fought many of the internal battles which the sect's leaders seem instinctively to understand should not be fought in public.

At the public level, extreme positions and disputes have seldom been in evidence from among the Orthodox leaders. (This was in stark contrast to the publicity with which the Maronites or Druze conducted their internal faction fights!) However, the generally liberal political attitude of the Orthodox allowed some community members, in Lebanon as elsewhere in the region, to play leading roles in various modern radical movements.

The *Greek Catholic* church is a group which split off from the Greek Orthodox in 1724, turning to the Vatican for overall leadership. (The local name for this group is slightly confusing for Westerners. Its members call themselves 'Roum Catholic' – harking back to the old days of Rome and Byzantium. But there are also a few congregations of mainstream pro-Vatican Catholics in the country as well: they call themselves not 'Roman Catholics', but 'Lateen'.)

The number of Greek Catholics in Lebanon today is around 200,000, or 6 per cent of the population. Many of the families who make up the church's present membership in Lebanon came from the Syrian interior, seeking refuge under the Maronite/Catholic umbrella which extended over Mount Lebanon in decades past. The Greek Catholics are overwhelmingly urban, concentrated heavily in Lebanon's largest cities and towns. They are probably the most prosperous religious community, per capita, in the whole country. Among many other succesful businessmen who came from this community was Henri Pharaon, majority shareholder in the company which operated Beirut's busy international port.

The *Armenians* are members of an ancient Christian nation who first came to Lebanon in great numbers after 1915. That was the year that Turkish regular and irregular military units launched a massacre of the Armenians in their ancient homeland, killing an estimated 1.5 million of them in all.

After the First World War, the Maronite leaders in Lebanon and their French backers were eager to boost the Christian population of the area under their control. They therefore encouraged the resettlement of Armenian refugees in Lebanon, offering them Lebanese citizenship as a further incentive.

The largest group of these Armenians settled around the northern outskirts of Beirut. Rapidly, they established themselves in the kinds of small manufacturing enterprise which were in great demand as the city's economic life expanded. Other Armenians settled in Tripoli; and an additional Armenian resettlement zone at the ancient site of Anjar, near Lebanon's principal border crossing with Syria, quickly grew into a flourishing Armenian-dominated town.

The Armenians were the only major group which had entered the Lebanese system without having Arabic as their mother-tongue, and without claiming early Arabian tribal origins. Once in Lebanon, moreover, they maintained their own linguistic and other traditions through a sophisticated network of community institutions.

By the mid 1960s, third- or fourth-generation Lebanese citizens of Armenian origin could be born in Armenian hospitals in Lebanon, educated in Armenian schools and the Armenian university there, work in an Armenian-owned business – and still not have to speak a word of Arabic!

The Armenians of Lebanon brought with them their existing divisions in both the political and the liturgical spheres. Politically, the dispute between the two traditional Armenian parties – the left-of-centre Hunchaks and the right-of-centre Tashnaqs – continued in Lebanon with little of its original ferocity dampened. The much more recent Armenian Communist Party also had some representation in Lebanon. In church matters, meanwhile, the Armenians were divided – like the 'Greek' group – into Orthodox and Catholic churches.

The *Jacobites* are a small group, also known as the 'Syrian Orthodox', which forms less than 0.5 per cent of the Lebanese population. Remnants of an old Orthodox sect from the south of present-day Turkey, the total world Jacobite community is today dispersed between Turkey, Syria, Lebanon, and the Americas. In 1957, the seat of its patriarchate was moved from southern Turkey to the Syrian capital, Damascus.

The *Syrian Catholics* were a pro-Vatican splinter from the above-mentioned church. As with many Middle Eastern Catholic groups, a high proportion of the members of this church migrated to Lebanon during the years of the Maronite ascendancy there. In 1932, the Syrian Catholics re-established their patriarchate in an eastern suburb of Beirut. They too form well under 1 per cent of the Lebanese population.

Lebanon's other small Christian minorities also included some *Nestorians*, whose origins lay in an early heresy from Byzantium's orthodoxy; some of the *Chaldaeans* who are the Nestorians' pro-Vatican counterparts; and some small *Protestant* communities descended from converts made by Western missionaries of differing persuasions. But all these groups remained extremely limited in number. Their members understood they could only ever have any effect at the national political level by relating to the politics of some larger group.

These, then, have been the actors in the drama which has unfolded in Lebanon over the centuries. It is true, that larger, outside actors have often also loomed over the Lebanese stage – prodding, prompting, jeering, or on occasion even making their own brief appearance in the country. But their intervention has always, in the end, given way to the re-emergence of internal forces. The sects and minorities described above were the only ones who stayed onstage in Lebanon.

Indeed, one fact which seems amazing to me is precisely the *continuity* of the presence of these internal actors over not just decades, but centuries – enough centuries, just about, to add up to a whole millennium! For that is the length of time the Maronites, the Sunnis, the Shi-ites, the Druze and the 'Greek' group have all persisted in Lebanon.

Ever since the Druze closed their 'Divine Call' in AD 1043 the single major addition to the cast-list of 'Lebanese' has been the Armenians. And the Armenians, by retaining so much of the community infrastructure they brought with them on their sad exodus, always remained slightly marginal to the interactions of the other large groups in Lebanon. (That marginality was underscored during the troubles of the late 1970s, which saw an out-migration of Armenians of far greater proportion than that of any other Lebanese group.)

So what is it that united the five groups which persisted in the country for nearly a millennium? Have they indeed, by virtue of this persistence, or of anything else, come to constitute a single Lebanese 'nation'?

This question has certainly never been easy to answer. Indeed, the disputes between the citizens of the country itself over precisely this point have lain at the heart of some of their most violent bouts of fighting.

'No!' protested Father Boulos Naaman, the influential Maronite cleric who became a close adviser to slain President-elect Bashir Gemayyel, when he was asked this question. 'We are two peoples, with two languages and two cultures! We Christians have nothing in common with the Muslims!'

'Yes!', the local leftists would reply. 'Of course we are all one nation! The divisions between the sects are mainly artificial, kept in existence only by the hostile forces of imperialism, who seek to exploit them to keep us weak.'

Certainly, at the purely anthropological level, the mainstream sects and minorities of Lebanon do seem to have much in common with each other – and, to a slightly smaller extent, with the people of the Syrian and Arabian interior.

The language used throughout Lebanon is still clearly a dialect of Arabic. As is the case with all forms of that language spoken as a vernacular outside the Arabian peninsula, the Lebanese dialect shows obvious signs of accretions from other, local sources. These accretions, in the case of Lebanon, often have some association with the Aramaic linguistic forms which predominated in the region before the advent of Islam.

Regarding their social traditions, too, most Lebanese still have a lot in common with the Arab environment in which they have lived for the past thirteen centuries. Male infants in Lebanon are still routinely circumcized in the early days or months of their lives. The single most common form of marriage, right down to modern times, has remained the marriage between first cousins. The Lebanese still exhibit many of the same traditions of courtesy, and of hospitality towards strangers which are on enduring mark of Arab social life.

It is important to stress that social and anthropological traditions such as these are shared by *all* the major religious groups in Lebanon, including all the major Christian groups with the sole exception of the Lebanese Armenians.

Certainly, many internal variations are found within Lebanon in the fine details of some of these social traditions. But such variations occur between Lebanese in different geographic regions, as well as between members of different religious groups. For example, the Druze can generally be recognized as such in any region, purely from certain peculiarities in their speech. But a Maronite from south Lebanon will talk much more like his Shi-ite neighbours than his co-believers in the Kisrawan (with their flat and twanging long 'a' sound). He will also probably share many of the details of the southerners' preferences in food.

Lebanese food! It just seems such a pity that one cannot really count cuisine as the factor which finally pins down the question of nationhood. For if one could – what a fine type of nationhood would be found in Lebanon!

Lebanon has a bountiful Mediterranean type of agriculture, producing a gourmet's dream of olives, lemons, aubergines, tomatoes, fresh fish and fresh herbs. However, these common Mediterranean ingredients are augmented in Lebanon by the fragrant soft fruits of its higher terraces and tempered by the other, spicier tastes of its continental Asian interior. Only in Lebanon would one ever dream of eating a dish such as *kibbeh nayyeh* – raw ground lamb, chopped with fresh Italian-style parsley and onion, then mixed with bulgur wheat which has been soaked in lemon juice, and seasoned with sumak, salt, pepper and other spices. Or the famous *tabbouleh* or *fattoush* salads – both best in the spring when the necessary fresh herbs are heaped in high mounds on the vendors' barrows.

And what feasts are put together by the hard-working women of the family, whenever there is an occasion! The unwary visitor may sit back after the first succession of delicacies – only to hear his or her Lebanese hosts say, 'That was just the hors d'oeuvre. Now here's the main course!'

Such complicated people, the Lebanese; so difficult for the outsider to fathom. The same people, the very same people, can be so overwhelmingly generous with their hospitality, so modern-sounding with their ideas one day. And the next they may be consumed with hatred for their neighbours: so irrational and, sometimes, so terribly brutal.

How can such a people be understood? Is there, indeed, any rhyme or reason to them? My contention is that there is, if one can just sort out what is persistent in their society from what is transitory.

That means taking a journey backwards in time, to the days of the height of the Renaissance in Europe. It was during the sixteenth century that the process of developing an inter-sectarian system in Lebanon was set in train. That process has continued since then, though it has still not produced a fully formed modern nation in the European sense. It has been a process of great dynamism, a process which has often been both exciting to its local participants, and of consuming interest to outside observers. It has been, and still is, the making of Lebanon.

Notes

1 Kamal Salibi, in his presentation to the Georgetown University Center for Contemporary Arab Studies' Ninth Annual Symposium, 'Toward a Viable Lebanon', Washington DC, April 1984.
2 For an estimate of the total population figures of the country, see Table 1.
3 Alamuddin and Starr (1980), pp. 99-105.

'Village life'

2   The emergence of inter-sect rule (1516–1920)

The Lebanese state, in the form which has been generally recognized throughout most of the twentieth century, gained its formal boundaries in 1920, and its constitution in 1926.

Yet a political system which was specifically *Lebanese* in nature – that is, both separate from the regime of its neighbours, and embodying important elements of internal, inter-sect coexistence – had been in the making inside Mount Lebanon since the sixteenth century.

What was it about life in Mount Lebanon at that time which encouraged such a system to emerge? *Something* must have happened to encourage members of the Maronite and Druze sects to move towards an inter-sectarian system, rather than the separate development their sects had been pursuing for the previous 500 years. What was it?

The first condition for the emergence of the system which developed in Mount Lebanon must, I think, have been a general aura of stability, both locally and at the level of surrounding region.

It was in AD 1516 that the (Sunni) Ottomans captured Mount Lebanon and the area around it from their Sunni co-believers in Egypt. For the following 300 years, the predominance of the Turkish Ottomans over that region met no serious threat. It was during those 300 years of regional peace that an inter-sectarian system struck its first roots within the Maronite and Druze communities of Mount Lebanon.

Then, in the early nineteenth century, a new regime in Egypt directly challenged Ottoman supremacy in the Lebanese/Syrian region; and an Egyptian army advanced into Syria and Mount Lebanon. There followed eight years of Egyptian occupation which rocked the system in Lebanon to its very foundations. However, the roots the system had developed during its previous 300 years under the Ottomans eventually proved strong enough to enable the inter-sectarian principle to prevail.

The precise nature of the inter-sectarian system emerged much changed from the decades of Ottoman–Egyptian rivalry of the nineteenth century. But inter-sectarianism did, after twenty-six years of strife, prevail. Furthermore, it provided a climate in which a veritable cultural renaissance flowered in Lebanon. That fact in itself provides an important pointer to the hardiness of the inter-sectarian idea in Lebanon.

It was not only regional stability which was important for the incubation of inter-sectarianism in Lebanon. Internal stability inside Mount Lebanon itself was also an important condition.

The percipient English-Lebanese historian Albert Hourani has written brilliantly about the emergence of the Lebanese system. He identified several important components of the internal stability of Mount Lebanon which allowed inter-sectarianism to develop there. 'By the early Ottoman period . . . three elements in the structure of Lebanon already existed: the population, the system of lordship, and the autonomy of the local ruler', he wrote. 'A fourth was also coming into existence: Arabic was becoming the common language, although some Syriac continued to be spoken among Maronites . . .'[1]

By 1516, the basic pattern of the population of Mount Lebanon had been stable ever since most of the Shi-ites were driven out of Kisrawan in the early 1300s (see Chapter 1). That had left just the Druze and the Maronites as the major 'sects' residing in the central part of the Mountain. These were then the two principal groups between whom the inter-sectarian system first developed.

By the time the Ottomans started consolidating their rule in the area, the system of local lordship was also quite well-developed among the people of the central part of the Mountain.

The cultivators and herders of this part of the Mountain were already, as described in Chapter 1, an independent-minded group. They could certainly not be held in thrall by a single large landowner or a military regime, as could the residents of flat plains or vulnerable cities.

The first guarantee of the security of an individual in the Lebanon Mountain was always the strength of his family. But Mountain families had long banded together in larger groupings, based on allegiance either to the village community, or to a local lord. In doing so, however, no one could stop them from continuing to exercise many rights *as families*: the right to shift allegiance to another group, for example; or the right, if necessary, to move to another part of the Mountain. The broader, inter-family groups were thus always, to a certain extent, voluntary associations in Mount Lebanon.

In the central parts of the Mountain, the strongest kind of inter-family grouping was the allegiance groups of families would give to a single lordship. Each lordship would generally be retained within a single family, passing sometimes from father to son, sometimes from brother to brother. Many of those lordly families have died out over the past 400 years – the one which has remained in continuous existence is the Shihab family. But the years from 1516 to 1711 saw little basic change in the system of lords in the Mountain. That element of local stability also contributed to the emergence of Lebanon.

The 'autonomy of local rulers' Hourani wrote of was always limited to some degree by the regional supremacy of the Ottomans in this period. But what *was* important for the emergence of an inter-sectarian system in the Mountain was that the various different lords were tied into a single system, by the maintenance of a single lordly family at their head. Moreover, this primacy of a single lordly family in the Mountain received general recognition throughout this period both from the Ottomans and from a majority of the other lords: neither side was able to undermine it during these 300 years.

The dynasty of local overlords, or 'princes' was founded by one of the chief lordly supporters of the Ottomans' advance into the region in 1516. His name was Fakhr al-Din al-Ma«ni; and it was as a reward for his help that year that the Ottomans then gave him overall responsibility for ruling the central parts of Mount Lebanon. In recognition of this responsibility, the Ottomans gave Fakhr al-Din and his successors from the Ma«n family the honorific title of 'Amir' (commander, or prince).

This title would have remained, empty, however – and intersectarianism would probably not have come into existence in Lebanon over the centuries which followed – if the Ma«ni lords had not also been able to retain the support of the other local lords for their own primacy. But this the Ma«nis did have the political skill to achieve. Surviving challenges both from the Ottomans and from lordly local rivals, they continued in power until the male line of their family died out in 1697. When this happened both the Ottomans and the other lordly families collaborated in founding a successor dynasty, part of whose recognized virtue was that it was descended from the Ma«nis through a female line.

The third of the Ma«ni princes was called Fakhr al-Din the Second. He was prince from 1585 to 1635. During those years he was able considerably to extend the area under the control of the princedom.

As his forces pushed north into Kisrawan province (see map, p. 8), they expelled the few remaining Shi-ite inhabitants and encouraged the settlement there of Maronites. This forced the Shi-ites to the edges of Mount Lebanon, both in the southern Jebel Amel region, and in the Beqaa. It also directly linked the principal areas of Druze and Maronite settlement in the Mountain, paving the way for the emergence of an inter-sectarian system between the two sects.

Fakhr al-Din II, who was probably a Druze, brought great benefits to his Maronite subjects. Until this time they, like all non-Muslims, had been treated as distinctly second-class citizens of the Sunni Muslim empire. Lacking the status of the dominant group, they had been explicitly forbidden from displaying many of the customary marks of honour within Muslim society. Fakhr al-Din II's last contribution to the emergence of the Lebanese system was that, for the first time, he elevated the Maronites to the same civil status as the group which was dominant in his own fiefdom, the Druze.

According to one nineteenth century Maronite historian, 'During the reign of Fakhr al-Din II the Christians raised their heads, they built churches, rode on saddled horses, and wore white turbans . . . for most of his armies were Christians and his advisers and servants were Maronites.'[2] None of those actions were, at the time, permitted to Christians who came under the direct rule of the Ottomans. By allowing them to the Maronites under his control, Fakhr al-Din was asserting a new principle of the civil equality of at least some of the sects in the Mountain. He was also asserting his own independence from the traditions of the Ottomans.

This assertion of independence may well have riled some of those in the Ottoman bureaucracy. But what finally forced the Ottomans to act against Fakhr al-Din were his attempts to expand the area under his control considerably beyond the Mountain; and to do so, moreover, in close collusion with the merchant princes of Italy who were the Ottomans' chief rivals in the East Mediterranean at the time.

Fakhr al-Din's successive military expeditions extended his domain as far north as the Syrian city of Palmyra, and southwards to the Sinai Peninsula. His Ottoman rulers were most definitely displeased by this. They mounted numerous expeditions against him and finally in 1635 he was captured and executed. The Ottomans then stripped the princedom of most of its new conquests. But significantly, they were forced to leave the institution of the princedom itself intact, along with the core of its domain inside Mount Lebanon. And, after a fierce power-struggle within the Mountain, the Ma«n family retained control of the princedom, and the new prince was Mulhim, the nephew of Fakhr al-Din.

Mulhim and his son ruled over a reduced and subdued Mount Lebanon. When Mulhim's son died heirless, the princedom passed relatively smoothly to his successor, who was the grandson of his sister. According to Hourani, 'When the last Ma«ni died it was with Ottoman permission that the lords of Lebanon met at Sumqaniyya in 1697 to choose a successor; and when they chose the house of Shihab it was the [Ottoman] government which decided which member of the family to recognise as prince.'[3]

From 1697 until 1842, the Shihab family provided a constant succession of princes for Mount Lebanon, an area which included nearly all of its Druze-peopled regions and an increasing proportion of its Maronite areas. Although this period was often a stormy one for Mount Lebanon, anybody – whether Ottoman provincial official or local Mount Lebanon rival – who sought to challenge the authority of the ruling Shihab prince found it wise to do so only in the name of, or with the support of, one of his numerous Shihab cousins.

The main political basis for the Shihab princedom, as for the Ma«ni princedom before it, remained the alliance of the lordly families of Mount Lebanon. Although the Shihabs were themselves Sunni Muslims, their traditional fiefdom had been the Druze area of Wadi al-Taym, so a generally convenient myth was for long upheld that the Shihabs were in some way really Druzes. The Shihabs were supported in power by five lordly Druze families and three Maronite families: together these families made up the class of the major lordly fief-holders in the Mountain.

The major trend of the Shihab dynasty was the gradual shift of power within it from its Druze to its Maronite components. Their Ma«ni predecessors had certainly had many Maronite subjects, in the Kisrawan region and other parts of their domain. However, the traditional heartland of the Maronites in the northernmost peaks of Mount Lebanon had generally remained outside Ma«ni control; and it had been chronically weakened by bitter feuds which raged across and around it. It was the Shihabs who were able to bring north Lebanon effectively under the control of the princedom, and restore many of the ravaged Maronite villages there to their previous vigour, introducing an era of sustained Maronite population growth. Thus, the Maronite component in the princedom grew stronger throughout the 145 years of the Shihab dynasty.

On the Druze side, meanwhile, the Shihab era saw successive

strong disputes dividing the Druze-dominated aristocracy. These disputes weakened the Druze politically; they also weakened the sect in the important population stakes in Mount Lebanon, sending successive waves of Druze eastwards into the Hawran. The first of these disputes divided one lordly coalition called the 'Qaysi' party from another called the 'Yemenis'. (These names harked back to the earliest days of Muslim history, and occurred over the centuries inside many other communities of Arabian origin.) The Ma«ns and the Shihabs had both been supporters of the Qaysi faction, but the Yemeni faction's opposition to the Qaysi ascendancy continued to fester inside Lebanese Druze society until 1711.

That year, the Yemeni faction was decisively beaten in the Battle of Ain Dara. Those 'Yemeni' Druze who survived the battle were forced to seek refuge in the Jebel Druze, in inland Syria.

The Qaysi faction barely had time to celebrate its own victory before it was itself riven by another dispute, which has continued as a live issue in Lebanese Druze society down to recent times. This was the dispute between the 'Jumblatti' and the 'Yazbeki' factions.

The Jumblatts are the descendants of a Sunni Kurdish chieftain who had successfully sought asylum with Fakhr al-Din II in Mount Lebanon during the seventh century. Exceptionally for the Druze, the Lebanese Jumblatts soon came to be accepted as members of their sect. They rose rapidly towards a position of pre-eminence within Mount Lebanon's Shouf heartland, the traditional fiefdom of Ma«ns.

When the Ma«ni dynasy ended in 1697 it was the Jumblatts who took over as Lords of the Shouf. Even after the Ma«ns had been succeeded in the princedom by the Shihabis, the Shouf still remained the heartland of the Druze community of Mount Lebanon: from there the Jumblatts were rapidly able to exercise wide influence over other regions of the princedom.

Not surprisingly, the Jumblatts's rise of influence excited the resentment of many of the longer-established Druze feudal families. They resisted the Jumblatts's rising influence in the name of an old-established lordly family called Imad, or Yazbek. Hence, they came to call themselves 'Yazbekis'.

The splits which continued inside Druze lordly ranks gave the Shihab princes ample opportunity to play one side off against the other. The Shihabs were also sensitive of the changing sectarian balance inside their princedom and in the mid eighteenth century one of the Shihab Princes, himself a devout Sunni, allowed his sons to succumb to the pleas of the Maronites to join their number. In 1770, one of these sons, Prince Yusuf, became the first Christian Shihab to take power. But like most of the other Shihabs who followed him in and out of power Yusuf still kept his religious allegiance open to much deliberate public confusion.

The most notable Shihab ruler in Lebanon was Prince Bashir II, who first came to power as a 21-year-old youth in 1788 and spent a total of seven distinct spells in power over a total period of fifty-two years.

Bashir's greatest asset in his rule over Lebanon was his generally recognized sense of religious tolerance: 'Christian by baptism, Moslem in matrimony, Druze through convenience rather than conviction' is how one Lebanese historian described him.[4] While generally fostering an inter-sectarian spirit, Bashir also paid attention to making his concept of an inter-sectarian regime attractive to his subjects. Under his rule, new roads were built to connect the villages to the coast and the ports. He enforced an early quarantine regulation on foreign boats entering Beirut harbour. He tried to rationalize the tax system and save the princedom's peasants from the sometimes excessive greed of their own lords.

But Bashir was not free to rule Mount Lebanon exactly as he pleased. Within the Ottoman system, Mount Lebanon formally came under the authority of two Ottoman provincial officials. Its northern parts came under the Pasha of Tripoli, and its southern parts under the Pasha of Sidon. In 1776, the Ottomans appointed as Pasha of Sidon a man called Ahmad Pasha, also known as 'al-Jazzar' (the Butcher).

The Butcher was often brutal in exacting the taxes due from his region to the central Ottoman authorities. In Mount Lebanon, he soon learned to play disgruntled Druze feudal chieftains or rival Shihabs off against their own Prince, and beyond the Mountain he was often able to extend his authority deep into the Syrian interior. In these ways he became the dominant figure in both Mount Lebanon and Syria in the years before his death in 1804.

After the Butcher's death, Bashir moved quickly to try to restore his own princely authority in the Mountain. He punished all the Druze lords whom he suspected of having connived in the Butcher's plottings, exiling them and confiscating most of their lands. Of all the fief-holding Druze families, only the Jumblatts retained their previous position. During the next fifteen years, Prince Bashir Shihab built up a position of unrivalled power in Mount Lebanon, in alliance with his strong Druze backer, Sheikh Bashir Jumblatt.

In 1820, however, a new Pasha in Sidon demanded extra levels of tribute from Prince Bashir. The prince could not risk offending his Jumblatti ally by trying to raise the new taxes from the Druze, so he demanded them instead from the community which he now perceived as weaker, the Maronites.

Jumblatt's counterparts in the group of Maronite lords had indeed grown weaker over the preceding decades. But the major threat to their power was coming from inside their own community, from an emerging peasant movement organized by egalitarian monks and priests from within the Maronite church. When Prince Bashir made known his demands for new high taxes from the Maronites, this movement erupted in a widespread challenge to feudal and princely power called the 'General Uprising'.

The driving ideas of the General Uprising were radical for their day, and harked back to many egalitarian themes of the Maronites' traditional society in the northern villages. The General Uprising movement proposed a general criterion of 'the public good' for social behaviour, as against entrenched privilege – whether in the lordly palaces or in the aristocratic hierarchy of the church itself. (Some of these ideas continued to permeate sections of Maronite society right down to recent times.)

Prince Bashir was able to outmanoeuvre the leaders of the 1820 uprising. But the Christian peasant movement it had generated continued to provide a counterweight to lordly power inside the Maronite community, particularly within the northern villages.

Then in 1825 Prince Bashir made a move which decisively signalled the end of the period of reliance on the Druze chiefs as the main buttress of his princedom, and his understanding that his Maronite constituency had now become more important.

That year, a growing power-struggle between Prince Bashir and the Jumblatti leader finally erupted into the open. Forces loyal to the two sides engaged in a pitched battle in the Shouf village of Mukhtara, Jumblatt's forces were routed. Thus ended – for a time – the influence of the last of the great Druze fief-holders. The Jumblatt family and their supporters were forced into exile, and their lands were sequestered and often handed over to Maronite cultivators.

In 1832, Prince Bashir's rule entered a dramatic new phase. He entered into an alliance with Muhammed Ali, the ambitious governor of Egypt who had set out with French backing to challenge the authority of his nominal Ottoman overlords. Muhammed Ali's son Ibrahim Pasha was sent on a military expedition to win the whole

Syrian province from Ottoman rule: Prince Bashir's support in this venture was a valuable key to its success.

The first years of the new Egyptian rule over Mount Lebanon – still mediated, as the Ottomans' rule had been before it, through Prince Bashir's offices – were generally perceived as good ones by its Christian inhabitants. The Egyptians encouraged Christian equality with the Muslims. Indeed, they often *favoured* the Christians in many of their transactions.

The Druze remnants in the Mountain, however, still harboured bitter memories of their leaders' recent fall from power and they looked askance at the new confidence of the Maronites. They were particularly appalled when the Egyptians demanded that Prince Bashir supply hundreds of Druze conscripts to serve for fifteen years in the Egyptian army because this would take many of the healthiest generation of Druze away from their remaining lands. From their places of exile in Wadi al-Taym and the Hawran, the deported Druze leaders started to plan for their comeback and their revenge in Mount Lebanon.

In 1838 the Druze mounted their first battles against Egyptian units, near the Hawran. Disaffection with the Egyptians was also growing rapidly among other communities in the region. In late 1839, the Shi-ites of Jebel Amil revolted. By the following year, even the Maronites had become wearied of the Egyptians' continuing demands for raised taxes and new conscripts: they, too, now swung against both the Egyptians and the man who had facilitated Egyptian rule, Prince Bashir. On 27 May 1840, Druze Maronite and Greek Catholic representatives met in Dair al-Qamar, the traditional Shihab capital in the heart of the Shouf. After the meeting, they declared their common opposition to both Prince Bashir and to the Egyptians.

The armed revolt which followed shook not only Muhammed Ali's administration in Egypt, but also the heart of the great European chanceries of the day. For Muhammed Ali's challenge to the Ottoman empire in Syria had added a significant new twist to the whole problem of instability in the Ottoman-ruled regions which was known in West Europe as 'The Eastern Question'. The French were heavily committed in their support of Muhammed Ali; but the British and Austrians, among others, did not want to see him rock the slender stability of the Ottoman empire in the East Mediterranean.

In July 1840, Britain, Russia, Austria and Prussia signed an agreement with the Ottomans known as the Convention of London, which warned Muhammed Ali to withdraw partially from his venture in Mount Lebanon and the other 'Syrian' province. These terms had not yet been presented to the Egyptian ruler, when British and Austrian gunships appeared off Beirut to back up their arguments. Muhammed Ali still refused to withdraw. So in September, troops from both Britain and France joined some Turkish troops units in open battle against the Egyptians in Lebanon, while British naval gunpower backed up their campaign. By early November the Egyptian forces had been driven out of their last foothold in the Levant.

Seeing the end of the army which had supported him in power for eight years, Prince Bashir left the Shouf, and a British ship took him to exile in Malta. Thus ended the fifty-two year period of his rule.

Prince Bashir II Shihab had done much, at various stages in his rule, to further the development of an inter-sectarian system in Lebanon. But he had also sown the seeds of his own downfall, when he totally alienated Mount Lebanon's Druze. For while it had long been the case that a Prince of Lebanon could generally remain inviolate inside his Mountain from any attacks launched from outside the inter-sect system, the Druze, even while they fulminated in the Hawran, were still not 'outside' the system. They were certainly prepared to pay the price no truly 'outside' group would ever willingly pay to make their voice heard again inside the Mountain.

Prince Bashir should probably have known this. But by the late 1830s he had become so heavily beholden to his Egyptian backers that he had to do as they asked, even inside his 'own' Mountain. He thus should have provided a salutary lesson to any Lebanese ruler who might in later years have sought to do the same: to throw himself totally on the mercies of a foreign power, rather than seeking to use the existing internal mechanisms of the Lebanon's inter-sectarian system. For in Lebanon, the 'inside' factors would always prevail in the end.

Prince Bashir II was succeeded briefly by a much weaker cousin of the same name. But Lebanon's newly-restored Ottoman rulers did not want to see the restoration of a strong Shihab princedom. Neither did the returning Druze lords and their followers. Flushed with the success of their recent victory, the Druze now reasserted their presence in the Shouf by force, challenging Bashir III at his palace in Dair al-Qamar. Surrounded by the Druze, Bashir III was forced to leave the country in his turn, in January 1842.

Following his departure the Ottomans introduced an intricate new form of governance for Mount Lebanon, called the double *qa'immaqamiyya* ('district presidency'). The new role of he West Europeans in Lebanese affairs which this signalled was underlined by the fact that the formula had first been drawn up by the renowned Austrian Chancellor, Prince Metternich.

The striking fact that external developments could have a great effect *within* the Lebanese system had been amply illustrated by the history of the country prior to 1810. It had been painfully evident in the 1630s, in the whole story of Fakhr al-Din II's expansion beyond his mountain domain, and then his subsequent downfall. For Fakhr al-Din had been pursuing his broader objectives in close collaboration with the Medicis of Tuscany, and other powerful Italian merchant princes. Earlier, during a period when the Ottomans had virtually exiled him from his home, he had spent a total of five years travelling between various Italian cities. *He* had presumably been impressed while there with the thrusting new wealth of the Italians. *They* had presumably been impressed with the access to the profitable trans-Asian spice routes which he might afford them. The Italians had thus apparently assured Fakhr al-Din of their backing in his territorial challenge to the central Ottoman authorities in the region. But when the Ottomans counter-attacked against Fakhr al-Din, the Italians reneged on their supposed promise. Overextended already, and without any hope of reinforcement from his Italian friends, Fakhr al-Din was thus left at the mercy of the Ottomans, who then brought about his downfall.

In the 1770s, the influence of distant European powers was once again to make itself felt in the region. This time it was in neighbouring Palestine, where a local chief called Dahir al-Umar carved out a strong base for himself in Galilee. The Russians, who were then at war with the Ottomans, backed Dahir in his challenge of Ottoman authority. When, in 1774, the Russians finally reached a formal peace with the Ottomans Dahir was left to his fate with his nominal Ottoman overlords, and was killed. The Lebanese historian Kamal Salibi has explained the significance of this episode: 'From 1770 onwards, there was scarcely an event in Syria or any other part of the Ottoman empire which remained the purely internal concern of local chieftains and Ottoman officials.'[5]

When the double *qa'immaqamiyya* regime was established in Lebanon in 1842, the intervention of the European powers in Lebanese political life became dramatically more direct. It had even reached a degree of institutionalization through the consultations between the Europeans and the Ottomans which grew out of the 1840 Convention of London.

Throughout the decades from 1840 until the defeat of the Ottoman empire in the First World War, the exercise of final power in Lebanon – still nominally a part of the empire – was in fact to be in the hands of an uneasy condominium between the Ottomans and a 'Concert of Europe' which was never itself playing in anything like harmony. However, a general pattern soon emerged in Lebanese-European relations: the Maronites and other Catholics were supported primarily by the French, but also by the Austrians, the Druze were helped by the British, and the Orthodox Christians by the Russians. As one Lebanese chief was soon to complain: 'Our affairs have become the concern of Britain and France. If one man hits another the incident becomes an Anglo-French affair . . . .'[6]

The double *qa'immaqamiyya* provided the major example history has given us of a cantonal, or heavily de-centralized political system in Lebanon. From the outset, it looked like an administrative nightmare. Mount Lebanon and the coastal areas adjoining it were to be divided into two districts, north and south of the main Beirut–Damascus highway. The northern district would have a Christian *qa'immaqam*, and the southern district a Druze one. Both would be responsible to the Ottoman Pasha of Sidon, whose seat was now transferred to Beirut.

This facile division of the country, however, took scant account of the demography of Mount Lebanon. Many Druzes lived in the northern district, and the Christians of the southern district actually vastly outnumbered the Druze living there. The uncomfortable issue of the Christians consigned to live under the Druze *qa'immaqam* and the Druze to live under his Christian counterpart contributed heavily to the widespread dissatisfaction with the arrangement.

In the first few years of the *qa'immaqamiyya*, the Pasha tried to finesse a solution to the problem. He proposed that each *qa'immaqam* have two 'agents' under him, one Christian and one Druze, to deal with the judicial and tax matters of their own communities. But even this did not fully resolve the representation problem.

Other problems faced by the Pasha in making the formula work included the intransigence of the Druze leadership, on the one hand, and the fractiousness of the Christian leaders, on the other.

The man appointed as Christian *qa'immaqam* was a purely honorific 'prince' of the Maronite Abillama« family. His appointment was bitterly criticized both by those Maronites who sought a restoration of the Shihab dynasty, and by followers of those early Maronite radicals who had sparked the 1820 General Uprising. The Christian *qa'immaqam* thus had great difficulties having his writ accepted in his region.

On the Druze side, things were very different. The Druze warriors who had swept Prince Bashir II Shihab and his Egyptian backers out of the country had then proceeded to try to regain their former lands by force. But over the preceding years, Bashir had distributed many of those lands to his Christian backers. The returning Druze then brutally dispossessed many of those Christian settlers in 1840–41.

The European consuls in Beirut insisted the Ottomans punished the Druze for these actions. Thirteen leading Druze chiefs were imprisoned in Beirut in 1841, and the Druze community was required to make a hefty reparation to make up Christian losses.

The Druze, however, still saw themselves as the prime liberators of Lebanon from Egyptian rule, and they resented these Ottoman demands. They reacted to the new pressures on their community with an impressive display of unity. The Ottomans did actually allow them to choose their own *qa'immaqam*: the man they picked was one of the thirteen prisoners, 'Prince' Amin Arslan. He was chosen precisely because his family was still neutral in the continuing Jumblatti–Yazbeki feud; and over the years wich followed the adherents of these two rival factions displayed a remarkable ability to work together.

In 1845, the contradictions underlying the *qa'immaqamiyya* formula all erupted. In February, the Jumblatti chiefs convened a meeting in their seat in Mukhtara, to which leading Yazbeki chiefs were also invited. Some Maronite leaders, fearful of what might be afoot, started mobilizing for war. Within weeks, inter-communal clashes were escalating throughout the Mountain. A new Pasha, more favourable to the Druze instructed his forces to give them some support on the ground. That, and the Maronites' continuing lack of unity, enabled the Druze to go on the offensive through Christian areas.

With Christian villages burning throughout the Mountain, the European powers pressed the Ottomans to do something. The Ottomans immediately dispatched their Foreign Minister to Beirut, and within six weeks he had implemented radical new reforms in the *qa'immaqamiyya* formula. Each *qaim'maqam* was now to have a council to advise him, consisting of representatives of all the significant sects, not just the Maronites and the Druze. The councils were to rule through unanimous agreement, and if this could not be obtained, the Ottoman Pasha was to have the final say.

These new arrangements were in line with a whole series of administrative reforms being introduced throughout the Ottoman empire in that period. But the lordly families of both the major sects in Mount Lebanon saw them as threatening to their own power and privilege. Missions sent out from Istanbul to organize a land survey of Lebanon and a census of its population both resulted in failure due to opposition from the local lords. The Druze chieftains, in particular, were able to maintain a virtual 'no-go' area in the regions under their control. They collected all the taxes due from their peasants and then kept the revenue for themselves. One contemporary observer wrote that when the Druze *qa'immaqam* sent emissaries to inquire after these monies they were either just kept waiting or 'unceremoniously ejected' from the fiefdoms.

This kind of behaviour did not improve the Ottomans' view of the Druze. So in 1852, the imperial authorities called for a general conscription of the Druze. In late spring that year, the Druze men therefore once again made their way out of Mount Lebanon, going back as usual to Wadi al-Taym and the Hawran. There, once again, they declared an armed revolt against the Ottomans.

The Ottomans sent an expedition against the rebellious Druze. But this was beaten back, and the authorities were forced to conclude, once again that, rather than antagonizing the Druze, it was probably better to work with them.

Momentous developments had meanwhile been stirring Maronite society. The populist style of peasant movement which had erupted in the General Uprising of 1820 had also played a part in the final fight against the Egyptians in 1840. And over the years which followed the movement continued to grow, its organization and ideology heavily shaped by its supporters in the monasteries and the other radical wings of the church.

The peasant movement was especially combative in the Kisrawan province in the central portion of the Mount Lebanon range, where it confronted the authority of a lordly Maronite family called the Khazens. Meanwhile, in relatively remote north Lebanon, a charismatic Maronite radical called Yusuf Karam exercised great sway throughout much of the nineteenth century. And in the southern parts of the mountain, the bitterness of the Maronite peasants towards their feudal masters was fuelled by the fact that these latter were all from the Druze community.

In the winter of 1858–9, this peasant movement started an open revolt against the Khazens in Kisrawan, expelling every member of that family from the region and redistributing their lands to the peasants.

The momentum of the peasant movement then rolled southward, towards the Shouf: but there, the Druze lords were ready to confront it. They had already warned the Druze among their peasants that the new movement was directed against the whole of the Druze sect as such. So the whole Druze community united in preparing for the kind of mountain fighting at which it had proved itself so adept over the preceding centuries.

Over the bloody months of fighting of 1859 and 1860, the Druze force estimated at 12,000 men was able completely to rout Christian forces totalling some 60,000 men. In the Shouf, the Druze managed to seize all the major Christian areas. In the Beqaa, they took all the Christian parts of Wadi al-Taym, and managed to burst through the staunch defences of the Greek Catholic town of Zahleh. In a single four-week period in the summer of 1860, the Druze killed an estimated total of 11,000 Christians throughout Lebanon.

The victorious Druze forces were then poised to push their offensive even further, into the Christian *qa'immaqamiyya* itself – to take advantage of the paralysis caused by its own internal social upheaval. With dazed Christian survivors of the Druze rout filling the streets of Beirut, the European powers once again urged the Ottomans to act.

An early attempt by the local Pasha to solve the crisis as an internal affair showed some signs of succeeding. The central Ottoman administration backed up his efforts by sending a frigate and troop reinforcements to Beirut. But three days after Lebanese Christian and Druze leaders had signed a peace pact in Beirut, the Muslim population in *Damascus* suddenly attacked that city's Christian quarters. On 9 July 1860 alone, some 5500 Christians were slaughtered in that ancient city.

This time the Europeans felt they could not stand aside. The French, British and others had all had warships steaming off Lebanon for some weeks. When they heard the news from Damascus, the French immediately landed troops just south of Beirut. Their ostensible purpose was to 'help' the Ottomans restore order in the area; but in fact they constituted a powerful threat to the Ottomans to get on with the job quickly themselves. Under this pressure, the Ottomans once again despatched their Foreign Minister to the scene.

In Damascus, the Minister dealt sternly with the Muslim offenders. He executed over 100 of the Ottoman officers and soldiers quartered there for dereliction of duty, and conscripted all of the male population of Damascus which was eligible for service.

In Lebanon, he found it much harder to apportion responsibility for the fighting. He had already arrested the local Pasha and his leading officials, as well as the Druze *qa'immaqam* and thirteen other Druze chiefs. (The majority of Druze chiefs, however, fled once again to the inaccessible Hawran.) The Lebanese Christians presented the minister with a list of 4,600 Druze and 360 Sunni and Shi-ite offenders: but no one was willing to testify openly against these suspects. Finally, a total of 245 Druze were exiled for a period to Libya. The minister then announced that no further complaints would be entertained relative to the fighting.

Meanwhile, a commission representing Britain, France, Russia, Austria and Prussia, with the Ottoman minister in the Chair, convened in Beirut to work out a *political* settlement for Lebanon. The commission finally completed its deliberations in June 1861. As a result, the French withdrew their troops from Lebanon, and four days later the Ottoman ruler announced a new regime for Mount Lebanon, which was to operate the guarantee of the five deliberating powers plus Italy. This regime, still nominally part of the Ottoman Empire, would be called the *mutasarrifiyya*, or provincial governorship.

The *mutasarrifiyya* arrangements brought to an end the turbulence which had racked Lebanon since 1820, inaugurating a period of civil peace in the Mountain which was to last for over half a century. Throughout that period, Mount Lebanon gained a widespread reputation as the 'best governed, the most prosperous, peaceful and contented country in the Near East'.[7]

The new arrangements included a number of changes designed to correct the mistakes of the *qa'immaqamiyya* formula. The idea of twin administrations for the southern and northern areas was dropped. Instead, Mount Lebanon was now re-united under a single *mutasarrif* (provincial governor). It was explicitly stated that this new official should be a Catholic Christian subject of the Ottoman ruler, who should *not* be of Lebanese origin.

Eleven successive provincial governors ruled Mount Lebanon under the *mutasarrifiyya* regime. Each was advised by a local administrative council. After some early adjustments, membership in this council was fixed in 1864 at four Maronite members, three Druze, two Greek Orthodox and one each from the Greek Catholic, Sunni and Shi-ite communities. The lordship system was formally abolished, and all Lebanese citizens were declared equal before the law.

The Ottomans signalled their commitment to making the *mutasarrifiyya* work by appointing governors of a high calibre, often distinguished former diplomatists. The first *mutasarrif* was Dawood Pasha, an Armenian Catholic from Istanbul. He moved swiftly to replace the former sectarian differences in Mount Lebanon with a new sense of political and administrative purpose.

In the early years of the *mutasarrifiyya*, the Maronites were still reeling from their defeats of 1860. In the traditional Maronite heartland of north Lebanon, an irredentist movement led by Yusuf Karam continued for a while to oppose any formula for coexistence with the Druze. But the movement gradually died out after Karam was exiled in 1867. The majority of Maronites, meanwhile, were gradually reassured by their relative power on the administrative council, and by the international guarantees governing the *mutasarrifiyya* formula.

For their part, the majority of Druze felt that the victories of 1860 had wiped out the indignities the Druze community had suffered over preceding decades. But they realized that restoration of the Druzes' historic domination of the Mountain was unattainable. And they felt that, because it did not explicitly endorse total Maronite supremacy but only a general Maronite primacy, the *mutasarrifiyya* formula offered them a dignified way to accept their reduction to second place with their honour intact.

The constituency of the irredentists in both camps thus shrank over the years and the remaining decades of the *mutasarrifiyya* saw only isolated cases of sectarian violence – and nothing at all on the scale of what had happened in 1825, 1841 or 1860.

Dawood Pasha had well understood that the abolition of the lordship system might leave many former lordly families disenchanted. So he tried to win over key lords to his side by giving them official responsibilities in his new administration. His success in this endeavour started a long tradition whereby members of the traditional lordly families served in key posts in the Lebanese administration.

Throughout the decades of stable government which the *mutasarrifiyya* brought to Mount Lebanon the creative energies of the Lebanese were largely turned away from political factionalism towards more productive fields. The successive *mutasarrifs* laid particular stress on the development of the Mountain's internal communications. In 1863, a French company completed construction of the cross-mountain highway which to this day links Beirut with the important markets of Damascus. Road-building over subsequent decades drew all of Mount Lebanon's major towns into the modern road network. In 1863 a first telegraph message passed from Beirut to Istanbul, and soon most Lebanese towns had been connected into the telegraph network. In 1895, a railway company opened a rail link between Beirut, Damascus and the Hawran.

Dawood Pasha was also able – unlike his predecessors in the *qa'immaqamiyya*! – to carry out a cadastral survey of Mount Lebanon, and to start to collect census data. The collection of taxes and customs duties was regularized, and in 1864 Dawood established a permanent Public Comptroller's Office.

Such measures as these set the scene for the steady growth of the Lebanese economy. Mount Lebanon's principle economic link with West Europe had for long come from one particular crop raised in the high mountain terraces: the many mulberry orchards tended there provided a constant supply of tender leaves on which generations of silkworms were fed. The silk from their cocoons was bought by local or French traders, and much of it was exported for sale in the silk market of the French city of Lyons.

The new stability of Mount Lebanon under the *mutasarrifiyya* now added to this silk export trade many other types of commercial transaction with the West. Import duties at Beirut port were kept attractively low; and the trading-house which mushroomed around the port could promise speedy cross-mountain access (legal or extra-legal) to the profitable markets of the great Syrian/Arabian interior. The commercial activity of Beirut thus multiplied throughout this period. And as Beirut and the Mountain became tied ever closer to the economies of the West, a growing stream of enterprising young Lebanese left their home villages for Europe and the New World.

The merchant and banking families of Beirut – many of them members of the Greek Catholic or Greek Orthodox sects – grew rich on the expanded trade, while many of the traditional feudal families of the Mountain fell heavily in debt to them. A similar situation arose in Tripoli, where Greek Orthodox bankers lent heavily to the feudal lords of the Akkar.

The coastal cities had, or course, been specifically excluded from political participation in the regime in the Mountain. But the economic links between the cities and the Mountain were considerably *strengthened* by the economic policies pursued by successive *mutasarrifs*. (This fact received administrative recognition in the fact

that the European consuls in Beirut were given commercial juris-
diction over the affairs of the Mountain.) The 'new money' of the city
traders generally took the economic initiative, while the stability and
relative independence of the regime in the Mountain gave them a
valuable political environment in which to operate.

The successive governors of Mount Lebanon also worked hard to
build up their region's educational infrastructure. Among his many
other innovations, Dawood Pasha established the first modern type
of school for boys in the Druze-dominated part of the Mountain, as
well as Lebanon's first government printing press. European and
American religious missions also continued, or expanded their
educational efforts in the country. Their motives in this may
sometimes have been less than totally altruistic; but the net effect was
further to fuel the educational and cultural renaissance in the
country.

The explosion of education and the new-found civil security caused
many new schools of thought to flourish in Lebanon. No fewer than
forty periodicals, including fifteen newspapers, started publication in
the country during the last three decades of the nineteenth century,
and numerous books were published. Lebanese scholars made a huge
contribution during these years to a region-wide cultural renaissance
which sharpened the classical Arabic language into a refined and
flexible vehicle for modern ideas. (The educational infrastructure
among the Christians in Lebanon was more developed than that in
Druze or other Muslim areas. So it was, in fact, the Christians among
the Lebanese who were pre-eminent in these Arabic cultural efforts.)

One key field in which the new generation of Lebanese scholars
were eagerly examining the ideas of the West was in political
thinking. The concept of Western-style nationalism attracted much
attention, but there was never a consensus on how it should be
defined in local terms.

Some Maronites and other Lebanese Christians were attracted to
the concept of a purely *Christian* Lebanese nationalism. Many
proponents of this idea were often heavily influenced by the
egalitarian social ideals which had been expressed in the Maronite
peasants' General Uprising in 1820.

Other Christians, generally from the mixed central and southern
parts of Mount Lebanon, argued instead for greater *Christian–*
Muslim co-operation. The Mountain could never reach economic
self-sufficiency on its own, they argued. So if a Lebanese entity was to
have enough food-growing capacity and its own access to the sea,
then the Christian majority in the Mountain must learn to live with

the Muslim majority on the coast and in some of the fertile plains abutting the Mountain on its other side.

Yet others, Christians and Muslims, looked to the wider community of the whole historic Syrian province (that is, present-day Syria, Lebanon, Jordan and Israel). This wider area included the birth-place of Christianity and many of its oldest continuously worshipping communities. So the Lebanese who advocated a strain of *pan-Syrian* nationalism included a majority of Lebanese Christians.

During the latter decades of the *mutasarrifiyya*, proponents of such ideas as these had to be prepared to defend them not only against defenders of the current Ottoman orthodoxy, but also against new currents of thinking circulating throughout the Arab-peopled parts of the Ottoman empire. New generations of thinkers in Lebanon, as in others of the empire's Arab provinces, started thinking in terms of a *pan-Arab nationalism*, which rejected the continued rule of the Turkish Ottomans.

But again, there was much disagreement over what form an Arab nationalism should assume. One strong current of opinion within the early definitions of Arab nationalism was an *Islamic* current. And within the whole world of Islam, too, there was an intense debate between rival revivalist and modernizing currents, centring on the precise role of the ruler and the nature of the ruling process.

Later, determinedly *secular* brands of Arab nationalism developed, in Lebanon as in the other Arab regions. Once again, Lebanese Christians played a large part in formulating these ideas.

Many of these latter kinds of debate raged with their strongest fury far from the intimate society of the Mount Lebanon villages. But the new generations of intellectuals who had grown up in those villages were still closely related to them, in a number of different ways.

It was, after all, largely the literary work of Lebanese scholars which had set the linguistic stage for many of the new debates throughout the Arab world. Many educated Lebanese Christians had meanwhile left their native region, fanning out throughout the Arab world – but particularly in Egypt, where a modernizing regime was hungry for their talents. The Lebanese *émigrés* in Egypt came into close contact with the ferment of ideas there, especially through the ambitious new newspapers and periodicals, the establishment of which they had pioneered. Finally, no proponent even of a purely Lebanese *Christian* brand of nationalism could ever think of putting his ideas into practice without thinking also how to deal with the powerful Sunni-dominated cities of the coast and the Syrian interior.

It was into this busy and busily developing society that the First World War burst like a bombshell. In October 1914, the Ottoman empire entered the conflict on the side of Germany. The whole East Mediterranean, with its web of competing Ottoman and West European interests, was plunged willy-nilly into the heart of the war.

In summer 1915, the Ottoman authorities abolished the *mutasarrifiyya* regime for Mount Lebanon and placed the whole area under direct military rule.

Immediately the new military authorities decreed that contact with the French, the British, or the British-backed Arab nationalist movement of Sherif Hussein of Mecca was seditious. On 6 May 1916, fourteen Christians and Muslims – a majority of them Muslims – were publicly hanged in Beirut for alleged treason to the Ottomans. Seven were hanged the same day in Damascus, for the same reason. In later years, that occasion would be publicly commemorated in both Lebanon and Syria, as an annual 'Martyrs' Day'.

The embattled Ottoman military requisitioned all it could to beef up its sagging war effort. The young men of Lebanon were rapidly conscripted, regardless of sect, and draft evaders were dealt with mercilessly at hastily-established military courts. Farm animals and food were either just taken from the farms, or paid for in useless Turkish paper money. Wide areas of Mount Lebanon's hillsides were denuded of trees, as Ottoman conscripts axed them to fuel the strategic railways.

Whole villages were reduced to penury, and disease set in to finish where hunger left off. Starving bands roamed the hillsides. Many of those who could, fled the Mountain for the Syrian interior. The Druze made for their traditional refuge, among their co-religionists in the Hawran. Other Lebanese threw themselves on the mercies of the beduin of the Syrian desert. By the end of the war, a staggering 100,000 of Mount Lebanon's previous population of 450,000 had died of starvation or disease.

By the end of summer 1917, the Ottomans were coming under severe pressure in the region. The British and their allies were pushing northwards towards Beirut from Palestine. On 1 October 1917 the Ottoman administration in Beirut collapsed.

At that point, the local notables of Beirut proclaimed the establishment of an *Arab* government there, hoisting Sherif Hussein's flag over public buildings. A Sherifian commander from the interior came with a token force to occupy the city. He then reconvened the same administrative council that had served the *mutasarrifiyya* in

Mount Lebanon, and which had been disbanded in 1915. Its Maronite president, Habib al-Saad, was called on to govern the area of 'Lebanon' in the name of Sherif Hussein.

The British and French were greatly displeased by this development. For back in early 1916, their two governments had reached an explicit agreement, called the 'Sykes–Picot agreement', on how to divide between themselves the Ottoman empire's provinces in the historical Fertile Crescent region – that is, broadly, the area lying between the Nile and the Tigris and Euphrates basins. Under the agreement, France would exercise its influence in Lebanon and Syria, while Britain would be predominant in Iraq and Palestine (that is, present-day Iraq, Israel and Jordan). Arab self-government in any of those areas was most certainly not part of their immediate plan.

Six days after the Sherifian regime was proclaimed in Beirut, the British and French armies finally reached the city. They took down all the Sherifian flags, and a French colonel was installed as military governor. Habib al-Saad's council was forgiven its momentary lapse, and allowed to remain in existence under firm French auspices.

In April 1920, when the victorious allies reached their final decision on how to dispose of the remnants of the vanquished Ottoman empire, it was totally in line with the earlier Sykes–Picot agreement. The newly-established League of Nations awarded France a 'mandate' to rule over Lebanon and Syria, until such a time as these two regions should be 'ready' for independence. (Britain won a parallel 'mandate' in Iraq and Palestine.)

The Sherifians were still in control in the Syrian capital, Damascus. So in July 1920, a French expedition was sent to oust them. It soon succeeded; and by August the French authorities were ready to publish a decree describing the boundaries of the two new states. Lebanon was now called 'The State of Greater Lebanon', and included all the area of the former *mutasarrifiyya*, plus the Beqaa Valley, the Wadi al-Taym region, Jebel Amil, and the coastal cities of Beirut, Tripoli, Sidon and Tyre – that is, the whole area which since then has been internationally recognized as 'Lebanon'.

Through their actions in Lebanon over the decades, from their redrawing of the boundaries in 1920 onwards, the French were to inject many new elements into the political system which had been evolving inside Mount Lebanon over the centuries. Nevertheless, significant other elements in the French-defined state had been inherited directly from those previous traditions.

Chief among these elements of continuity was the very principle on which the new state – like the regimes which had preceded it in the area – was founded. This was the principle that 'Lebanon' should imply a form of coexistence between the religious groupings of which its population was composed, such that these groupings would retain much of their internal independence within the framework of a unitary political regime.

By the 1920s, this inter-sectarian principle had been predominant in a considerable part of Mount Lebanon for well over 300 years. And the actual regimes founded there on the basis of that principle had displayed a remarkable degree of continuity: only two historically significant changes of regime had occurred in Mount Lebanon since AD 1516.

The first of those changes of regime occurred during the transition period from 1842 to 1861. It was in 1842 that the Shihab dynasty – which had in many important respects been merely a continuation of the previous Ma«ni-dominated system – came to an end when Prince Bashir III was deposed. That event signalled the end, not only of the rule of the Shihab family as such, but also of the whole system of princedom through which Lebanon had been ruled since 1516.

The years from 1842 to 1861 were transition years in many important respects. They were the years in which the previously unitary political system was replaced, for a while, by a decentralized system; but this rapidly proved to be unworkable. They were years, too, in which the cacophonous Concert of Europe – which had been brought to play in Lebanon on the coat-tails of its previous Egyptian maestro – was still casting about for a way to collaborate with the Ottomans.

Remarkably, all the major problems of those stormy transition years were resolved through the establishment of the *mutasarrifiyya* in 1861. The Europeans found a new overall harmony among themselves – at least, as far as concerned most of their dealings in Lebanon. They had found a satisfactory way to join their efforts with those of the Ottomans in a virtual condominium of rule over Mount Lebanon. And the Ottomans played their part by appointing what seems to have been some of the most skilled of their officials to serve in the post of *mutasarrif*.

The general stability evident during the *mutasarrifiyya* years was also based on the emergence of a new balance *within* the Lebanese system. The Shihabs may themselves have been Maronites in the latter decades of their rule, and may in the end have come to represent a new Maronite primacy within Mount Lebanon. But the lordly system which they headed, and from which they derived their legitimacy, was still deeply rooted in social traditions which were essentially (in their Mount Lebanon context) Druze in origin. It was thus understandable that, if the Druze lords were loath to submit to Maronite primacy at all they were particularly loath to see this primacy expressed through the very same lordly system they themselves had dominated through the centuries.

From the last decades of the eighteenth century onwards, powerful demographic and social trends were building up the pressure on the Druze leaders to relinquish their political power to the Maronites. The Druze population, which had been relatively stable for centuries because of the sect's opposition to conversion, and its general social conservatism, registered several sharp declines as a result of successive waves of emigration to the Hawran. With most Druze villages still locked into the old-style system of feudal loyalties, relatively few Druze were able to take advantage of the new economic opportunities which accompanied the growth of European influence in the country at this time.

By contrast, the egalitarian atmosphere of Maronite villages and the spread of modern schooling in Maronite areas allowed many Maronites to take part in new forms of economic activity. The cultivation of cash crops such as wheat or mulberry leaves (for the silk industry); the growing trade associated with such crops; the birth of new manufacturing centres: all these were activities in which Maronite participation far outstripped that of the Druze.[8] And alongside these circumstances of economic growth, the Maronite population increased rapidly, posing an additional challenge to the primacy of the Druze.

Understandably, however, the Druze were reluctant to give way to the new Maronite challenge; and equally understandably, the thrusting new forces within Maronite society grew increasingly impatient with their reluctance. Behind all the violence and turmoil of the years between 1825 and 1861 there thus lay that deep-rooted power-struggle between the two communities.

In particular, the high degree of Druze violence against the Maronites and other Christians in that period can be viewed as the last desperate protest of the previously-dominant group against their inexorable reduction by the unstoppable march of history.[9]

By 1861, the primacy of the Maronites had been clearly enshrined in the provisions of the *mutasarrifiyya* formula – although it should be noted that the new power of the Maronites was still subject to important checks: the *mutasarrif* himself, though a Catholic, was still a non-Maronite, and an Ottoman official; and his actions were still subject to external, European ratification. On this basis the Druze came to accept the new order. Indeed, over the years which followed, they carved out for themselves quite an honourable role within the Maronite-dominated system, ensuring that they would continue to play an important role within it.

The next major break in the regime in Mount Lebanon came during the First World War. The Ottomans' summary ending of the *mutasarrifiyya* regime in 1915 ushered in another period of transition in the area, which only ended with the establishment of the 'State of Greater Lebanon' in 1920.

The major change brought about by that period was, of course, the total dissolution of the Ottoman empire. That empire had, for the previous four centuries, provided the general regional environment in which an inter-sect system had grown up in Lebanon. Could Lebanon now survive the removal of the Ottoman umbrella?

The other major change evident in the Lebanon of 1920 was the inclusion of significant new population groups within its borders, which might threaten to undermine the whole basis of Maronite–Druze entente in the Mountain.

Was the inter-sect principle already deeply enough enshrined in Lebanon in 1920 that it could survive all these radical changes? This was the basic question the system had to face as it entered the next act in the drama of Lebanon.

Notes

1 Hourani (1981), p. 126. Some of Hourani's best writings on the emergence of Lebanon are found in the four essays on Lebanon which were re-published in this book.
2 Istfan Duwayhi, quoted in Harik (1968), p. 20.
3 Hourani (1981), p. 129.
4 Hitti (1957), p. 417.
5 Salibi (1977), p. 16
6 Quoted in ibid., p. 79.
7 Quoted in Khalaf (1979), p. 85.
8 For details of these economic changes, see Paul Saba, 'The creation of the Lebanese economy – economic growth in the nineteenth and twentieth centuries', in Roger Owen (1976), pp. 1–5.
9 The parallels with the period of Maronite violence against the Shi-ites and other Muslims, from 1976 and 1984, are striking. See Chapters 5 to 7 below.

Beirut, showing the shanties of the Dikwaneh refugee camp in the foreground

3 Foundations of the modern state (1920–43)

In 1920, the French found themselves on their own in ruling Lebanon and Syria, free from the constraints of the condominium-type arrangement which had limited Ottoman power in Lebanon for the past century. Certainly, the League of Nations was too amorphous, and too far away, for its 'Mandate' to the French to have much effect on what the French actually did in the two countries.

French rule in Lebanon was to continue until – like Ottoman rule before it – it came under threat from the broader geopolitical developments of a world war. The Second World War (like the First World War before it) was to cause a significant 'break' in the system of rule in Lebanon, throwing the country into yet another transition period. This fact once again underscored the extreme vulnerability of a political system located, like the Lebanese system, in an area of enduring strategic importance to huge outside powers.

French rule in Lebanon, then, both started and ended in the region-wide turmoil of great wars. Nevertheless, during the inter-war years, the French were able to provide an environment in Lebanon in which the principle of inter-sect collaboration survived. And more than that, during the years of French rule the inter-sect system in Lebanon also *developed* in ways which were to have a lasting impact.

The French sponsored two developments in the Lebanese system which were to prove to be of major, lasting importance. The first was their drawing of new borders for the Lebanese entity, which from 1920 onwards drew significantly new population groups into it. And the second was their introduction, in 1926, of a modern-style constitution to govern the system's political life.

The principal author of the constitution was a wealthy Lebanese Roman Catholic banker called Michel Chiha. In it, he explicitly stated that positions in the country's administration should be divided equally between the different religious groups (although he did not, at that stage, specify any precise proportions for this).

This principle of explicit, inter-sect power-sharing became known in Lebanon as 'confessionalism'. However, in advocating the application of this principle, the 1926 constitution also stated that it should be applied only 'temporarily', until a fully *non-sectarian* system could develop in the country. Some fifty years later supporters of a non-sectarian system were to mount a significant challenge to the 'temporary' application of confessionalism in Lebanon. But their challenge was beaten back (see Chapters 6 and 7). The confessional principle, and most of the rest of the 1926 constitution in which it had been included, thereby proved its hardiness.

The 1926 constitution also enshrined many other principles which were to have a lasting impact within the Lebanese system. It declared that the country should be firmly *republican*, with all citizens enjoying equal rights under the law. And it inaugurated a system of formal *democracy* in Lebanon, based on elections to a single legislature.

Indeed, the electoral system for which the constitution provided cut right across the boundaries between the country's sects. It thus played a significant role, at various times, in helping to create a truly *national* political life. This provision did not succeed in fully eradicating the importance of the sects. Nevertheless, it is probably true, as the historian Albert Hourani has written, that this electoral principle, 'might indeed be regarded as the most important contribution made in the Mandatory period to the political life of Lebanon'.[1]

Many Lebanese would probably also agree with this assessment. The constitution and its electoral system continued to stand as bastions of continuity – however symbolic – until at least the middle of 1985 (see Chapter 1). The intra-Lebanese violence which had, by that point, plagued the country for nearly a decade had truly tested the hardiness of the constitution's electoral provisions! Yet, thus far, they had still passed that test.

The constitution pretty rapidly proved itself an enduring factor, which strengthened the inter-sect system in Lebanon. (Moreover, it achieved this despite the fact that the French actually suspended it for three and a half years during the 1930s, and again with the outbreak of the Second World War.) The other major change introduced by the French – the inclusion of new areas and new populations in the system – did not, in the first decades after 1920, always seem to act in favour of a stable inter-sect system.

The new areas included in the 'State of Greater Lebanon' were the coastal cities, the Akkar plain, the Beqaa Valley and Jebel Amil. The first two of these had strong Sunni Muslim majorities within their population, while the latter two had strong Shi-ite Muslim majorities.

How would these two groups react to being brought into a system which for centuries had been dominated by Maronites and Druzes? And conversely, how would the system react to their inclusion?

The transition proved to be particularly difficult for the newly-included Sunnis. They had long been linked by vital ties of trade, politics and family to the other great cities of the Ottoman empire. Now, they had to shrink their horizons dramatically, to relate to the very different politics of their own mountain hinterland. For many of them, the transformation from being part of the ruling majority in a vast empire, to being a second-class minority in the much smaller new state, was to prove particularly difficult.

A few of the Sunnis had remained loyal to the Ottomans until the last days of the empire. Many more had been fired with enthusiasm by the Sherifian revolt, and continued to call for a restoration of their traditional links with the Syrian interior. For whichever of these reasons, much of Sunni public opinion rejected the whole concept of Greater Lebanon for many years after 1920. But a gradually increasing trickle of Sunni personalities took the initiative in extending co-operation to the Mandate administration throughout the 1920s and 1930s.

Meanwhile, the Shi-ite communities of the Beqaa, and of Jebel Amil, had their own transition to make when they were included into the Lebanese system. The Beqaa had had some traditional links with the Maronite and Druze areas of Mount Lebanon although often, too, it had come under the domination of nearby Damascus. And Jebel Amil may have been, geographically, an extension of the Mount Lebanon range. But it had spent most of its time prior to First World War more closely linked to the ports and uplands of northern Palestine, than it had been to the developing entity in Mount Lebanon.

Shrewdly, the French offered community leaders in the two Shi-ite areas a positive inducement to make the transition to rule from Beirut. For the first time, they agreed to recognize the Shi-ite sect as a separate group within the system. The country's previous rulers, the Sunni Ottomans, had not seen fit to grant any dissenting Muslim groups the same kind of 'separate' status they gave to Christian or Jewish communities. So the French move offered Shi-ite community leaders an important new way to participate in political life.

For a number of the large landowners who still dominated the Shi-ite areas, this inducement soon proved sufficient to win their commitment to the regime in Beirut. And throughout the Mandate years, these landowners were able to beat off the few challenges which started to be raised within their communities, to the near-absolute right they claimed to speak for the communities as a whole.

But still, the French were attempting an enormous task as they tried to integrate into the inter-sect system, which had emerged over the centuries in the Mountain, not just one but *two* entirely new local partners.

The first president elected under Lebanon's 1926 constitution was Charles Dabbas, a Greek Orthodox. The French had proposed his candidacy primarily to allay the fears of the various Muslim groups that the Maronites, long-time allies of the French, might dominate the new system. And Dabbas certainly did much to establish the norm that the president should stand above the country's sectarian divisions, and act in the light of a truly pan-Lebanese national interest.

Throughout his six years in office, Dabbas did appoint prime ministers who were Maronites. But he also maintained his pan-Lebanese credentials since his presidency received the continuous backing of the new Republic's first prominent Sunni supporter, the jurist Muhammad al-Jisr from Tripoli. Jisr was the Speaker of the Republic's first Chamber of Deputies.

Two of the men who served Dabbas as premier had their own ambitions to become president. These were Emil Eddé, from Byblos, and Bishara al-Khoury, from further south. The contest between these two was much more than a clash of personalities. It was a continuation in modern times of one of the most fundamental debates about the nature of Lebanon which had raged inside the Maronite community throughout the previous century.

Eddé held to many of the specifically *Christian* nationalist ideas which had traditionally been prevalent among the hardy Maronite villagers of northern Lebanon (see Chapter 2). Khoury, for his part, was a typical representative of the Maronites of the mixed southern regions. From the outset, he based his political strategy on the idea of building a strong Christian–Muslim coalition to ensure the stability of the nation.

The contest between these two men – and thus between the conflicting views of Lebanon which they stood for – was to dominate much of the politics of the Mandate period. Khoury's view was eventually to prevail in the country, once French rule had come to an end. But the stress on *Christian* supremacy which Emil Eddé had advocated was to continue to be attractive to a substantial number of Maronites.

As Dabbas's second three-year term came towards its end in 1932, it became clear that Khoury could win a presidential election against Eddé. So bitterly opposed was Eddé to Khoury's candidacy that he withdrew from the contest, and supported the candidacy of the Sunni, Muhammad al-Jisr in the presidential campaign.

Eddé was presumably hoping that this action would force the French to intervene in his favour in the election. But Jisr was apparently serious about his chances. In early 1932, in his capacity as Speaker of the House, he quickly organized a census of the country in an attempt to prove the existence of a Muslim majority which would bolster his claim to the presidency. He failed. The census – the first and last ever organized in the country's modern history – revealed that the Christians still enjoyed a slim majority. The French then went ahead and pre-empted the presidential election by suspending the constitution.

For the next three and a half years, Lebanon was ruled by a president who was an appointee of the vastly more powerful French High Commissioner. At the end of 1935, the High Commissioner announced that the local Chamber of Deputies would once again be allowed to vote for a president. The same two contestants, Eddé and Khoury, once again entered the fray. This time, Eddé won by a single vote.

One of Eddé's first acts was to dismiss the Sunni politician who had been serving as a sort of prime minister, and appoint to the premiership a Protestant Christian. The Sunnis and other Muslims might have expressed some opposition to this move. However, their attention was not at that stage focused on the affairs of the Lebanese Republic, but on a massive independence movement which was then underway among their co-believers in neighbouring Syria.

In March 1936 an unofficial body called the 'Conference of the Coast' convened in Beirut. Its participants represented a broad majority of Lebanese Muslim opinion – with the notable exception of those Sunni and Shi-ite Muslim politicians who had already been drawn into the formal parliamentary system. The Conference almost unanimously demanded the re-integration of Lebanon's Muslim districts with Syria.

This demand was not as unthinkable at that time as it might later have come to appear. For Lebanon was not the only part of the

Mandated area in which the French had established a regime separate from that in the historic capital of Damascus. Indeed, the French had originally established another wholly separated 'State' in the north Syrian city of Aleppo, with a semi-autonomous subsection of that carved out around Alexandretta. And they had designated the area around the Syrian Mediterranean port of Latakia as a 'State of the Alawis', and had established in the Hawran a 'Druze national Government'.

In 1925, the states of Damascus and Aleppo were combined into the single 'State of Syria', from which the Alexandretta area was excluded. Further unionist agitation in 1935–6 resulted in the formal annexation of the Hawran and Latakis 'states' to the central Damascus regime in 1936. Those Lebanese who pursued parallel aims for union with Damascus during those years thus viewed them as perfectly realistic.

In Lebanon, the 1936 movement for union with the Damascus regime met no success. But the nationalist movement which was then active inside Syria managed to put so much pressure on the left-leaning 'Popular Front' government now ruling in France that, in September 1936, the French concluded a formal treaty allowing for the phased termination of the direct French administration in Syria.

Almost immediately afterwards, the French opened negotiations with President Eddé for a smiliar agreement with Lebanon. By November 1936, the two sides had arrived at an agreement by which France would recognize Lebanon's independence and sovereignty. In return for this, the Lebanese would commit themselves to military co-operation with the French, and to giving the French other special economic and political concessions in their country. In an annex to the treaty, the two sides concurred in the principle that the Lebanese Republic should guarantee 'the fair representation' of all the country's sects in the government and high administration.

The treaty was quickly approved by all members of the Lebanese Chamber of Deputies, both Christians and Muslims. But Muslim opinion outside the Chamber was outraged by the treaty's supposed confirmation of the country's existing borders, and by the special privileges France would continue to enjoy even after 'independence'. The fierce debate over the treaty sparked widespread demonstrations in the major Muslim areas. In the rapidly growing Beirut suburbs, this debate took on serious sectarian overtones, as Maronite activists hastily organized in paramilitary groups to defend the treaty's terms. The Maronite militants called their *Ketaeb* ('phalanges' – the singular is *katiba*): they were a harbinger of things to come in the suburbs.

In January 1937, in accordance with the ideas expressed in the treaty's annex, President Eddé called on a Sunni Muslim to form a government. This appointment set an important precedent in Lebanese public life. For just as all the elected presidents from Eddé on were Maronites, all the prime ministers after 1937 on, were Sunnis.

The *Ketaeb* groups which made their first public appearance during the troubles of the end of 1936 were part of a movement which was still in its fragile infancy in those days. But in later decades it was to grow to have a formidable influence within the Maronite community, and in 1982 the seventh president of independent Lebanon, Amin Gemayyel, was a Ketaeb Party member.

That the Ketaeb was able to gain such strength was the result both of the leadership provided by the party's founder, Pierre Gemayyel and also of the circumstances which he exploited so adroitly. The most significant of these circumstances was the rapid movement of large numbers of Maronites from their mountain villages to the sprawling suburbs of Beirut.

Pierre Gemayyel had been born in the Mount Lebanon town of Bikfaya in 1905, to a strongly pro-French family of some stature in that town. After the outbreak of the First World War the family was forced to flee to Egypt. There, and later in Beirut, young Pierre gained his education in Jesuit schools and colleges, eventually graduating as a pharmacist from the French School of Medicine in Beirut.

From his early youth, Pierre harboured a strong interest in sports. One early picture published by the Ketaeb Party archives shows him as referee in a 1927 soccer match between a local Beirut team and a Labour Zionist 'Ha Poel' team, from nearby Palestine. Nine years later he was to follow up his sports interest in another way – he flew to Germany to see the 1936 Berlin Olympics.

Those Olympics were a source of world-wide controversy because they were being hosted by Adolf Hitler's Nazi Party which had ruled Germany for the previous three years. Gemayyel was apparently not daunted by the controversy: he enjoyed the Games, but especially, he enjoyed seeing how his Nazi hosts had organized their paramilitary youth groups. After his return to Beirut, he set about emulating their example. The name of the groups he set up was borrowed from the appellation of General Franco's fascist groups in Spain – 'les Phalanges libanaises'.

In November 1936, the first 'Phalanges' (or in Arabic, *Ketaeb*) started practising their formal marching drill in the East Beirut sports field used by the 'Railway and Port Club'. From the beginning, betraying its origins, this drill was punctuated with Nazi-style salutes. Over the years which followed, Gemayyel united the 'Phalanges' into the single political party which bore their name. From its earliest days onwards, the movement was always to retain its strongest base among the newly-urbanized Maronites of the East Beirut suburbs. It also retained its emphasis on physical fitness and military training: one constant feature of Ketaeb Party life was its holding of prolonged annual summer camps, at which members would hone their para-military skills.

Gemayyel's emerging movement stood aside from the major debate which was raging inside the Maronite community in the 1930s – that between Emil Eddé and Bishara al-Khoury. The young Phalangist boss rejected Khoury's stress on the need for co-operation with the Muslims; and he rejected Eddé's reliance on the French. Rejecting some of the traditions within his own family, Gemayyel sought to build a movement which was determinedly Lebanese rather than French – although he himself always spoke French much better than Arabic.

The Phalangists – and later the Ketaeb Party – generally presented themselves as opposed to the entrenched power of all the sect leaders in Lebanon, including those within their own Maronite community. Indeed, they often swore that they were opposed to the whole institutionalization of sect differences, such as had resulted from the application of the constitution's confessional principle.

However, the Ketaeb Party was seldom able to present a persuasive picture of itself as non-sectarian. Sometimes, in its public posturing, it appeared to be trying to do so. And at some stages it was able to attract a limited following within the Shi-ite Muslim community. But at times of particular crisis its actions always seemed to reflect merely the sectional vision of the Maronites who formed its backbone. Nearly always their net effect was to defend against any inroads into the Maronite ascendancy in Lebanon.

Most of Gemayyel's early lieutenants were, like him, young professional people who were first-generation immigrants to the suburbs. Over the years after 1936, many of them peeled away from the movement. But a hard core stuck by Gemayyel, even through the long decades when a majority of Maronites would continue to think of them as little more than a lunatic fringe. Thus, at moments when the Lebanese system was going through a period of stress – as was to happen in 1945, in 1958, and then from the 1970s onwards – Gemayyel and his disciplined core were there, ready to take advantage of the circumstances.

Under the terms of the 1936 treaty, France was supposed to support Lebanon's application for membership of the League of Nations, as a fully independent nation, at the end of 1939. However, only weeks before that deadline was reached the Second World War erupted. Once again, the hopeful course for Lebanese politics was to fall hostage to the broader strategic interests of the imperial power.

On 21 September 1939, the High Commissioner suspended the Lebanese constitution. Then, as had happened in 1932, the sitting president was retained as a president by appointment.

In June 1940, Germany invaded France, where they backed the government with the collaborator Marshal Philippe Pétain set up in Vichy, well away from Paris. In December, the Vichy regime appointed a General to the High Commission in Beirut. (This move was ominously reminiscent of the Ottomans' establishment of military government in Mount Lebanon in 1915.)

As in the earlier world war, food supplies became increasingly scarce throughout Lebanon. In April 1941, popular dissatisfaction with president-by-appointment Eddé came to a head, and the French were forced to remove him from what was by then only a very nominal presidency of the Republic.

Meanwhile, French patriots throughout the world who called themselves the 'Free French' were working with the Allied armies to undermine the Vichy regime and its German backers. In June 1941, British and other Allied forces made their way up from Palestine into Lebanon and Syria. As they did so, their aircraft dropped thousands of leaflets, in which the Free French proclaimed their commitment to the sovereignty and independence of the two countries. And after the Allied takeover of Lebanon and Syria was completed the following month, the new Free French administrator who was installed in Beirut repeated that undertaking.

However, the actual regime in Lebanon changed little with the Allied takeover, and the Free French appeared reluctant to move with any speed towards their stated aim of Lebanese self-rule. But it was the British, not the Free French, who had provided most of the manpower for the move into Lebanon and Syria. It was thus the British who had the most at stake in the military security of the region. One of their primary concerns was to prevent any upsurge in local opposition sentiment in the two countries which might undermine the military security of the region. So the British were for ever prodding the Free French, in private and in public, to move faster towards self-rule in Lebanon and Syria.

In February 1942, Major-General Sir Edward Spears was appointed British Minister to Syria and Lebanon, with his headquarters in Beirut. Two months later he began to urge that elections be held in the two countries. The local and British pressures then mounted on the French to concur in this, until in March 1943 the French Delegate-General finally agreed to restore the Lebanese and Syrian constitutions.

The French continued to aim for a favourable outcome from the elections, supporting a move which would have given the Christians thirty-two seats in the Chamber of Deputies and the Muslims only twenty-two. But under British pressure, the composition of the House was finally fixed at thirty Christian seats and twenty-five Muslim seats. Elections were held on this basis in late summer 1943 and Bishara al-Khoury was elected president.

Khoury had established good contacts with the British over the preceding months, and had consolidated his longstanding links with the Lebanese Muslims. In the spring of 1942, several prominent members of the Sunni Sulh family, based in Beirut and Sidon, had advocated a new formula for Christian–Muslim coexistence in Lebanon which came to be known as the National Pact.

Almost immediately after his election as president in 1943, Khoury called on Riyadh al-Sulh to be his first premier. The National Pact then became an unofficial but pivotal part of the Lebanese constitution throughout the first forty years of the life of the independent Lebanese Republic. The fact that the Pact's terms were never formally spelt out or publicly defined generally gave the agreement the strength of some flexibility – but the studied ambiguity involved also proved a weakness at periods of extreme political tension.

Already, under the French Mandate, the principle had been established whereby the president would be a Maronite, and the prime minister a Sunni Muslim. The National Pact was further to formalize this division of the top posts within the administration. It was now also agreed in the Pact that the Speaker of the House should be a Shi-ite; and that whereas the commander of the army should be a Maronite, his chief of staff should be a Druze.

The National Pact also endorsed the principle already established, whereby the country's Christian sects should have six representatives at any given level of government to every five Muslim representatives. Thus every Lebanese Parliament elected throughout the forty years following 1943 contained a number of members which was a multiple of eleven, divided in these proportions. And these same proportions were to be observed throughout all levels of the country's administration.

No sooner had Sulh formed his first government than the Lebanese opened negotiations with the French for the total termination of the mandatory regime. The Lebanese government was aiming to reach an amendment of the 1926 constitution which would remove all the special privileges granted therein to the French. But the Free French leaders huffily replied that they would not allow unilateral Lebanese moves against the mandate. As a result of this the Lebanese, probably still supported by the British, convened a special session of parliament in November 1943, at which the proposed constitutional amendments were unanimously accepted (in the notable absence of Emil Eddé).

On 9 November, President Khoury countersigned this parliamentary bill. Two days later, French troops arrested him and his leading ministers in a midnight raid, and the French administrator announced the total suspension of the constitution. This action united Lebanese Christian and Muslim opinion against the French. Two members of Sulh's cabinet had escaped the arrests, and made their way to a village in the Shouf where they proclaimed the continued legitimacy of their government. The French imposed a rigid curfew in Beirut. But this was not enough to prevent massive demonstrations, organzied by both the Ketaeb and by parallel Muslim organizations.

Finally, on 22 November 1943, the French had to give way. President Khoury and his ministers, who had all become national heroes, were released from jail. The French Mandate over Lebanon was over.

During the year that followed the ending of the French Mandate, the political powers which the French High Commissioner had previously exercised were gradually turned over to the Lebanese president. The French retained only certain military prerogatives in the country.

In May 1945, the Allies finally won the war in Europe. The Lebanese then expected that the French would renounce their remaining military powers in the country. But instead, the French immediately set about reinforcing their garrisons in both Lebanon and Syria. And they told the governments in the two countries that they wanted to reinstate the special treaties which had formerly given France such wide powers over their foreign, defence and economic policies.

The behaviour of the French outraged local opinion in both countries, and a number of open clashes erupted between the local population and the arriving French reinforcements. Finally, at the end of May, the French went as far as bombarding some particularly nationalist parts of Damascus. At that point, the British stepped in. Forcefully, they told the French to abandon their ambitions in Syria and Lebanon, and to promise to evacuate their troops from them.

The French had only recently won their own liberation from Nazi Germany. So they were still very dependent on the British military, in the Middle East as elsewhere. Once they had understood the seriousness of the British demands, they rapidly agreed to comply. They left Syria during that same summer of 1945 and by the end of 1946 had completed their withdrawal from Lebanon. And though the British had succeeded in persuading the French to withdraw from the two countries, they did not themselves immediately try to replace them there.

Ever since November 1943, Lebanon had enjoyed many of the elements of political independence. To this was now added – for the first time ever in modern times – the full sovereignty of the local government.

The Lebanese Republic's attainment of independence and sovereignty in the 1940s was possible because of a lucky combination of external and internal factors.

Externally, the Lebanese were indeed fortunate that their moves towards independence had been viewed with favour by Britain, which throughout that decade remained the single strongest power in the East Mediterranean region. Of course, the main motivation of the British was probably little linked to any intrinsic desire to do the Lebanese a good turn. The first British priority in Lebanon in that period is much more likely to have been their reluctance to see the re-emergence of French influence in the region.

But whatever the motivations of the British, their decision proved a happy one for the Lebanese. And more particularly so, since it soon became clear in the post-war years that the major regional concern of the British was to trim down a colonial presence which had become over-extended and burdensome there, rather than to seek aggressively to expand it. For the Lebanese, this meant that the crucial first years of the country's independence were spent under the general umbrella of a world power which, happily for them, sought to keep its own intervention in their system to a minimum.

The principal internal support on which independence had been built was the 1943 National Pact. This Pact represented a significant new phase in the inter-sect system which had evolved inside Lebanon over the centuries. For while it did not challenge the clear primacy within the system which the Maronites had enjoyed since 1861, it now for the first time allotted the 'second place' in the system to the Sunni Muslims. Moreover, the *kinds* of Maronites whom the Pact brought into first place were now predominantly the urban merchants and bankers, rather than the Mountain clan leaders who had dominated the historical collaboration with the Druze. The principal Sunni parties to the Pact, meanwhile, represented the urban merchant interests which had always dominated the Sunni community. The Pact therefore signified an important sociological change in the content of the principal inter-sect coalition in Lebanon. The coalition was now primarily one between mercantile city interests, rather than an entente between clan leaders in the inaccessible Mountain.

The mercantile city interests were certainly on the upswing in Lebanon in the latter years of the Second World War. As one scholar has noted, 'During World War I Lebanon had suffered as much as most of the belligerents but World War II brought it nothing but gain. From 1940 to 1944, inclusive, allied expenditure in Lebanon and Syria totalled 76 million pounds sterling and from 1939 to 1945, inclusive, these countries had a surplus of 607 million Lebanese-Syrian pounds in their current account.'[2] It is probably safe to bet that a high proportion of those military expenditures had been made in Beirut, whose port played a vital role in the Allied armies' supply operations in the region.

The National Pact explicitly dislodged from 'second place' the Druze, whose original compact with the Maronites had formed the historical basis of the inter-sect system itself. But the Druze, whose weight in the population had continued to dwindle, could probably live with this, so long as they felt that their position in their Mount Lebanon heartland would not come under threat. Their continued strength within the national army, as enshrined in the National Pact, seemed to offer them sufficient guarantees of this.

The other main 'losers', or rather 'non-winners', from the National

Pact system were the country's Shi-ite Muslims. But back in the 1940s the Shi-ites still seemed little able to pose any significant threat to the National Pact system.

The Shi-ites, after all, did not have much significant presence in either Beirut or central Mount Lebanon, which were the two key areas able to affect the political process in the capital. Indeed, isolated in their remote villages, the great mass of Shi-ites had yet to participate directly in *any* national political system. For the present, the right of the feudal landlords to lead the whole Shi-ite community remained barely questioned by their constituents. And the big Shi-ite landlords themselves posed no threat at all to the National Pact. For like French Mandatory rule before it, the Pact served to strengthen, rather than weaken, their hold over their own community.

The major problem inherent in the National Pact, indeed, arose not from its 'reduction' of the Druze or Shi-ite role, but from the elevation of the Sunnis. For the Sunnis were a group whose commitment to the principle of separateness from its neighbours, on which the inter-sect system had historically arisen inside Lebanon, remained as yet untested.

As recently as 1936, the consensus expressed within the Sunni community had supported integration with Syria. What had happened between 1936 and 1943 to make the Sunni leaders change their minds on this issue?

Some Sunni leaders, especially those in Tripoli and other 'outlying' parts of the country, had never really done so. These Sunnis had many long family and business links with the Syrian interior. They had agreed to go along with the National Pact not because they had any great commitment to its vision as such, but primarily as a means of getting rid of the French. And once the French had gone, agitation in support of union with Syria resumed in many Sunni-populated parts of Lebanon (as it did among much smaller numbers of radicalized Shi-ites, and members of other sects).

The Sunni merchant-leaders of Beirut had much more at stake in the national pact than their counterparts in Tripoli. They had a long and profitable history of business collaboration with the Maronites and other Christians, and could certainly share in the vision of an ultra-liberal merchant republic which President Khoury held out to them.

For over a century already, Beirut's port had been expanding its operations at the expense of Tripoli's historically much busier harbour. Then, in the early 1940s, the business the Allied armies had brought to Beirut port had caused it far to outstrip its previous local competitors. The wave of super-profits Beirut's large Sunni trading-houses accrued in those years must certainly have helped them to decide in favour of keeping their operations well out of the reach of the socialist and statist political movements which were active at that time in the Syrian interior.

For the Sunni leaders of Beirut, compromise with the Maronites – even conceding the Maronites' political primacy – was a small price to pay for keeping their environment safe for the untrammelled operations of merchant capitalism. Inside Maronite society, meanwhile, the National Pact had been championed by similar kinds of social forces. Maronite bankers and traders, and the smaller kinds of Beirut business people who were the backbone of the Ketaeb Party, provided President Khoury with a key base of support in his own community. In vain might some traditional Maronite politicians from the Mountain express reservations about the Sunnis' partnership in the Pact.

The economic boom Beirut had experienced during the years the Allied armies were there offered a foretaste to the whole Beirut business community of the future which might await them under continued British auspices. Already, during the war, the explosion of Beirut's communications with the Arabian interior had opened up many new horizons for the city's businessmen. They saw clearly that in the post-war world it would be Britain, rather than France, which would be the prime power throughout the region. How wise it must have seemed, then, to continue to put their bets on the British.

Notes

1   Hourani (1981), p. 138.
2   Charles Issawi in Binder (ed.) (1966), p. 73.

'Town life'

4 The experience of independence (1943–67)

In late 1946, the final evacuation of the French left Lebanon nominally 'independent' for the first time in the modern era. From the beginning, the Lebanese politicians themselves well understood the economic and geopolitical limitations on the 'independence'. In this, they were perhaps luckier than leaders in other Third World countries, who often came to learn about these limitations only well after the first hard years of political independence. The Lebanese also had another asset. By the time they attained political independence, they already had more of the fundamentals of a national political community than were evident in many other newly-independent 'nations'.

By 1946, a specifically 'Lebanese' system had been emerging inside the Mount Lebanon interior for 350 years. The basic components of this system were twofold. The system was *separate* from those of its neighbours. And it involved some kind of *co-operation* between the different sects which participated in it.

By 1946, too, further refinements had been built on the basis of those long traditions. In 1926, the country had acquired a constitution, which specified that it should have a political system which was both *republican* and *democratic*. The constitution had further specified that the opportunity to participate in the administration should be *divided fairly* between members of the country's different sects.

The constitution had built a first political storey on top of the foundations provided by the older, inter-sect traditions. A second storey was then added on to the first: this was the National Pact of 1943, which gave precise definitions of how the *fair division* of posts in the state apparatus, as advocated in the constitution, should be implemented. The country's pesident should be a Maronite; its premier a Sunni Muslim; the Speaker of the House a Shi-ite Muslim; parliamentary seats should be divided between Christians and Muslims in a 6-to-5 ratio; and so on.

These three levels of internal agreement which had evolved inside

Lebanon over the years certainly provided the country with a firm basis on which to face the challenges of 'independence'. Moreover, during the late 1940s and early 1950s Lebanon witnessed a continuation of the kind of heightened economic activity which the Allied armies had first brought during the Second World War. So the country was not – as were so many of its newly-independent counterparts elsewhere – immediately plunged into a kind of economic anguish which might strangle its effective political system at birth.

Independent Lebanon, thus, had both a democratic constitution, and some experience of democratic practice. But in the workings of Lebanese democracy, many traces of the country's older political traditions continued to be evident.

The constitution had provided for a French-style system in Lebanon, with the prime emphasis laid on the role of a strong president. (During the French Mandate, of course, he had always been subject to an ultimate French veto, which was vigorously applied at various stages.) But the constitution also provided for the holding of regular elections to a parliament which had to vote its approval for the major actions of the president.

Parliamentary elections were held on schedule in Lebanon, from independence right down to 1976, when the sitting parliament started extending its own term. They were in general remarkably free of presidential or army interference – though the president could always influence participants strongly, by promising the many political favours at his disposal to this or that grouping. Despite many relatively promising starts, however, a Western-style party system never really took deep root in Lebanon. Neither modern ideologies, nor modern-style economic interests, ever became the voters' prime concern. Instead, time and again, the much older traditions, family and sect, re-emerged at the ballot box.

Candidates for election would always base their campaigns on a specific kind of local leader called a *za«im* (leader, the plural is *zu«ama'*). A *za«im* could win over key family-heads to his campaign. Or, he could try to hinder the efforts of rival *zu«ama'*, by force, if necessary.

The activities of rural and urban *zu«ama'* differed slightly. But the main appeals of both kinds of *za«im* were always to ancient clan or sect loyalties. A successful *za«im* could win a wide reputation as effective in a certain district. Candidates would vie for his backing with offers of jobs in, or contracts from, a victorious administration. It was a self-perpetuating system.

The situation which resulted from the continuation of the *za«im* system in Lebanon was brilliantly summed up in a paper written in the mid 1960s by the percipient American sociologist Edward Shils. 'The Lebanese Parliament', he wrote, '. . . cannot educate Lebanese public opinion both because it cannot debate with a view to decision, and because there is no public in Lebanon. There are only consti-tuencies defined by primordial attachments and beliefs, and parliamentary discussion can play little part in the definition of their interests.'[1]

In that same paper, Shils concluded that, twenty years after independence, Lebanon's political system still remained very fragile indeed. Two vital conditions were needed, he added, if it were to develop into 'a genuinely democratic system'. The first of these was 'the continuation of Lebanese prosperity', and the second was 'the quiescence of the political life of the Middle East'.

Shils's words were published in 1966, and already, dark storm-clouds were gathering over Lebanon's horizons in both the fields he mentioned. But those same factors – local prosperity and regional quiescence – had also played a key role twenty years earlier, in prompting the relatively smooth emergence of the independent Republic of Lebanon.

Lebanon's regional environment had always, as we have seen in earlier chapters, been able to exert strong influence on the local political system which emerged inside the Mountain over the centuries.

Throughout the period from 1946 to 1976, Lebanon's principal environment in the East Mediterranean was dominated by apolari-zation between the West and the Arabs. (Just as, in an earlier era, it had witnessed the intense competition between Western Europe and the Ottomans.)

In 1946, the Western pole in the region was represented by Britain, whose troops had dominated the East Mediterranean since the end of the Second World War. However, following the abortive invasion of Suez in 1956, in which Britain participated, British strength in the region was rapidly replaced by that of the United States. In a slightly different way from the British, the US thereafter upheld the Western end of region's polarization.

If the Western pole in the region was occupied by first one and then another Western power, the Arab pole was meanwhile under multiple occupancy. In the preceding century, the 'European' interests that had confronted the Ottomans in the East Mediterranean had constituted a Concert of Europe which was often lacking in internal harmony. Similarly, the Arab interests which formed one pole of the post-Second World War environment were an oft-disharmonious Concert of Arabia.

The Arab states in the region were still, in the mid 1940s, emerging from colonial pasts towards their national independence. In March 1945, Lebanon had been one of the five founder members of the League of Arab States, also called the Arab League. From the first days of its independence it was thus tied into the Arab state 'system', and affected by developments within it.

It soon became clear that Syria would be the Arab power wielding the most direct influence over Lebanon. Syria's influence over Lebanon was enormous, not least because of the stranglehold it could exert over Lebanon's important land communications with the Arab interior. (From 1949 until 1976, Lebanon's southern border with Israel remained closed.)

Successive Syrian regimes did not hesitate to demonstrate their power over Lebanon. In periods when they were displeased with the policies of Beirut, they would underline their displeasure by closing the entire border. Lebanese agricultural produce, expressly raised for profitable sale in the Arabian interior and suitable for no other market, would start to rot in the ground, or in its vast refrigerated wagons. The government in Beirut had better listen to Damascus!

Lebanon's relations with independent Syria were further complicated by the fact that it had long been a basic tenet of Syrian nationalists that Lebanon *was an integral part of Syria*. In the days of the French Mandate, unionist agitation throughout Syria had resulted in the integration of three other separate administrations, which the French had originally established there, into the regime run from Damascus. Successive post-independence regimes in Syria continued to demand that Lebanon be likewise integrated – and this demand was echoed by many voices within Lebanon.

The Syrians expressed their ideological stand on this issue by doggedly refusing to establish formal diplomatic relations with Beirut. The two countries were joined in a Customs Union until 1950, and continued to be bound together by many other practical and administrative links even after that.

Syria was clearly the Arab regime with strongest influence over Lebanon. But it was not the only Arab regime influential there. Indeed, at the level of the whole East Mediterranean region as such,

Egypt was much more powerful than Syria; and it, too, had many means of influencing Lebanon. Many Lebanese – often those who raised the slogan of 'Arab nationalism' – were happy to encourage the Egyptians and other Arab states to counter-balance Syrian pressures. Syria and Egypt were thus the first and second violins in Lebanon's post-independence Concert of Arabia.

When those two outside regimes were at peace with each other, and with the power which occupied the Western pole of influence, Lebanon could find the regional quiescence it needed. But when, as often happened, they were not all at peace, their rivalry (and the supplementary interventions of all the other, less powerful, Arab regimes) could result in a cacophony in Lebanon reminiscent of the worst days of the Concert of Europe (see Chapter 2).

How lucky for Lebanon, then, that the first few years of its independence coincided with a period when neither of the major poles of its regional environment was able to maintain a very aggressive policy there. The power then occupying the Western pole, Britain, was finding it hard to adjust to the harsh facts of post-war life, and was in no mood at all for new imperial adventures. And the Concert of Arabia had no sooner started tuning its international instruments in the mid 1940s, than most of them were smashed in the disastrous Arab-Jewish fighting in Palestine in 1948. That fighting left the Arab regimes humiliated and confused.

The 1948 war also affected Lebanon. But it never had the same terribly de-stabilizing effect there that it did in Egypt or Syria. For centuries, Lebanon had been marching to a political tune which was separate from, though still strongly influenced by, that of its Arab neighbours.

Indeed, rather than suffering along with its Arab 'sisters', Lebanon ultimately profited from the instability they lived through in the late 1940s and early 1950s. Their instability kept the Concert of Arabia weak, at a time when the East Mediterranean's Western pole was weak anyway.

Moreover, the Arabs' instability in those years sent to Lebanon a vast flow of fugitive Arab capital. Fleeing the rampant statism which threatened to prevail in Cairo, Damascus and Baghdad, that capital found safety in the determinedly free markets of Beirut.

It also provided independent Lebanon, at its birth, with the 'prosperity' which Shils was later to identify as necessary for the smooth development of the country's democratic system. It was a very particular kind of economic boom, dominated by bankers, gold traders and local investment experts, that Lebanon experienced in the late 1940s and early 1950s. It was on the crest of that wave of prosperity that independent Lebanon began its history.

In 1943, Bishara al-Khoury began his term as Lebanon's first president with a broad base of popular support. He had won this primarily because of the political alliance which he, a Maronite Christian, maintained with his first premier, the Sunni Muslim leader Riyadh al-Sulh. Sulh had been one of the authors of the 1943 National Pact, which had put the Maronites and Sunnis in first and second places in the Lebanese political firmament.

However, several developments worked to erode Khoury's popularity towards the end of the 1940s. These centred around accusations that his friends and relations had acquired large amounts of wealth throughout the early years of his presidency.

In 1947, the independent Republic held its first parliamentary elections. Afterwards, Khoury was accused of having used undue influence to try to secure a Chamber favourable to his own ambitions. Sure enough, a year later, the parliament passed a bill allowing Khoury a special renewal of his presidential term, which would otherwise have expired in 1949. This move alienated some of Khoury's closest supporters, especially Camille Chamoun, a Maronite member of his bloc who had hoped to succeed him to the presidency.

Instability was meanwhile growing throughout the East Mediterranean region, and this denied the infant nation an easy environment for its first steps in independence. In 1948, Britian's withdrawal from Palestine led to a full-scale war, in the course of which the Palestinian Jews declared the establishment of the new State of Israel.

Lebanon had been a founder member of the Arab League in 1945, so there was some pressure on the Lebanese government to join the other Arab states which despatched their armies in an ill-fated attempt to 'save' Arab Palestine. The Lebanese authorities were able to resist these pressures. But they could not prevent the efforts of those Lebanese and other volunteers who made their way through south Lebanon to join the fighting against the new Jewish state.

By March 1949, Lebanon had become one of the first of the Arab governments to sign an armistice agreement with Israel. But the armistice did not provide for the return to the Israeli-held areas of the scores of thousands of Arab Palestinians who had fled to Lebanon to escape the fighting at home. Many of the refugees, in Lebanon as in the other countries ringing Israel, were destitute. As they crowded round Lebanon's cities looking for work or aid, they were gradually settled into vast refugee camps ringing the major urban areas, which were administered by a specially-created United Nations agency, UNRWA.

In March 1949, the army in Syria overthrew the constitutional regime there. Thus, Lebanon's weighty neighbour was plunged into a series of coups and counter-coups which was to last throughout most of the 1950s and 1960s.

As though inspired by events in Syria, in July 1949 the members of a conspiratorial grouping called the Parti Populaire Syrien (Syrian Popular Party, or PPS) tried to mount a coup against the Khoury regime in Lebanon. The coup failed. But the Lebanese government then tried to suppress all the country's paramilitary organizations, along with the PPS. This forced the Maronite-dominated Ketaeb group and a parallel Sunni paramilitary organization to withdraw their former support for the regime.

1949 was also the year that Kamal Jumblatt, youthful scion of the powerful Druze clan leaders of the Shouf, organized his followers into the Progressive Socialist Party (PSP), which agitated strongly for administrative and political reform. By the time the next parliamentary elections came round in 1951, there were thus powerful opposition forces arrayed against the president, which made their influence felt in the new Chamber. The opposition to Khoury was still extremely heterogeneous, but the main opposition groupings allied themselves in a loose front which they called – with no great accuracy – the Socialist Front.

However, as long as Khoury could rely on the support of his Sunni Muslim ally Riyadh al-Sulh, his presidency did not seem in jeopardy. Then in the summer of 1951, plotters of the PPS were able to assassinate Sulh while he was on a visit to Jordan.

By 16 September 1952, the Socialist Front was ready to move. Khoury was facing yet another of the string of cabinet crises that had occurred since the killing of Sulh, when the Front declared a general strike, demanding his resignation. Khoury asked the army to step in to break the strike. But the army commander, a descendant of Lebanon's former princely Shihab rulers called Fuad al-Shihab, refused to do so. On 18 September, Khoury resigned, and five days later parliament met and elected Camille Chamoun to succeed him.

Chamoun had been born in the Shouf town of Dair al-Qamar in 1900. In 1916, his father had been one of those exiled from Lebanon by the

Ottomans on suspicion of harbouring pro-French sympathies. Once the French regained their influence in Lebanon after the end of the world war, the family was able to return. Camille Chamoun was first elected to the Chamber of Deputies from the Shouf constituency during the early years of the French Mandate, in 1929.

He held that seat continuously from then until his election as president in 1952, and then again from 1968 right through to the early 1980s. During the crises of the late 1970s and early 1980s, Chamoun thus stood out as the oldest and longest-lasting – as well as one of the most intransigent and feisty – of the major Maronite leaders.

Chamoun did not come from one of the old-established ruling families. Back in 1952, he was still known mainly for the close links he was thought to enjoy with the powerful British. He had been Ambassador in London from 1944 to 1947, and then after a brief period at the United Nations he became Lebanon's representative on the Council of the Arab League.

Throughout his six years as president, Chamoun adopted foreign policy positions staunchly in line with his pro-Western leanings. In 1955, he supported the conclusion of the Baghdad Pact, a British attempt to tie up an anti-Soviet military alliance between the countries along the central section of the USSR's southern flank. (He did not enrol Lebanon into the Pact, however, for fear of antagonizing Arab public opinion.) The same year, he disapproved the move taken by Egypt's new military ruler, Colonel Gamal Abdel-Nasser, to nationalize the British-owned Suez Canal. And when, in 1956, Britain, France and Israel joined in a military campaign against Egypt, he resisted Arab pressures to break off diplomatic links with Britain and France

These policies in the field of external affairs had grave consequences for President Chamoun's ability to conduct internal affairs, for they alienated a growing tide of Lebanese Muslim opinion. In the case of the Shi-ite Muslims, Chamoun was relatively successful in maintaining enough alliances with the Shi-ite feudal leaders to ensure him of the community's overall support. But from the more powerful Sunnis and the Druze he quickly came to face opposition.

None of the group of Sunni politicians who had become contenders for the premiership after Riyadh al-Sulh's death had inherited his broad command of the Sunni constituency. So for a while, Chamoun was able to make his choice between four or five second-echelon Sunni leaders. This gave him great power to 'divide and rule' his Sunni subjects. For example, in November 1956, when Chamoun refused to join other Arab heads of state in breaking off relations with Britain and France, his Sunni premier resigned. But Chamoun was almost immediately able to replace him with another Sunni contender.

The self-confidence of the Sunni community at the level of its important public opinion – the 'Sunni street' – was meanwhile on the upswing. Sunni confidence had been badly battered since the break-up of the Ottoman empire after the First World War. Now, it was becoming buoyed up especially by Nasser's rise to power in Egypt in 1952–4, and by the defiance with which he stood up to European powers. Sunni public opinion, including many of those sectors which had previously agitated for union with Syria, was now riveted on the blunt and youthful leader in Cairo, and on his voice as transmitted regularly on Egypt's powerful 'Voice of the Arabs' broadcasts.

Chamoun may have been able, at the formal governmental level, airily to dismiss the demand which Sunni politicians raised for more Muslim 'participation' in governing Lebanon. But, meanwhile, a combination of internal grievances and the appeal of Nasserism was setting the Sunni community as a whole on to a collision course with him.

In the Druze community, Kamal Jumblatt discovered only too soon after the 1952 elections that the victory of his temporary ally Chamoun would not bring him any additional power. Indeed, Chamoun seemed determined to cut his Shouf neighbour right out from any real influence under his presidency. Jumblatt thus redoubled his calls for political reform; and he spent the years Chamoun was in power planning his revenge against him. Chamoun rubbed further salt into Jumblatt's wound by according new political favours to another Druze leader, Emir Majid Arslan. Arslan's family had by now assumed the leadership of the 'Yazbeki' faction of the Druze – historic rivals of the Jumblatts.

In 1957, all these developments came to a head. In March of that year, Chamoun announced his acceptance of the 'Eisenhower Doctrine', which enabled friendly governments overseas to call in the military help of the US in the face of outside threats. Both Syria and Egypt had derisively rejected the Eisenhower Doctrine, which they considered aimed against themselves. Chamoun's acceptance now placed Lebanon in open opposition to these two influential Arab states.

Within Lebanon, the Sunni sympathizers of Nasser's ringing pan-Arabism were not the only critics of Chamoun's move. Jumblatt was also extremely hostile, as were many influential voices even inside the

Christian communities. Within the Maronite community, no less a figure than the Patriarch, Boulos Méouchy, openly deemed it folly for the Lebanese government to align itself against Syria and Egypt in this way. So too did serious political rivals to Chamoun such as former President Khoury and the northern Maronite figure Hamid Frangieh. Frangieh was one of seven parliamentary deputies who resigned in protest of the government's position during a debate on the Eisenhower Doctrine.

Chamoun's main bases of support were now found in two Christian groupings which were still relative outsiders to the traditional Lebanese game of lordly power-broking. These were the Ketaeb Party, and Bishara al-Khoury's old opponents in the PPS.

The PPS had acquired its appellation as the 'Parti Populaire Syrien' from the description given it by the French in the days of their pre-war mandate in Palestine. The name the party itself preferred was the Syrian Social Nationalist Party, but in Lebanon they were known generally as either 'the PPS' or just 'the Nationalists'.

The PPS had been founded in 1932 by a Greek Orthodox emigrant who had just returned to Lebanon after a period in Latin America. As implied by their name for the party, party members held to the idea of the existence of a pan-Syrian nation. This nation, they said, was made up of the original inhabitants of present-day Syria, Lebanon, Jordan, Israel, Iraq, Cyprus and parts of Turkey.

Viewing the concept of this nation with near-reverence, PPS members believed all other interests should be subordinated to trying to bring about its full political realization. They opposed pan-Arabism, communism, sectarianism and individualism all with equal vigour; and British imperialism only slightly less than French. Tightly organized in close-knit cells, down to the early 1980s party members retained a near-fascist type of salute as their personal greeting, accompanied by the intonation of a ritual 'Long live Syria'.

The main bulk of PPS membership was always in Lebanon, but it also had active groups of adherents in Syria and Palestine. While the PPS drew some members from nearly all the region's many religious groups, the core membership mainly belonged to the founder's own Greek Orthodox church. The PPS was the heir to one of the longest-standing trends of thought in the Lebanese Christian community, as described in Chapter 2.

The Ketaeb saw themselves as heir to another longstanding Lebanese intellectual tradition – that advocating a specifically

Lebanese nationalism, and involving some implied degree of Christian domination.

The PPS had amply demonstrated its power in Lebanon when it killed Riyadh al-Sulh in 1951. But for a long time thereafter, the Ketaeb remained more on the fringes of Lebanese political life. In the Maronite villages it was largely irrelevant to the continuing age-old patterns of brokering local power, and among the Maronite upper-crust of the cities it was deemed thuggish and unsophisticated. The main power-base of the party was among the middle and lower classes of the newly-urbanized Maronites. Throughout the 1950s, these new city-dwellers were growing rapidly in number. And they were slowly breaking away from the traditional political ties of their villages.

It was with some strong-arm help from members of these two parties that Chamoun staged the parliamentary elections in June 1957. Groups and individuals opposed to the president lost out badly in the elections. Kamal Jumblatt and former Premier Abdallah Yafi were among the many popular opposition leaders who lost their long-held seats. The opposition then immediately accused Chamoun of having manipulated the voting in order to obtain a Chamber that would renew his presidential term, due to expire the following year.

Denied an effective platform in the parliament, some strands of the opposition turned to violence. In the Shouf, Druze followers of Jumblatt started blowing up roads and bridges. In Beirut, unexplained bomb explosions shattered the calm of many neighbourhoods.

In February 1958, a further spark was thrown into what was already an incendiary situation in Lebanon. Towards the end of that month, Syrian officials travelled to Egypt to ask President Nasser for union between their two countries. When the formation of the resulting 'United Arab Republic' (UAR) was announced on 22 February, Nasser's power in the whole East Mediterranean region soared to new heights. The influence he could now exert over Lebanon had multiplied dramatically, overnight.

Wisely, Chamoun did extend formal congratulations to President Nasser on hearing news of the merger. But at the same time, he had to brace for the almost inevitable demands he would now face that Lebanon too be included in the new union. The weeks which followed saw pro-union agitation escalating throughout Lebanon, radiating especially from the Sunni-dominated coastal cities.

Then in early May 1958, a prominent Maronite journalist close to the opposition was killed, and his friends assumed government agents were responsible. The loose opposition coalition with Druze, Sunni and other leaders had first put together to fight the elections the previous year now declared a general strike, and demanded the president's resignation. Almost immediately, the strike call triggered violent demonstrations in the heavily Sunni-dominated northern city of Tripoli. With clashes mounting throughout the country, on 13 May Jumblatt's partisans attacked the presidential palace near Dair al-Qamar. The general strike had turned into an insurrection.

The civil war which racked Lebanon in 1958 saw the opposition forces quickly gaining control of a majority of the country's physical area. The demand that the president step down won the support of a broad spectrum of political figures from all the different communities, including his own.

Yet Chamoun, who was probably honestly convinced that he was 'saving Lebanon for Western-style democracy', still hung on in power. As the opposition's threat to the legal forces at his command mounted, in many case Chamoun's legality could be maintained only through recourse to the harassment the rebels met from armed partisans of the Ketaeb or the PPS.

The 1958 civil war did not, however, see a total breakdown of the Lebanese political system. In the immediate theatre of events, this was due as much as anything to the 'neutrality' which Army Commander Fuad Shihab adopted between the pro- and anti-Chamoun forces on the battlefield. But at a deeper level, the ease with which – once Chamoun had resigned in September – a political consensus was re-established among the country's political forces pointed to the persistence of the inter-sect idea inside Lebanon.

When the rebellion started in May 1958, Sidon, Tyre and Tripoli all quickly came under rebel control. In Beirut, the city was divided along largely sectarian lines, with the Sunni-dominated areas held by the rebels and the Christian-dominated areas in the hands of the loyalists. Jumblatt's forces battled Chamoun supporters in the Shouf, and even at one stage looked set to advance victorious from the Shouf highlands down to the foothills immediately overlooking Beirut airport. In many outlying areas of the Beqaa and the Akkar, rebel forces were easily able to take control, backed up by a stream of logistical help from across the border in Syria.

From the beginning of the rebellion, Chamoun and his pro-Western foreign minister accused the UAR of having fomented it – ignoring its many domestic causes completely. The Lebanese government's accusations were taken first to the Council of the Arab League, and then to the United Nations Security Council in New York. On 11 June, the Security Council decided to despatch an observers' mission to Lebanon, to be called UNOGIL (for UN Observation Group in Lebanon).

By early July, UNOGIL was able to make its first report back to the Security Council, in which the Lebanese government's allegations against the UAR were found to be 'not proven'. But because of the complexity of the situation in Lebanon UNOGIL was unable ever to operate effectively.

On 14 July 1958, the crisis in Lebanon suddenly became over-shadowed by a development of much greater moment in the life of the region. This was the republican revolution which overthrew the pro-British monarchy in Iraq. Iraq's King Faisal had been a key pillar of the anti-Soviet Baghdad Pact, which was named after his own country's capital. Now, Faisal and his family were killed, and his Crown Prince's body was dragged through the streets of Baghdad, as the leaders of the revolution tried in vain to hold back the passions of an angry crowd.

The next day, about 2000 US Marines disembarked from the American fleet that had been building up in the East Mediterranean, landing on the beaches south of Beirut, alongside the international airport. Over the next few days, the total Marine presence in Lebanon was to mount to 15,000.

American officials were later to explain that this deployment was connected far more closely to the events in Iraq, and the possible need to intervene there or in pro-Western Jordan, than it was to events in Lebanon. But the ostensible reason for the marines' presence in Lebanon had been provided by Chamoun. He had been horror-struck to hear the first reports of the fate of his close ally, King Faisal. It was under the terms of the controversial Eisenhower Doctrine that he then immediately asked for US intervention in Lebanon.

Chamoun had not, however, thought to notify his own army commander, General Shihab, of his request for US help. On 16 July, some Marines units moved towards Beirut itself, but they found Lebanese army units blocking their way! When he learnt of the confrontation, Shihab hurried to the presidential palace at Baabda, where he found Chamoun already pleading with the American Ambassador to hasten the dispatch of marines to protect government installations in Beirut.

The ensuing negotiations revealed the real mission of the Marines in Lebanon. The final agreement that day allowed marines units of limited size to enter the city in order to protect the US Embassy and other American installations there. Other small marines units could also enter the city and mount patrols in government-held areas there, but only under constant escort from the Lebanese army.

Under the terms of this agreement, the stipulated deployments of the marines took place in Beirut without further incident. But by his intervention, Shihab had made it clear to the Americans that their forces were in Lebanon primarily on his sufferance rather than on Chamoun's. He thus became the man they had to deal with to ensure the security of their forces in Lebanon – whose regional mandate was, after all, far wider and more important than to guarantee merely the survival of Chamoun's already shaky regime in tiny, fractious Lebanon.

When the US Marines landed in Beirut in mid July 1958, Chamoun had just given his first, reluctant promises that he would not try to renew the presidential term which was due to end that September. But the broad consensus of Lebanon's traditional political figures were still not convinced of this. The principal cause of their opposition to him was thus still alive.

An American Under-Secretary of State, Robert Murphy, had been in Beirut trying to untangle the political impasse there since the beginning of the marine deployment. He quickly became convinced that Chamoun should not seek a renewal, and came to favour the succession of Shihab, as did many sections of the Lebanese opposition.

However, it was the same Chamber of Deputies which had been elected under Chamoun's auspices the year before which had the constitutional authority to elect the president. The events of the first half of 1958 had persuaded many of the deputies to move away from the totally pro-Chamoun views they had professed on election. And shortly after the landing of the marines, even the President of the Chamber, Adil Osseiran – formerly a key Chamoun ally – had protested. He called the landing 'an encroachment on Lebanon's independence and sovereignty'.[2]

By 24 July, a session of the Chamber had been scheduled expressly for the election of a new president. But some of Chamoun's supporters were still wary of switching allegiance completely to Shihab. So Osseiran postponed the electoral session a further week, during which time even Chamoun came to be reluctantly convinced to put his weight behind the army commander's candidacy. The opposition privately assured Chamoun, meanwhile – through the mediation of Shihab – that they would allow him to remain in office for the last months of his term.

But amazingly for Lebanon, the last major obstacle to Shihab's election remained the reluctance of the preferred candidate himself to run at all! Certainly, Shihab had already played a politically decisive role as army commander both during the events of 1952 and now throughout the 1958 crisis. Perhaps he was genuinely convinced that it was more important to be the military president-maker than to be the president himself. (And indeed, the contribution made by the generally dismal track-record of successive army commanders to the breakdown of political order during the crisis of the late 1970s might tend to vindicate this belief.) It was not until the eve of the scheduled parliamentary meeting that Shihab finally agreed to run. By then his victory was a foregone conclusion. The following day he was elected by forty-eight votes. The sole opposing candidate, Emil Eddé's son Raymond, garnered a mere seven votes, one bailot was left blank and ten seats in the Chamber remained unfilled.

On 23 September, Shihab took the oath of office as planned. The next day he announced the formation of a government under the premiership of the youthful Rashid Karami from Tripoli. Karami had been the prime candidate of the anti-Chamoun forces for the post, and the first government he put together contained six other opponents of the former president and only one figure who had stood neutral during the weeks of the rebellion.

Chamoun's former supporters had more or less conceded their own defeat before Shihab had been elected. But the first Karami government met with sharp opposition from Chamoun's former allies in the Ketaeb. They feared that the pro-Nasser forces would now use their position in government to dominate the whole country, and perhaps even take it into the Egypt–Syria union.

The Ketaeb had already been upset by the kidnapping of a prominent journalist on the party's daily. On 20 September, they had declared a protest strike against the kidnapping in those parts of Greater Beirut where they were strong. On hearing the composition of the new government, they then extended their strikes and demonstrations in an immediate challenge to the authority of the Shihab regime.

The three weeks which followed saw many of the bloodiest incidents of the whole 1958 events. Many regions of the country became polarized along sectarian lines. Travellers or residents in the 'wrong' areas were kidnapped, and then often tortured or killed. The

Ketaeb showed themselves well able to mine the rich lode of sectarian fear which runs just under the surface of much of Maronite society, and Muslim extremists in some areas retaliated in kind.

By mid October, Shihab had finally worked out a solution, which was based on the inclusion of the Ketaeb for the first time ever in the Lebanese government. On 14 October, Karami announced the formation of a new four-man government, in which he and another Sunni minister would be joined by Ketaeb leader Pierre Gemayyel, and failed presidential candidate Eddé.

This movement the Ketaeb would later laud as their 'counter-revolution'. But the formula through which Shihab had solved the problem soon became described as the 'no victor, no vanquished' principle. This principle was then incorporated as an additional tenet of Lebanese public life. Its status as such was to remain unchallenged until 1982.

On 27 October, in a footnote to the Lebanese crisis, the last American troops left Lebanon. Their broader mission in the region had been achieved. In Lebanon itself, the skill of American diplomacy had kept them well clear of any direct involvement in the fighting. They had suffered one casualty, killed by a sniper's bullet.

The Shihab presidency ushered in a new era in Lebanese politics. The descendant of the former princes of Lebanon who now occupied the presidential palace tried to forge a new national identity not based on allegiance to individual leaders. In later years, the epithet 'Chamoun-ist' was used to describe persons loyal to Camille Chamoun himself. The epithet 'Shihabist', by contrast, came to describe those loyal to the whole nation-building outlook which President Shihab brought to his task.

The era when 'Shihabism' was in control in Lebanon covered both Shihab's own term (1958–64), and that of his successor and disciple, Charles Hélou (1964–70). Throughout most of those years – at least, up until the regional disruptions of the 1967 Middle East War – one central concern of the government was the renewal and upgrading of the country's infrastructure at both the physical and the political levels.

Nothing better typified the ethos of 'Shihabism' than President Shihab's own refusal to become the focus of personalized loyalties. In 1960, a new round of parliamentary elections replaced the former pro-Chamoun Chamber with a new Chamber in which 'nation-building' influences dominated. Claiming that his political aims were now amply fulfilled, President Shihab immediately tried to resign – unheard of previously in the Lebanese system! Loyalist demonstrations soon swirled around Beirut and other cities, begging the president to stay in office. Shihab was then prevailed upon to stay out his full six-year term.

It was never fully known whether Shihab actually stage-managed the 1960 resignation. Certainly, the whole affair considerably strengthened his popular mandate. But in 1964, he was adamant that he would not seek an extension of his term.

By then, the administrative machinery Shihab had worked for was nearly all in place. This machinery included a considerably expanded military intelligence apparatus, called in French style the 'Deuxième Bureau'. To the immense chagrin of most of the older-style politicians, many of the Bureau's operations in the Shihabist era focused on the close surveillance and control of their activities. But such was the continuing popularity of Shihab's methods – as well as the effectiveness of his Deuxième Bureau – that in 1964 his disciple, Hélou, was elected by an easy majority.

As President Shihab moved to implement his ideal of administrative reform he came increasingly to rely on the political support of the two groupings whose ideas about the modernization of the country were closest to his own. These were the odd combination of the Ketaeb and Kamal Jumblatt's Progressive Socialist Party (PSP). The Ketaeb, for many years after their 1958 'counter-revolution', gave Shihab a valuable base inside the Maronite community, while Jumblatt brought to his support many of the modernizing forces within the Druze and other Muslim communities.[3]

These two parties differed widely on many issues connected with Lebanon's regional and international alignment. The Ketaeb were deeply opposed to the identification of Lebanon with Arabism, the spread of Nasserism, and the influence of the Soviet Union – all of them things that the PSP supported.

But from 1958 until just after the Middle East War of 1967, Lebanon was fortunate in that it was the subject of an informal agreement between the two powers which then were strongest in the Eastern Mediterranean – Egypt and the USA.

Despite the fears of pro-Western personalities such as Camille Chamoun or Jordan's King Hussein, the tumultous events of 1958 in Iraq and Lebanon had not hugely strengthened Nasser's hand in the region. The republican regime which emerged in Iraq quickly adopted an overtly anti-Nasser position. And in Lebanon, the

Americans seemed content to accept some increase in the UAR's influence over the government, provided the UAR leaders did not insist on incorporating Lebanon into their union. (Nasser, anyway, quickly ran into trouble in his unionist schemes with Syria, and in 1961 the Egypt–Syria union broke up.)

An all-out confrontation between Nasser and the Americans was thus avoided in both Iraq and Lebanon. And both Nasser and the US apparently remained convinced that a breakdown in Lebanon was not in their interest. Both had seen at first hand, in 1958, the huge potential that a minor imbalance inside Lebanon had to draw them towards a major regional confrontation.

The years from 1958 to 1967 thus saw an informal but none the less effective Egyptian–US condominium over the government in Lebanon. The UAR Ambassador in Beirut was so powerful throughout those years that he was often referred to half-jokingly as the 'High Commissioner'. But the US Ambassador was equally influential, if in a generally more low-key style.

The Shihab presidency was thus assured the support of both these powers and considerations of regional alignment were largely removed from the effective agenda of the internal Lebanese body politic. Thus it was that the differences which divided the Ketaeb and the PSP on regional issues never, until after 1967, seriously eroded their ability to reach agreement on the government's modernizing policies at home.

As mentioned above, one primary concern of the Shihabist governments was the economic development of the country. In fact, Lebanon had already been experiencing a marked economic upswing since before it attained independence in 1945. This had been fuelled, first by the Allied armies' local expenditures, and later by the vast amounts of capital which had fled to Beirut from instability elsewhere in the Arab world.

The administrations of Presidents Khoury and Chamoun had both seen these big businessmen – mainly, trade and financial entrepreneurs – retaining their predominance in the Lebanese economy. The silk industry which had brought prosperity to much of Mount Lebanon in the nineteenth century had long since faded away, in the face of competition from cheaper producers and the new synthetic fibres. But the tradition of commercial and financial expertise which had also grown during the nineteenth century still remained.

This expertise was well able to take advantage of the Second World

War bonanza, and of the arrival of the fugitive Arab capital. By the early 1950s, Beirut had been transformed into a trading and financial centre for a wide region covering most of the Middle East as well as areas far beyond. The big trading families of Beirut acquired vast fortunes from third-party transactions. A Beirut merchant could buy wheat in Chicago, sell it to Kuwait, arrange for the shipping, insurance and financing of the consignment, and all before opening his mail in the morning. According to one estimate, by 1951 no less than 30 per cent of the world's gold trade passed through Lebanon![4]

Presidents Khoury and Chamoun had both proved themselves responsive to the needs of Lebanon's vast new mercantile interests and both were, indeed, closely connected to them. In office, they had lifted foreign-exchange controls, enacted banking secrecy laws, and taken other similar steps to facilitate the speedy movements of trade and finance.

President Shihab was also concerned to keep Lebanon safe for capitalism. But he recognized that the free workings of the market economy were not enough to hold Lebanon together for ever. Beirut, unlike Singapore or Hong Kong, had a hinterland which could still exert its own powerful influence on the system. And during his tours of the country as army commander, Shihab had seen at first hand that the hinterland was not getting much share at all of the country's new wealth. While socialites in Beirut were acting as an extravagant extension of the new international 'jet set', many villages in the outlying regions had still not been connected into the national road system; they lacked fresh water supplies, electricity, schools, hospitals.

Shihab had seen that one significant underpinning to the violence of 1958 had been the anger of the have-nots in the Lebanese system. So an important part of his national reconstruction effort after 1958 concerned focusing attention back on the adequate development of the country's infrastructure.

By 1959, Shihab's public-investment plans had increased the government's share in new investment to 30 per cent from a total of 15 per cent only a few years before. After the concession on the old French-run Banque du Syrie et du Liban ran out, he established a new Lebanese Central Bank, in an attempt to provide more control over Lebanon's unruly financial system. He set up a central planning organization, and brought in French experts to prepare a comprehensive economic plan for the country. He brought even the most remote villages into the national road system, and increased spending on government schools, a social security system and the army.

The Shihabist programme of national renewal attracted the loyalties of a new generation of Lebanese nation-builders. But from the beginning, it also met with opposition from many parts of the old coalition of mercantile businessmen and conservative politicians which a leading historian described as a 'ousiness oligarchy'.[5] The business oligarchs had certainly prospered under Presidents Khoury and Chamoun. But President Shihab did not rely on exchanges of political favours, patronage and influence with the oligarchs, as his predecessors had done. Instead, Shihabism relied on the get-things-done attitude of the modernizers of the PSP or the Ketaeb and their ilk, and on the Deuxième Bureau.

It was an inescapable feature of the era of Shihabism in Lebanon, that the Shihabists felt they could only achieve their ends through exercising a pervasive control over the political life of the country. And the main instrument through which they hoped to achieve this was the same instrument through which Fuad Shihab had regulated his own much smaller domain during his previous term as army commander – the Deuxième Bureau.

While serving as army commander, Shihab had built up a trusted corps of intelligence operatives. They had kept him well abreast of national political developments, enabling him to steer the army intact through the political crises of 1952 and 1958. Small wonder then, that when he took over as head of a state administration which had been filled with his predecessors' clients, he turned to the political reporting organization he knew best to help him put the administration in order.

Throughout the years the Shihabists were in office, they continued to feel themselves under attack from members of the former 'business oligarchy'. When, in 1961, the Deuxième Bureau was able to foil a coup attempt by Chamoun's old allies in the PPS, this further reinforced the Shihabists' fears. They therefore continued to rely on the Deuxième Bureau – to infiltrate groups suspected of loyalty to the business oligarchs, to set up rival groups at street level to attract support away from the oligarchs, and generally to maintain a heavy-handed control over the whole political system.

If Shihab's confrontation with the former ruling groups had been only political, perhaps he could have won it. But his economic programmes very rapidly attracted the opposition of the powerful merchant class.

They did not see why the fabulous riches they were able to acquire in Beirut should provide the taxes to pay for infrastructure schemes in remote Lebanese villages. They objected again and again to measures proposed to protect Lebanon's infant industries from competition with the imports from which they prospered so hugely. Tax evasion became as much a national habit as eating the fragrant *tabbouleh* salad. And the pattern of industrial investment remained stunted despite the Shihabists' best intentions to lay a viable basis for industrial development.

The Shihabist governments were able to register some limited successes for their economic plans. They gave Lebanon an international airport, an upgraded road system, new municipal arrangements and the beginnings of a modern irrigation system. In two rural regions distant from Beirut, the Shi-ite heartlands of the Beqaa and Jebel Amil, the school-building programme increased enrolments from 62,000 in 1959 to more than 225,000 in 1973. Because of the continuous blocking activities of the business oligarchs, the Shihabists were never able to put their economic policies fully into practice. But until the far-reaching regional upset of 1967 they continued to try to do so, battling away against the entrenched power of the tax-evaders, the gold merchants, bankers and other large traders.

The continuing contest between the Shihabists and their opponents did little to dampen the ebullience of Lebanese social and cultural life in those years. Beirut was not just a banking centre for the other countries of the region; throughout the first thirty years of independence it became an important focus of cultural and ideological concern for all the Arab countries of the region.

The intense cultural ferment in Beirut in those years grew directly out of the climate of nearly unfettered political freedom. Nearly everywhere else in the Arab world, creative expression was severely limited by comparison, whether through rigidly statist official ideologies or through the traditionalism of monarchies. Beirut may not have been endowed with the centuries of tradition which would keep Cairo in the forefront of Arab culture; and European residents in Lebanon in those years might have been struck primarily by how European many of the local cultural activities seemed. Nevertheless, Beirut did become virtually the only Arab city where artists, writers and thinkers from the Arab countries – including Egypt – felt able to express themselves freely. From Beirut, through the coming and going of artists, businessmen, and those Arab tourists who liked to spend their summers in the mountains behind Beirut, the city's cultural influence spread widely throughout the Arab world.

Publishing houses multiplied, until by the late 1970s (and despite the travails of those years) the number in active operation still exceeded eighty. Newspapers and small periodicals sprouted irrepressibly, pushing the cost of an official publishing licence to dizzy heights; further periodicals struggled to survive outside the limits of legality. Theatrical productions ran the gamut from the Europeanized glitz of the annual Baalbek Festival to a plethora of small experimental groups working on local transplants of the dramas of despair and the absurd. The great Syrian poets Adonis and Nizar Qabbani became habitués of the Beirut cultural scene.

Hand-in-hand with all the cultural activity, an Arab-wide marketplace of political ideas developed rapidly in the city in those years. The burgeoning periodicals and newspapers resounded to the clash of battles between the Nasserists and the communists, the conservatives and the Arab socialists, the Baathists and the Syrian nationalists, or any other combination of the above. One important incubator of all these ideologies was the American University of Beirut (AUB), which staunchly held to the educative value of critical thinking, and whose student body came from throughout the Arab world. From the AUB campus, the Palestinian George Habash and the Syrian Hani al-Hindi laid their plans to establish the Arab Nationalists' Movement. In the small cafés which ringed AUB, political exiles from Iraq, from Egypt or Yemen would meet to do deals or plot their ultimate revenge.

At a broader level, the major Arab governments were all active in trying to steer Lebanon's chaotic democracy towards their own alignment. The most important players in this game were undoubtedly Egypt and Syria, with Saudi Arabia, Jordan and Iraq always in the background. But at the end of the day, there generally seemed to be a consensus among even the most statist of them, that the solid economic services which Beirut provided were too valuable to be stifled in any major assault upon the country's freedom.

By 1967, Lebanon had lived through three decades of independence, in which the entire apparatus of state, its separation from its neighbours, and its inter-sect nature, had all been retained intact. Given the enormous potential the country had had, in those years, for the growth of secessionary or revolutionary movements, that was no mean feat.

Moreover, the country had weathered two serious internal crises in those years – those of 1952 and 1958. The way those crises had been resolved had done much to show that the borders the French had drawn for 'Greater Lebanon' in 1920 were viable even after their foreign authors had withdrawn from the country.

In 1952, a consensus of Maronite and Sunni business interests had decided that the country should not be run as the virtually exclusive fiefdom of the Khoury family. Then in 1958, the big Sunni bosses of Beirut opted for Lebanon rather than the United Arab Republic, and a consensus of Maronites again came out against one-family rule. Those various decisions had all proved vital to the country's stability.

In both 1952 and 1958, Fuad Shihab's wisdom in his role as army commander had added ballast to the generally wise decisions reached by the politicians of the various communities. Shihab had then further demonstrated his wisdom during the total of nine years of Shihabist rule from 1958 to 1967.

During those years, the Shihabists tried to find a new balance between the urban interests of Beirut and the older traditions of the Mountain. Fuad Shihab and Kamal Jumblatt, who was one of the two main pillars of the Shihabist system, were both descendants of ancient and respected Mountain families. Both cared deeply about the viability of life in the regions outside Beirut. Yet the merchant interests of the city were still so powerful that Shihab and Jumblatt were forced to coexist with them – though this coexistence was seldom happy.

Shihabism achieved much in Lebanon. But it was unable to find a final resolution to many basic questions about political and economic power in Lebanon. It failed to resolve the conflict between the Mountain and the city. It failed to resolve the disparity between the ultra-rich and the urban and rural poor. It failed fully to replace sectarian identity with a new loyalty to the pan-Lebanese nation.

The Shihabists made great efforts to resolve all these interweaving problems. But they still needed much more time.

However, time was one thing they did not have. In June 1967, the continuing battle between the Shihabists and their internal opponents was rudely interrupted by the outbreak of another war in the Middle East. That war changed the patterns of power throughout the whole East Mediterranean region.

In 1967 Middle East War shattered the fragile atmosphere of general regional detente which had allowed Shihabism to flourish in Lebanon. It certainly ended the 'quiescence of the political life of the Middle East', which Edward Shils had determined was necessary for the development of 'a genuinely democratic system' in Lebanon.

Over the years that followed 1967, the regional instability which resulted from the war was to bring the Shihabist era to an end in Lebanon, and to threaten the very foundations of the modern state there.

Yet the experiment in nation-building which the Shihabists had undertaken had already had an important impact inside Lebanon. Shihabism had not only brought the country sucessfully through the crisis of 1958, it had also built an important third storey of national political practice on top of the edifice already provided by ancient inter-sect traditions, the 1926 constitution, and the 1943 National Pact. By 1967, a whole new political generation had grown up, with the viability of a modern-style Lebanese state daily demonstrated before their very eyes.

After the 1967 war, new regional rivalries raged unabated inside, over, around and through Lebanon; and those issues the Shihabists had not had time to solve exploded inside the Lebanese system with a vengeance.

Once again, a period of some hope for the system in Lebanon was ended by the intrusion of strife between other parties in the region.

Notes

1   Edward Shils, in Binder (ed.) (1966), p. 3. The quotes in the next paragraph are from p. 11 of the same work.
2   Quoted in Qubain, (1961), p. 118
3   Even in those years the PSP had a strong Druze bias in its membership, though it still attracted the support of many socialists and modernizers from other sects, including the Christian sects. Towards the end of the 1970s, the PSP acquired a much stronger identification with the Druze. See Chapters 4 and 8.
4   Ibid., p. 74.
5   Kamal Salibi, 'Lebanon under Fuad Chehab 1958–1964', in *Middle East Studies* (London) (April 1966), p. 214.

5   The breakdown starts (1967–75)

In early June 1967, tension mounted rapidly between Israel and her Arab neighbours. Nasser ordered the removal of UN troops who had monitored the Sinai front since the 1956 hostilities, and imposed a naval blockade on shipping bound for Israel's southern port of Eilat. The Israeli air force then launched quick raids against Egyptian and Syrian air-bases which left the air forces of these two states in tatters on the ground. With the Israelis in clear command of the air-space of the whole region, Israeli ground units quickly advanced against Syrian, Egyptian and Jordanian ground positions. Within six days it was all over.

At the end of those six days, Israel emerged as clearly the strongest single power in the East Mediterranean. It had swept away the power-balance between Egypt and the United States which had previously dominated that region.

In the wake of Egypt's resounding defeat, President Nasser had to grapple with keeping his own 40-million strong population together. He was no longer able to pursue dreams for region-wide influence.

As for the USA, US navy ships had steamed right alongside some of the Israel–Egypt fighting in Sinai. But unlike 1956, the US did nothing directly to affect the outcome of the fighting. In the harsh new era of Israeli-Arab power politics which ensued from 1967 onwards, the US presented itself as a neutral arbiter between the parties, rather than as a direct participant in events.

In Lebanon, President Hélou's administration had expressed formal solidarity with the Arab parties to the war. But it took care not to entangle the Lebanese army in the fighting, and not to allow the other Arab armies to utilize Lebanese territory in their efforts either.

However, not even the smartest Shihabist thinkers could prevent the effects of the war from playing themselves out inside the Lebanese body politic. For the non-threatening regional environment which had removed regional issues from the Lebanese political agenda since 1958 no longer existed. After 1967 the Ketaeb and the Jumblattists were unable to set aside their very real differences in regional issues in an earnest Shihabist effort at Lebanese nation-building.

After 1967, the regional issue which most deeply penetrated the Lebanese system was no longer the question of alignment for or against Nasser, given his seriously weakened regional position. Rather, the key issue was now that of alignment for or against the Palestinian guerrilla movement which exploded on to the scene after 1967.

Throughout the Arab world, including in Lebanon, the common people witnessed directly, in 1967, the humiliation of the vast regular armies which the Egyptian and Syrian governments had been building up for a decade. Those governments, those armies, and those people, all shared the bitter feelings of the Arabs' dishonour in those days.

Then, in the weeks and months following the war, the whole Arab world saw a surge of popular support for the idea of guerrilla action against Israel, as propounded by the re-emerging Palestinian nationalist movement. Guerrilla action, it was generally felt, might not on its own suffice to tip the strategic balance back in the Arabs' favour. But at least, it could 'redeem the honour of the Arabs', which the regular armies had so disgracefully lost.

This wave of support for the infant Palestinian guerrilla movement occurred within Lebanon as in the other Arab countries. But Lebanon was the one Arab country in which a significant group – a section of the Maronites – expressed their reservations about the Palestinian movement openly, from the beginning. The Palestinian issue was thus brought to the very heart of the Lebanese political system.

The Lebanese could not as easily set aside their differences on this new issue as they had, after 1958, over the whole question of Nasserism. For the Palestinian guerrilla movement existed right within Lebanon itself, among the quarter-million Palestinian refugees who formed at least 10 per cent of Lebanon's total population.

In the late 1950s, Nasser had been able to agree to certain limits on his ambitions in Lebanon, in return for a certain amount of ill-defined 'influence' in the country. He had been able to do this because his nationalist movement already had its firm home-base in Egypt. But the Palestinian exiles had no such home-base: in the 1967 war, the Israelis had completed their occupation of all of historic Palestine. In their hundreds of thousands, in Lebanon as elsewhere in their diaspora, the Palestinian refugees now saw the issue of nationalist guerrilla action as a life-or-death imperative.

In the months following the war, the Palestinian guerrilla movement erupted among the Palestinians in Lebanon – and the resulting Palestinian *issue* then erupted inside the Lebanese system itself. That issue rapidly eroded the internal coalition on which the Shihabist edifice had been built in Lebanon. Three years after the end of the war, the Shihabists were to be defeated in the presidential elections. And the combination of new and ancient forces which had overthrown them was then to throw the country into ever greater turmoil, which reached its first major *dénouement* with the outbreak of the civil war in 1975.

By 1975, it looked as though Shihabism might not be the only Lebanese casualty of 1967. The events of 1975 and the years which followed made it seem that the 1943 National Pact, and even the 1926 Constitution itself, might be in danger in Lebanon. But first, we must travel back and see precisely how it was that the Palestinian issue brought Lebanon to that fragile situation.

The Palestinian refugees were mainly Sunni Muslims. Their homeland had been a religious focus for Muslims since the days of the Prophet Muhammed. (It already was such before that, of course, for both Jews and Christians.) For the Lebanese Muslim communities, support of the Palestinians in their fight to return to their homeland was, at the beginning, almost automatic. And it proved remarkably durable. For example, it was not until the late 1970s that the constant pressure the Israelis maintained against south Lebanon started to turn significant numbers of the Shi-ite Muslims living there against the Palestinians.

The deciding factor on the Palestinian issue in Lebanon was not so much whether one was actually Lebanese or Palestinian, or Christian or Muslim, as whether one considered oneself 'an Arab' or not. Most of the Lebanese Sunnis and Shi-ites instinctively did feel so. So did Kamal Jumblatt and his many supporters among the Druze. So did most Greek Orthodox Christians, and sectors within most other Christian communities in Lebanon.

In their thousands, members of all these Lebanese groups signed up to join the emerging Palestinian guerrilla formations. In their scores, political leaders from these groups took to the hustings to publicly defend the Palestinians' right to mount guerrilla actions against Israel from Lebanon. In their scores of thousands, ordinary people from these communities took to the streets in repeated demonstrations from 1968 to 1975 to try to force this position on a wary government.

These developments horrified the Maronite heartland. Many strands of traditional Maronite thinking were totally opposed to the Palestinian guerrillas' armed presence. Whether one looked to the well-being of a totally Christian Mountain, or of a confessionally mixed 'Greater Lebanon', the consensus of traditionalist Maronite thinkers was that this entity should not be dragged into the Palestinian issue. And this popular consensus was soon, after 1967, translated into a consensus among the major Maronite politicians.

The backing which the Muslim 'street' expressed for the Palestinians kept up a constant pressure on the established Muslim leadership to support the guerrillas' presence in Lebanon. But by the late 1960s the established leaders of both the Sunni and the Shi-ite communities had gained a vastly increased interest in maintaining a series of alliances with the Maronite leaders. For it was these alliances – whether within the orbit of the Shihabist machine, or in opposition to it – which had kept Lebanon together, and kept the super-profits flowing into the massive service industry centred in Beirut.

Thus, so long as the presence of the Palestinian guerrillas was an explosive issue inside the Lebanese body politic, the established Muslim leaders found themselves caught in the heart of a dilemma. Some of them, mainly the more feudal-style leaders of the Shi-ite community, came to opt for maintaining their links with their Maronite counterparts. Others, like Druze leader Jumblatt, veered towards the Palestinian leadership. But a majority of the old-style Sunni bosses found themselves caught unhappily in the middle, virtually immobilized by the contending stresses and strains thrust upon them.

These Sunni bosses were thus unable to take much effective action in any direction, either to shore up their alliance with the Maronites or to give much effective backing to the Palestinians. The Sunni leaders were further hampered by the political traditions of their own community, which had seen itself throughout the centuries more as a legitimate part of a larger state structure than as a sect pursuing its own interests. This resulting paralysis of the traditional Sunni leaders in the years following 1967 harmed the Lebanese system far more deeply than did the 'mere' crumbling of the Shihabist coalition between 1967 and 1970.

For it was always conceivable that a new governing coalition could be found to replace the Shihabists' formula. But the long-term paralysis of the traditional Sunni leaderships after 1967 struck at the heart of the whole National Pact system on which the country's very independence had been based. For the Sunni leaders had been one of the two main parties which had contracted that Pact back in 1943. Their paralysis now thus opened the way for the emergence of new political forces not envisaged in, or necessarily consistent with, the National Pact.

The first contender to fill the vacuum left by the paralysis of the old Sunni bosses was the Druze leader Kamal Jumblatt. A member of the powerful Jumblatt family which had dominated Druze politics since the seventeenth century, Kamal's father had been the governor of the Druze heartland of the Shouf when Kamal was born – two months after the British and French forces captured Lebanon from the Ottomans, in 1917. Four years later, his father died, but the youngster's right eventually to succeed to the leadership of the Druze community was fiercely defended over the following years by his powerful mother, Nazira.

Kamal was elected deputy for the Shouf before his 26th birthday, in 1943. Three years later he was made a minister, and had thus 'caught up', in the formal political race at the national level, with his much older Shouf neighbour Camille Chamoun – though since birth he had far outstripped Chamoun in the tribal power stakes in the Shouf.

Relations between these two Shouf neighbours – the one the strongest tribal leader within the compact Druze, and the other a wily Maronite politician with a necessarily broader national base – were to form a contant theme of Lebanon's politics until Kamal Jumblatt was killed in 1977. In 1952, Jumblatt's backing was an important factor in Chamoun's success in ousting Bishara al-Khoury from the presidential palace; and Jumblatt's subsequent opposition to Chamoun then helped to remove him, in turn, from the palace. Throughout the Shihabist era, Jumblatt had been well able to strengthen his bases of power through his near-constant association with the regime.

Kamal Jumblatt was never just another Lebanese politician. Eclectic, energetic, and often personally crotchety, in 1949 he had founded the Progressive Socialist Party (PSP). Thereafter, the PSP provided him with a powerful tool for organizing his (mainly Druze) base within the complex manoeuvres of the electoral system in those early years of independence.

But Jumblatt always remained eager to achieve more than just this with the PSP. He wanted to establish it as a genuinely socialist party, on a West European model. He meanwhile tried to reconcile the conflicts between his roles as feudalist and socialist by introducing complicated co-operative arrangements between himself, the tenants of the many Jumblatt family lands and the workers in the Jumblatt-owned factories.

The lanky Druze leader also pursued a broad range of intellectual interests with some dedication – in fields as diverse as socialist theory, French literature and Indian mysticism. The traditionalist Druzes who were longstanding family retainers at the rambling family palace in Mukhtara became used to hoisting an eclectic panoply of specialists in these and other fields. And as Jumblatt's stature also increased on the pan-Arab political stage, he became a valued intermediary between all kinds of disputing parties throughout the Arab world, and beyond.

After June 1967, Jumblatt became a firm ally of the Palestinian guerrillas. He was still, until 1970, also a supporter of the Shihabist regime. (There was some evidence to suggest that these two positions which Jumblatt adopted were not totally contradictory. For throughout at least some of the period between 1967 and 1970, the Shihabist military intelligence itself was also giving covert support to the guerrillas, in pursuit of its own power-struggle with Maronite hardliners.[1] So Jumblatt's behaviour was not, at that point, completely at odds with the Shihabists' aims.)

The support which Jumblatt gave the Palestinians after 1967 won him broad popular support in the Lebanese Muslim communities. In the immediate post 1967 fervour of Muslim support for the Palestinians, all the other Muslim politicians had also mouthed some support for the guerrillas. But most political activists within the Sunni and Shi-ite communities sensed the deep reservations entertained by their traditional bosses on this issue, and on other local issues which were also starting to concern them in that period.

Indeed throughout the series of government crises which plagued Lebanon from 1968 onwards, the Palestinian and the internal Lebanese issues appeared inextricably intertwined. Student radicals on the campus of the American University raised the Palestinian banner during their strikes against the university administration. Shi-ite villagers protesting the savage Israeli retaliations against south Lebanon raised it. Factory workers protesting inflation in Beirut raised it.

Those very varied movements, as well as many others equally as radical, threw up a whole series of new, radical leaderships within the Sunni and Shi-ite communities from 1968 onwards. Practically a whole new political generation within both those Muslim communities deserted their traditional leaders, for the new leaders who were radical on internal issues, and also pro-PLO.

At the level of ideas, these new leaders propounded a wide variety of views, whether 'Nasserist', leftist or Islamic fundamentalist in colour. They were united only by the directness of the support they offered to the PLO, and by the radical challenge they threw out to the status quo of the Lebanese political system.

In 1969, Jumblatt was able to group most of these radical organizations, along with his own PSP, into a coalition which came to be known as the Lebanese National Movement (LNM). Through its member-groups, the LNM had a broad constituency within all the country's major sects, except the Maronites. It thus provided Jumblatt with a powerful vehicle through which to organize a nation-wide constituency.

Kamal Jumblatt was uniquely placed, and perhaps uniquely motivated, to draw this new radical coalition together. He was, of course, still an important part of the political status quo in the 1960s. Indeed, his position in successive Shihabist and post-Shihabist governments enabled him to give important protection to members of the radical groups. In 1970, for example, he was able to withdraw a longstanding ban on the activities of the Lebanese Communist Party.

But for all that Jumblatt was a part of the status quo of the late 1960s, he never had to feel himself whole-heartedly committed to it. For the credentials he derived from his family and the Druze community far preceded Shihabism, the National Pact, and the modern-day Lebanese constitution itself. He was a valuable ally for the Shihabists, and had gained much from his alliance with them over the years. But he never felt he had to be totally loyal to the National Pact system on which the Shihabist edifice had been built.

Under the National Pact's rules, after all, Jumblatt could always be – as he had been since 1952 – the chief of the kingmakers. But as a non-Maronite, he knew he could never be king. There thus remained a question mark over his motives, in his constant call for the secularization of the Lebanese system.

Was it really the modernizing move he proclaimed it to be? Or was it simply a part of his own undeniable hunger for power – a device which would one day give Lebanon a President Jumblatt? One could never tell for sure. But this was always a favourite accusation of Jumblatt's many political foes.

Regardless of what the enigmatic Druze leader's personal motives really were, the fact remains that the post 1967 years saw him steadily increasing his influence outside the Druze community. And the main victims of this rapid growth in his constituency were the long-established political bosses of the Sunni and Shi-ite communities.

The first indications of all these developments were not long in appearing after the guns of the 1967 Middle East War fell silent. Early in 1968, the Palestinian guerrillas and their Lebanese allies held a massive public funeral for the first Lebanese national to be killed in action with the guerrillas (he was, actually, a Christian). Caught up in the swirl of pro-guerrilla enthusiasm, even the prime minister, Abdallah al-Yafi, declared that Lebanon should lift all existing restrictions on the guerrillas' activities.

In 1968, the country was just entering a new round of parliamentary elections. Ketaeb Party leader Pierre Gemayyel sensed the mounting wave of Maronite unease at the Palestinian guerrillas' growing powers. Now, he made his greatest step since 1958 to distance himself from a regime which he considered too conciliatory in the face of the threat he saw the Palestinians posing. He took the Ketaeb bloc into the elections against the Shihabist supporters of President Hélou, and into a new alliance with Camille Chamoun's 'National Liberal Party', and Raymond Eddé's 'National Bloc'.

This coalition of the three major political leaders of the Maronite community was known simply as 'the Alliance'. Significantly, it received the backing of the Maronite Patriarch, Boulos Méouchy. (In 1958, Méouchy's had opposed President Chamoun, and had thereby denied him much of the legitimacy he sought within the Maronite community.) The inclusion of the Ketaeb in the new anti-Shihab coalition was equally portentous. For it marked the crumbling of the first of the Shihabists' two traditional pillars of political support.

The Alliance was unable to secure a parliamentary majority in 1968 against the well-oiled Shihabist machine. But it was able to make sufficient gains to force President Hélou and his Shihabist followers to pay careful attention to Alliance demands.

At the end of December 1968, the Israelis intervened directly in Lebanon, for the first time on a large scale, to try to force the Lebanese government to clamp down on the guerrillas. Palestinian guerrillas had fired rockets at an Israeli plane on a runway in Athens.

The Israelis responded by landing commando units at Beirut airport and blowing up no less than thirteen Lebanese and Arab airliners on the tarmac there.

As the Israeli commando units effected a totally loss-free withdrawal from Beirut, the Palestinians and their supporters in Lebanon raised angry questions as to how the government had allowed the country to become so vulnerable. Further accusing the administration of complicity in the raid, angry pro-Palestinian demonstrations forced Premier Yafi to resign.

Thus, from the beginning of 1969, Lebanon was plunged into the first of a series of deep, Palestinian-related crises. President Hélou saw the last two years of his term deteriorate, as the Shihabist political coalition was eroded even further by each additional confrontation. The 'Palestinian issue' was to continue to wreak havoc on the country's delicate political system right down to the outbreak of the civil war in 1975.

Throughout the summer of 1969, there was a steady escalation of clashes between the Lebanese army and the Palestinians. The new premier – once again, the old Shihabist stalwart Rashid Karami – was proposing that the army command and the PLO 'co-ordinate' their activities, rather than fight each other. For many months the Maronite politicians kept up their insistence that such a dilution of Lebanese sovereignty was unacceptable, and President Hélou publicly supported their position. But Karami kept up his insistence on 'co-ordination', and in October 1969 he finally announced his refusal to form a government without it.

Hélou solved this new government crisis by acceding to Karami's demand. His army commander was sent rapidly to Cairo, to negotiate an agreement with the man who had only earlier that year taken over as Chairman of the five-year-old 'Palestinian Liberation Organization' (PLO) – Yasser Arafat.

The 1969 Cairo agreement allowed the guerrilla groups within the PLO coalition to maintain a military presence. But it also supposedly laid down strict limits for this presence, as well as close guidelines for how the PLO military command should 'co-ordinate' with the Lebanese army.

For the Palestinians in Lebanon, the Cairo agreement ushered in a whole heady new area in which they felt exuberantly free to express their nationalist sentiment. Ever since they were first established in the early 1950s, the Palestinian refugee camps had been kept under the tight control of the Lebanese military intelligence. Now, the Cairo agreement handed over this control to the PLO leadership – 'without compromising the overall sovereignty of Lebanon', whatever that might mean.

For the Shihabists, the concessions involved in concluding the Cairo agreement sounded the death-knell of the control they had maintained over the Lebanese administration since 1958. In the presidential elections which were held the following year, Shihabist candidate Elias Sarkis finally lost out by one vote to a relatively new face – that of the northern Maronite clan leader, Suleiman Frangieh.

Ironically, the final nail had been hammered into the Shihabist regime's coffin by Kamal Jumblatt, who until then had been one of the Shihabists' most stalwart supporters. Angry at demands from the army command that he, as interior minister, send security-police units into action against the Palestinians, Jumblatt finally authorized four of his eight supporters in parliament to vote for Frangieh. It was their votes which brought Frangieh into power.

Suleiman Frangieh was unlike any of the train of polished Maronite politicians who had preceded him into the Lebanese presidency. He was the anomalous heir to a long tradition which had grown up in Lebanon, according to which the first son of any family with political aspirations would be groomed as the patriarch's political successor; while the second son would do whatever might be necessary to 'look after the home-base'.

In modern times, this division of responsibilities was to be followed by the sons of both Pierre Gemayyel and Camille Chamoun. But in that older generation of the Frangieh family, Suleiman was a second son.

The Frangiehs were one of the five major clans from the northern mountain village of Zghorta. Suleiman's elder brother, Hamid, had indeed shown himself a promising political figure in the early 1950s, while Suleiman had busied himself at the younger brother's more traditional concerns. His most egregious achievement in that period was his connection with an inter-family feud in Zghorta, during which eleven people were gunned down in a church.

Then, in 1957, Hamid Frangieh suffered a stroke which left him badly paralysed. As it became clear that he would never wholly recover, political leadership of the clan passed to Suleiman. Continuing to use his traditional 'ward boss' techniques in his new political role, Suleiman rapidly built a reputation as a quirky but authentic Maronite strong man.

And in 1970, a Maronite 'strong man' was just what the veteran Maronite politicians of the Alliance had been looking for in the man they wanted to run against the Shihabist machine in the presidential elections. In Frangieh, with his cossack-style hat, his engaging grin and his wily successes in the clan politics of the northern Maronites, they certainly found a man of independent spirit.

Many of Frangieh's first acts delighted those old-style politicians of all sects who for twelve years now had chafed under the Shihabists' attempts at modernization. Saeb Salam, the most powerful Sunni politician in Beirut, delightedly ripped out of his wall the telephone lines which he said the Deuxième Bureau had been bugging for years.

Back in 1936, Salam's father had been the host at the 'Conference of the Coast', at which Sunni leaders from throughout Lebanon had called for union with Syria. But in 1970, Saeb Salam was the first man the 'strong Maronite' from Zghorta turned to, to form a government.

Salam's trademark was the dapper carnation in the buttonhole which bespoke an easy affluence and long familiarity with the burdens of leadership in Beirut's powerful Sunni community. But he had also built himself a strong and effective modern-style power-base, which bolstered the claims of Salam family tradition. The mainstay of this power-base was a network of Sunni charitable institutions called the 'Maqasid Association'. The Maqasid ran a high school in Beirut which was recognized as providing the best Arabic-language instruction in the country – many Sunni technocrats had been its graduates. It also ran a large hospital, orphanages and other social projects. Through it, Salam could influence many segments of the Sunni community, in Beirut and throughout the country.

Salam's first idea in 1970 was to form a technocratic 'Youth Cabinet' to symbolize the country's liberation from the controls of Shihabism. For a short while, this approach provided an appearance of dynamism.

However, even this appearance of dynamism could not hide the very real political differences which continued to divide the country. Although Salam himself may have been in favour of a carefully balanced patronage system in the administration, many other members of the Youth Cabinet saw in the overthrow of Shihabism an opportunity to return to the kind of favours system which had preceded Shihabist rule – and to do so with a vengeance. This seemed particularly true of Frangieh's son, Tony, who as telecommunications minister throughout his father's presidency became tarred with repeated accusations of corruption.

Finally, just after the Frangieh regime held its first set of parliamentary elections in the spring of 1972, Salam gave up the idea of the Youth Cabinet. The next government he formed was far more traditionalist in its approach.

The ninety-nine-member parliament elected in 1972 was to remain unchanged throughout at least the following dozen years. The bulk of the membership continued to be provided by the traditional families, blocs and alliances. However, activists of both the pro- and the anti-Palestinian radicals who were now growing within Lebanese society found a slightly increased voice in the 1972 Chamber. Meanwhile, true to the previous pattern, the supporters of the previous president found their representation in the Chamber considerably diminished under his successor.

1971 and 1972 had both seen a continued aggravation of the Palestinian issue within Lebanon. From September 1970 to July 1971, King Hussein's regime in Jordan cracked down heavily on the PLO guerrillas who had set up bases there. The regimes in Syria and Egypt may both have professed their separate commitments to a formal Arab nationalism, but both states insisted on maintaining full control of their own frontiers with Israel.

For the Palestinians, this left only Lebanon as a potential site from which they might strike Israel and many of the PLO survivors from the fighting in Jordan made their way to Lebanon to inflate the PLO's presence there.

In April 1973, Israeli retaliation against Palestinian targets in Lebanon once again shook the heart of the Lebanese political system. That month, an Israeli commando unit landed in Beirut, and killed three PLO leaders in their homes in the prosperous Verdun quarter, before making a nearly clean getaway.

Once again, the horrified Palestinians and their Lebanese allies accused the Lebanese security forces of complicity in the raid. Premier Salam immediately demanded the resignation of the Lebanese army commander, a key Frangieh ally. When Frangieh refused to accede to this demand, Salam felt himself obliged to resign.

President Frangieh had difficulty finding any Sunni politician of stature to replace Salam. He was finally able to persuade a second-echelon protégé of Rashid Karami's called Amin al-Hafez, to try to fill the post.

The fact that Saeb Salam, and all other Sunni leaders of his stature, had found themselves unable to deal with the conflicting pressures of April 1973 signalled the beginning of the era of weak premiers. This represented a considerable weakening of the National Pact tradition, based as it was on a near-equal compact between the Maronite president and the Sunni premier.

The security crisis continued even after Premier Hafez's appointment. Once again clashes escalated between PLO units and the Lebanese Army, right into the outskirts of Beirut. As in 1969, these clashes were only finally brought under control once the PLO and the government had reached a formal accord, whch formed an annex to the 1969 Cairo agreement.

In 1969, it had been President Hélou's conclusion of that previous agreement with the PLO which had finally persuaded the leading Maronite politicians that he should be replaced by a 'strong Maronite'. Now the fact that even this 'strong Maronite' president was forced to make a deal with the PLO leadership convinced them that there was little that anybody could do within the existing state structure in Lebanon to ensure Maronite interests. So long as deployments of the national army were subject to the agreement of a Muslim premier, they felt, the army would never be able to act decisively against the PLO's armed presence in Lebanon.

The Ketaeb and the followers of both Camille Chamoun and President Frangieh now therefore resolved that they would have to achieve this by themselves. So from mid 1973 onwards, these Maronite parties started preparing for their own eventual military showdown with the Palestinians.[2]

Nor were the big Sunni political bosses happy with the outcome of the spring crisis. They still remained unwilling to face the huge pressures involved in themselves agreeing to replace Hafez. But they also soon became dissatisfied with the fact that the Sunnis were now represented in the premiership by someone considered to be of only second-echelon standing within the community.

In June 1973, the big Sunni bosses were able to force Premier Hafez to resign. President Frangieh was finally able to find a mutually acceptable replacement in the person of Taqieddine al-Sulh. The ageing Sulh, it was thought, would make no waves. His principal trademark was that he still wore a Turkish-style fez though it was decades since this had been the general fashion in Beirut. As a member of the prominent Sulh family which had produced the famous Sunni co-author of the 1943 National Pact, no Sunni could challenge his community credentials – but at the same time, Taqieddine al-Sulh was a long-time political ally of Frangieh's.

With the formation of the first Taqieddine al-Sulh government, it looked as though a total breakdown of the political system had been averted. But deep sectarian, economic and political disputes continued to bring strife to Lebanon throughout the fifteen months of his premiership.

The 'Youth Cabinet' of technocrats which Saeb Salem had brought into power in 1970 had been unable to grapple with Lebanon's social and economic malaise, and certainly none of the cabinets which succeeded it were able to turn the system round. What was the nature of this malaise, which together with the presence of the Palestinian guerrillas acted to turn a whole generation of Lebanese against their own political system?

Certainly, no problem was immediately apparent in Beirut's smart Hamra Street, where elegantly-coiffured ladies could find the latest in European chic, or café intellectuals could endlessly debate the Arab issues which reverberated through Lebanon's ebulliently free press.

A bare three or four miles from Hamra, however, there festered vast unplanned suburbs which were home to hundreds of thousands of Lebanese citizens, new immigrants to city life from the Republic's furthest corners. These suburbs grew up between and beyond the string of Palestinian refugee camps which ringed Beirut. 'Suburbs' often in name only, many of these areas had more the aspect of ill-served shanty-towns: together with the refugee camps, they made up what came to be known as 'the poverty belt' surrounding the city. Similar, smaller 'poverty belts' ringed some of Lebanon's other cities. But by the late 1960s, the population of Greater Beirut already totalled well over a quarter of the population of the whole country; and the banks, trading houses, hotels and small manufacturing industries of Beirut easily dominated the entire Lebanese economy.

From the late 1950s onwards, the planning teams brought in by President Shihab had aimed both to rationalize the Lebanese economy as a whole, and to introduce planned development to all the country's regions. The Shihabists had been markedly successful in providing some of the basic infrastructure needed for these trans-formations. They had taken the national road network to the most remote regions – not, after all, a hugely difficult task in a country as small as Lebanon – and had made a good start on building government schools in most parts of the country.

But that was about as far as the momentum of Shihabism had been able to take the planners. In the face of the stiff opposition of the big Beirut trading and services community, neither Shihab nor Hélou had been able to follow through effectively with the subsequent steps towards balanced regional development. Few factories or agricultural development schemes ever materialized to stimulate economic life in the outlying regions, so the roads and schools the Shihabists had so proudly built eventually had the reverse effect to that originally intended. They simply funnelled people even more efficiently than would otherwise have been the case from the outlying regions down into the orbit of the service economy of Beirut.

Another factor that made an increasing contribution to the migration of many Lebanese villagers towards Beirut from 1968 on was the terrible pressure which the Israelis maintained against south Lebanon through their constant retaliations against the Palestinians and their allies. Israeli air raids were mounted not only against suspected PLO bases, but also against suspected PLO supply lines. In most cases these were the same roads and bridges the southern farmers used to take their produce to market. Lebanese farmers or fishermen suspected of being PLO supporters had their houses or boats arbitrarily blown up by Israeli raiding parties; or they were kidnapped and taken to Israel for interrogation.

In 1972, the Israeli army launched the first of a series of massive ground invasions of southern Lebanon which they would undertake at intervals throughout the succeeding decade. As Lebanese army units stood idly by, or made only the most perfunctory display of resistance, Israeli tanks rolled into most of the Shi-ite-inhabited parts of southern Lebanon, and stayed there for some days before withdrawing.

In Beirut, the inaction of the Lebanese army on this occasion caused yet another of the political uproars which were becoming almost routine. But in the south, the net effect of the Israeli action was further to intensify the economic and social dislocation of the area which had already been underway for four years. Streams of southern villagers took to the roads, heading towards the hope of a better life in Beirut.

Throughout the 1960s and early 1970s, the services centre in Beirut was booming, and could provide jobs, either directly or indirectly, for most of the newcomers who wanted them. As hundreds of thousands of internal Lebanese migrants flocked to Beirut in those years, smaller numbers of unskilled labourers from the Syrian interior were also sucked into the Lebanese economy. (They either worked on the construction sites which mushroomed around Beirut and other cities, or they took the places in the agricultural sector which the Lebanese internal migrants had deserted.)

If the job market of Beirut was ready for the stream of new migrants, the municipal services sector most certainly was not. As the Shihabists panted behind them waving useless 'urban development' plans in their hands, private-sector developers transformed the entire coastal plain around Beirut, whose agricultural produce had once fed the whole city, into an extended suburb-slum within the space of about twelve years.

Electricity, telephone and water lines were hurriedly hooked on to existing systems. Officials in these and other service sectors grew rich overnight by expediting certain requests for new services. This was, of course, at the expense of those who failed to pay the necessary bribe, whose requests would get lost in the system for years. And it was at the ultimate expense of all consumers of the vital services, who ended up with water rationed to a few hours every other day in summer, frequent power blackouts, and an often inoperable telephone system.

The rapid urbanization which took place in Lebanon in the 1960s and early 1970s affected more than just the new migrants' physical quality of life. It also radically changed their socio-political frame of reference.

A high proportion of the new urban-dwellers came from the Maronite and Shi-ite communities. Back in their native villages, political attitudes had been dominated far more by considerations of family than by considerations of sect. 'In contrast to family, sect has little importance in village politics', Lebanese anthropologist Fuad Khuri noted in a study of the urbanization process in Lebanon.[3]

However, when the former villagers moved to the suburbs, they suddenly found themselves cut off from the extended families which had been the mainstay of their social and political allegiance in the villages. The family credentials they had enjoyed back in the villages counted for nothing in the new environment. The new urban-dwellers thus felt themselves little able to participate in the politics of their new home areas on the basis of the family politics which already existed there. And neither did the original 'natives' of these suburbanized areas, who had seen them transformed from small villages into vast suburbs within half a lifetime, much welcome the newcomers' participation.

The way the newcomers eventually overcame these barriers was to switch their allegiance from their now splintered families to the broader group of the religious sect.

In the case of the new Shi-ite urban-dwellers, this shift was summed up in their expansion of annual public observances of the Shi-ite holy day of 'Ashura'. (In many of the Shi-ites' home villages, these observances had been performed only in the privacy of the home.) In the case of the Maronite migrants, in the mid 1950s these other new urban-dwellers had found that they could participate effectively in local community politics by allying themselves with the Ketaeb party apparatus. This act also had very distinct sectarian overtones.

By the early 1970s, the enormous groundswell of support which had mounted for the Ketaeb in most of the Maronite suburbs of Beirut was already apparent. But the growing adherence of many of the Shi-ite urban-dwellers to their own sectarian identity was less evident, for it was still masked by the much more overt signs of an ideologically leftist radicalization.

This shift towards the left became apparent in the post 1967 period throughout Lebanon's Shi-ite community, in the Beirut suburbs, as in the south and in the Beqaa. During that period, the leftist parties also registered a huge growth of membership and support within the Greek Orthodox and the Armenian communities, as well as much smaller gains among some of the Maronite intelligentsia.

The influence of the various radically Arab nationalist parties was, meanwhile, spreading like wildfire through the mainly urban Sunni population during these years. Thus, a majority of the new generation of activists in all Lebanon's major communities *except the Maronite community* were gravitating, in the late 1960s and early 1970s, through their participation in the various parties which made up the LNM, into Kamal Jumblatt's constituency.

In October 1973, yet another Arab-Israeli war was fought. The two key Arab states which had planned the war, Egypt and Syria, registered notable successes in the early days of their assault against Israel. But it soon became clear that Egypt's new President Sadat was much more interested in using the momentum of the war to obtain a diplomatic settlement with Israel than he was in pressing for full military advantage. As the fighting ground to a halt on both the Egyptian and Syrian fronts, the previous alliance between these two Arab states was replaced by a furious jockeying for position as each sought to assure for itself the most favourable bargaining position.

Each of these two powerful Arab states sought to strengthen its bargaining position by lining up outside Arab support. One place where they found they could easily play out their power-struggles was in Lebanon, since Lebanese society was already deeply divided over the Palestinian issue.

The intra-Arab contest for influence in Lebanon in the years following the October 1973 war also drew in other Arab participants such as Iraq, which 'rejected' any thought of talking peace with Israel. In addition to competing for influence within the Lebanese system as such, the Arab parties were also competing in Lebanon for control over the Palestinian national movement, which had found its last nearly independent base there. Control of the PLO's military presence could be a valuable negotiating-card for those Arab states which came to exercise it in Lebanon.

For the Israeli government, the new prospect of comprehensive peace negotiation which opened up after the war strengthened their resolve that the PLO should not be part of such a settlement. Thus, long after Israel's front-lines with Egypt and Syria had been formally disengaged, the Israeli army continued to launch punishing raids against installations of the PLO and their allies in Lebanon.

The intra-Arab disputes and the Israeli-Palestinian dispute thus all came home to roost in Lebanon in the aftermath of the 1973 Middle East War.

The heavy arming and training of all direct parties to the power-struggle in Lebanon, meanwhile, continued apace. In July 1974, a quarrel between two smugglers set off a two-day pitched battle between Ketaeb militia units and PLO fighters from the sprawling Tel al-Zaatar refugee camp in East Beirut. Two months later, a 'territorial' dispute between the Jumblattists and the *Ketaeb*, led to battles in the mountains east of Beirut, in which three were killed.

By the middle of 1974, Kamal Jumblatt had succeeded so well in tying together his radical LNM coalition, and in his co-ordination with the PLO leaders, that he found himself stronger than ever before. At the government level, his support was a vital factor in keeping President Frangieh's old ally Taqieddine al-Sulh in the premiership. He was thus in a relatively good position to indulge his dream of secularizing and modernizing the Lebanese system – with who knew what end?

The old Sunni bosses, led by the Beiruti former Premier Saeb Salam, had bitterly resented Jumblatt's growing power. In September 1974, Premier Sulh finally confessed himself unable to deal with the deteriorating security situation in the country and resigned. Saeb Salam then responded enthusiastically when Frangieh called on him to replace Sulh. But he also insisted forcefully that he now be allowed to form and run his government exactly the way he thought best.

However, Frangieh was not about to give Salam this kind of power. So, just as he had done in 1972, Frangieh once again turned away from Salam, to try to show him that he could form a government with a second-echelon Sunni premier who did not need Salam's support.

The man chosen to succeed to the premiership was yet another Sulh cousin, younger than Taqieddine, called Rashid al-Sulh. Rubbing salt into Saeb Salam's wound was the fact that Rashid al-Sulh owed the seat he formerly occupied in parliament directly to the support he had received from none other than Salam's arch-rival, Kamal Jumblatt. Frangieh was trying to prove that he and Jumblatt could still, between them, sustain someone in the prime political position held by the Sunnis, in open defiance of that community's established political leaders.

Towards the end of February 1975, another series of developments occurred which sent shock-waves through the Sunni community. The fishermen of Sidon – mainly Sunnis – had for some time been worried by the establishment of a new commercial venture called the Proteine Company, whose aim was the highly mechanized exploitation of Lebanon's fishing resources. Heading the company was none other than the old Maronite stalwart and ex-president, Camille Chamoun. The Sidon fishermen feared he would do them out of a job, and campaigned heavily to have the government withdraw the operating licence it had granted the new company.

On 26 February, the fishermen and their supporters held what was billed as a peaceful march through the crowded city-centre of Sidon. The march was led by a popular local deputy, a long-time Nasserist called Maarouf Saad. As the marchers came up towards lines established by police and army units an unknown gunman shot Saad fatally in the head. Immediately, intense fighting erupted between the marchers and the security forces. Over the next few days, strikes and demonstrations in support of the Sidon marchers spread throughout most of the coastal towns. In a clash near a Palestinian refugee camp on the outskirts of Sidon on 29 February, five soldiers and eleven civilians were killed.

This series of open confrontations between the Nasserists and their LNM and Palestinian supporters on the one hand, and the army and other security forces on the other, opened up all the political disputes which had been festering in Lebanon since 1967. The old-guard Sunni leaders were delighted with the discomfiture of Premier Sulh, whose orders the army commander had ignored completely. They kept up the pressure in the following weeks, in their call for the dismissal of both the army commander and Sulh. But Jumblatt and Frangieh were between them able to weather this storm.

Meanwhile, most sections of the Maronite community rallied around in defence of the army. When the Ketaeb organized demonstrations in East Beirut to 'express support for the army', scores of thousands of the Maronite suburbanites took part.

The atmosphere in the country thus remained highly polarized for some weeks. Then, on 13 April 1975, another unknown gunman shot four of Pierre Gemayyel's bodyguards in East Beirut and outraged Gemayyel supporters ambushed a bus carrying Palestinians to the nearby Tel al-Zaatar refugee camp. Twenty-seven of the bus passengers were killed, and a further twenty were wounded. From this further crisis, the Lebanese system could no longer recover. The whole country was henceforth drawn into the sinkhole of civil disorder from which it was unable to emerge for many long years thereafter.

The regional disruption caused by the 1967 war had acted with cumulative effect on the Lebanese system. The arming of the Palestinians in Lebanon after 1967 had brought regional issues to the heart of the Lebanese system. This denied to the Shihabists the relative insulation of Lebanon from regional power-struggles on which their rule had been based. And it brought out into the open the broad differences on regional issues which divided the Shihabists' two main internal pillars, the Jumblattists and the Ketaeb.

But it was not only the Shihabist ruling consensus which felt the effects of the instability of the East Mediterranean region after 1967. The new regional imbalance also brought the 1943 National Pact system itself under considerable strain.

The Pact had been based on a power-sharing agreement between two principal parties, the Maronite and the Sunni communities. Its maintenance thus always depended on the continuation of support for it within each of those two groups.

Under the multiple shocks of the post 1967 years, much of Maronite opinion hardened into support of the Maronitist exclusivism with which the hard-line Ketaeb supporters of the new suburbs were imbued. Many leading Maronite politicians swayed with these new winds.

In contrast, most established leaders within the Sunni community did continue to identify their interests with the National Pact system.

But in doing so, they lost much of their own constituency to the new radicalism spearheaded by Kamal Jumblatt. As the pressures on them grew inexorably stronger, from the Maronites' leaders on the one hand and from Jumblatt on the other, their role became dramatically weakened.

The combination of a strong Maronite leadership and a weak Sunni leadership did not provide a stable platform for the National Pact system. As the political crisis worsened in the country all its major communities and parties were arming themselves heavily, from the early 1970s onwards.

On the surface, the Lebanon of early 1975 might have looked as though it were prospering. The oil-producing Arab countries of the Gulf had just experienced 1974's fourfold rise in oil prices; and they looked poised to become a vast market for Lebanon's many goods and services. Between 1964 and 1974, the total assets of Lebanon's commercial banks had climbed from 3.5 billion to 11.4 billion Lebanese pounds, with non-resident deposits contributing a high proportion of this increase. (Throughout this period, the Lebanese pound generally held its own, or even appreciated, against major international currencies.) Beirut port, which was already operating near capacity in 1973, became clogged with additional business the following year, with some ships waiting for weeks for their turn to enter. The value of the country's principal exports leapt from 446 million pounds in 1973 to 836 million in 1974.[4]

Beneath this façade of prosperity, however, the country had become a political tinderbox; and its inequalities and instabilities had only been aggravated, not lessened, by the sudden inflow of new oil wealth. In April 1975, the spark of political violence was struck in earnest.

Notes

1 Salibi (1976), p. 27.
2 ibid., pp. 69-70.
3 The findings and quotations referred to here and in the following four paragraphs are taken from Khuri's article, 'Sectarian loyalty among rural migrants in two Lebanese suburbs: a stage between family and national allegiance', in Antoun and Harik (1972), pp. 198–209. Khuri's findings in this field were most completely documented in his own book, *From Village to Suburb: Order and Change in Greater Beirut* (Chicago and London: Chicago University Press 1975).
4 For further details, see *Fiches du monde arabe*, nos. 119 (6 November 1974), 1393 (3 October 1979), and 1625 (2 July 1980).

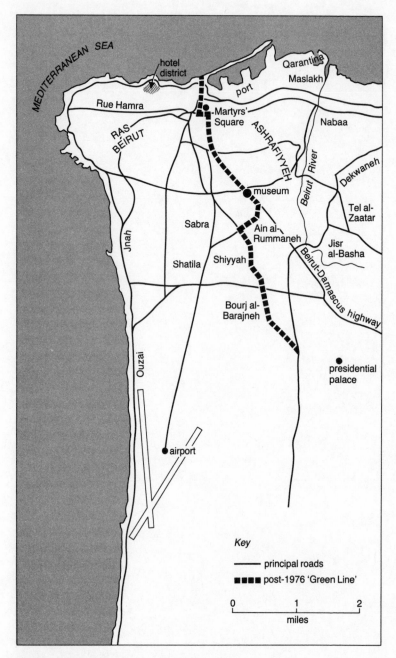

Map 2 The principal areas of Beirut

6 Eighteen months of civil war (1975–6)

The shots which rang out through the East Beirut suburb of Ain al-Rummaneh on 13 April 1975 brought a bloody death to twenty-seven Palestinians travelling to the nearby Tel al-Zaatar refugee camp. They also acted as the starting-gun for the series of armed confrontations which came to be known as the 1975–6 Lebanese civil war.

Ain al-Rummaneh; Tel al-Zaatar: the very names gave a clue to the recent rural nature of these two areas. Tel al-Zaatar means 'Hill of Thyme'. Ain al-Rummaneh means 'Well of the Pomegranate'. But by 1975, the only agricultural produce seen in these two places was that sold from hawkers' barrows, as they plied the narrow streets and alleys of these densely-peopled suburb-slums.

Ain al-Rummaneh and Tel al-Zaatar were two links in the 'misery belt' which by 1975 threw a thick noose of poverty right around the jet-set glamour of Beirut's city centre.

Ain al-Rummaneh was an older suburb, whose serried apartment blocks were peopled mainly by Maronites who were second- or third-generation city dwellers. By the early 1970s, these people had grown increasingly fearful about their own future. For to the east of Ain al-Rummaneh lay another suburb-slum, Shiyyah, which had also originally been a Maronite area. But during the 1960s, the older generation of Maronite residents of Shiyyah had become swamped with an influx of new Shi-ite immigrants, fleeing the poverty and instability of their home villages in south Lebanon and the Beqaa.

The new Shi-ite urban-dwellers might well have been hard-working and upstanding folk. But to their Maronite predecessors they represented a threat. They brought to the suburbs many of the rural habits – the easy camaraderie! the large families! – which the older Maronite townsfolk had left behind a generation or two back. In Shiyyah, the bells of Mar Mikhail church became drowned by the call to prayer blared from the minarets of a half-dozen new mosques.

The Maronites of Ain al-Rummaneh were determined that this

should not also be their fate. By 1976, the hard-line Maronite Ketaeb Party had quite a strong base there. So, too, did Camille Chamoun, whose views had become, if anything, even more toughly 'Maronitist' since he had lost the presidency in the civil war of 1958.

Over the Beirut River in Tel al-Zaatar, meanwhile, more than 30,000 people were crowded into one-storey cinder-block shelters. Since 1952, the area had been a registered refugee camp, administered by a United Nations relief organization. But since the conclusion of the Cairo agreement between the PLO and the Lebanese government in 1969, security inside the camp had been in the hands of the PLO. By 1976, camp residents included the Palestinian families who had lived and multiplied there since the early 1950s, and many poor Lebanese migrants from south Lebanon – mainly Shi-ites.

The Palestinians of Tel al-Zaatar, like those elsewhere in Lebanon, had given an effusive welcome to the Palestinian nationalist movement whose popularity had erupted after the Arabs' 1967 defeat. After the conclusion of the Cairo agreement, they had enrolled in the PLO militias in their thousands. They also found themselves able to relieve the horrendous pressures of population growth inside the camp by spilling outside the camp's original perimeters, into some of the apartment blocks which had grown up around them.

This spreading of the camp population brought the Tel al-Zaatar residents right up against the resentment of the Maronite majority in the densely-packed neighbouring suburb of Dekwaneh. Ever since 1969, relations between the two neighbouring areas had been tense: between 1969 and 1975, they had several times erupted into open armed clashes.

On 13 April 1975, after the shooting in Ain al-Rummaneh, the whole area around Tel al-Zaatar and Dekwaneh exploded into large-scale battles. In the course of these, for the first time, heavy artillery fire was also brought into play by the two sides.

The pro-Palestinian Druze leader Kamal Jumblatt accused the Ketaeb Party of having organized the Ain al-Rummaneh ambush and then of supporting the Maronite fighters of Dekwaneh against the Palestinians. Jumblatt tried to use this accusation to cut the Ketaeb completely out of access to political decision-making in Lebanon. On 26 April, the left-leaning Lebanese National Movement (LNM), which he led, passed a resolution calling for boycott on any dealings with the Ketaeb.

The Ketaeb responded by calling Jumblatt's bluff. The two Ketaeb ministers in Rashid al-Sulh's six-month-old cabinet resigned. Soon after, they were followed by nine other anti-Jumblatt ministers.

This posed an open challenge to Premier Sulh, who was generally regarded as little more than a Jumblatt protégé. So on 15 May, he offered his own resignation. The major issue then became whether he or another Jumblatt ally could form a successor cabinet without having to include the Ketaeb.

Jumblatt soon discovered he could not find any substantial Maronite politicians who would participate in a government from which the Ketaeb was banned, so no solution to the government crisis could be found on his terms. But the Druze leader exercised such considerable sway over the Muslim community at street level, that no Sunni politician could be found who might try to form a government which was *not* based on them.

On 23 May 1975, President Frangieh made a surprise move by naming a cabinet made up mainly of army officers. As premier, he named a retired Sunni brigadier called Nureddin al-Rifai.

This move was no mere 'technical' device to break out of the impasse caused by Jumblatt's anti-Ketaeb ultimatum. The 'strong Maronite' president must have known most Lebanese Muslims would oppose the formation of a military cabinet, just as his own 'strong Maronite' allies would welcome it. For the Muslims of all sects still recalled with bitterness the steps the army had taken against the fishermen's strike in Sidon the previous February (see Chapter 4). And the Maronite hard-liners meanwhile scarcely veiled their hope that the Maronite-dominated army might soon be pulled into the continuing inter-communal fighting, on their side.

The Muslim leaders responded to Frangieh's challenge with a rare display of communal solidarity. Kamal Jumblatt even got together with his main opponent in the Sunni community, Saeb Salam, in a joint denunciation of the cabinet. It took Brigadier Rifai precisely three days to find out that no one in his own Sunni community would back his premiership. So he resigned.

President Frangieh's little cabinet stratagem had failed, and intra-Lebanese violence of an ugly new sectarian mould was mounting throughout the Beirut suburbs. Frangieh thus felt forced to call on a Sunni leader of some substance, to try to form a government which could bring the situation back under control. The one he chose was Rashid Karami, scion of the leading Sunni family in the northern port city of Tripoli. Karami had served several previous terms in the premiership with some competence – including a total of four years under President Fuad Shihab.

Karami worked for the next month to try to line up a government list which could hold the country together. (As he did so, inter-communal clashes multiplied around the country.) On 30 June, he finally announced the formation of a six-man cabinet which included neither Jumblatt nor the Ketaeb. So traditionalist was the cast of the new government that no fewer than three of its six members had been ministers in Lebanon's very first cabinet after independence, back in 1943! One of these, ex-President Chamoun, was named Minister of the Interior, and given control over deployments of the police and paramilitary security forces.

For his part, Karami insisted on being his own Minister of Defence. He had a very real fear that the hard-line Maronites would try to draw the army into the fighting on their own side. This, he felt sure, would split the army, and damage the hopes of subsequent national reconciliation. So he wanted to make sure he retained some control over army deployments for himself.

The day after Karami announced his new cabinet, a cease-fire agreement was signed between the Lebanese army commander and the Chairman of the PLO, Yasser Arafat, in the presence of the Syrian foreign minister. From then until the end of 1975, Arafat was able to keep all those PLO units loyal to him – which included most of its heavier fighting units – largely out of the battles in Lebanon.

The cease-fire brought a much-needed peace to the Beirut suburbs for the following two months. But few Lebanese thought their country's deep political problems had been resolved. The Lebanese militias, and most of the Palestinian factions involved in Lebanon, spent the truce period re-arming for the battles to come.

The first drum-rolls of these battles sounded towards the end of August 1975, from outside Beirut. The Greek Catholic town of Zahleh in the Beqaa Valley became locked into clashes with some of its Shi-ite and Palestinian neighbours. A long-simmering confrontation between the Nasserite militias of Karami's home town, Tripoli, and the Frangieh family's militia from nearby Zghorta, erupted once again.

The major Maronite politicians repeated their call that the army be sent in to separate the Zghortawis from the Tripoli militiamen. Karami agreed that this would be the only way to bring the situation under control, but he shared the common Muslim view that the Maronite General who was then army commander was too close to President Frangieh to be able to be neutral between Zghorta and Tripoli.

Finally, Karami and Frangieh did a deal. Frangieh agreed to replace the army commander with another Maronite officer considered less partisan. Karami then agreed that the army be sent in to separate the warring militias in the north.

On 13 September, army peacekeepers in the north shot and killed thirteen Nasserist fighters thought to be infiltrating their lines. The Nasserists' national patron, Kamal Jumblatt, decided that the LNM should stage a nationwide strike to protest the army's partisanship in the north.

With every hour that passed towards the hour of the planned strike, the capital grew ever more tense. Militia units from both the Maronite and the Muslim parts of the city had been training heavily throughout the summer. Now, members of these militias took up battle positions on street corners, on top of high buildings, and commanding strategic road bridges.

At the very last minute, Jumblatt cancelled his strike call. But he was too late to halt the violence which was unleashed upon Beirut. This was particularly harsh in the city's labyrinthine downtown market area, which for a century now had been the principal meeting-place of Christian and Muslim interests in the city.

As clashes resounded throughout the Beirut suburbs, on 17 September Ketaeb units stationed in the downtown sector started a four-day-long bombardment of the market area. The markets were left lying in smoking ruins. With them, too, went all hopes of effecting speedy return to normalcy in the country.

The Ketaeb's motivation in launching this destructive action was hard to fathom. One prominent Lebanese historian said that it, 'indicated a determination by the Party . . . to demonstrate the readiness of the Christian Lebanese to destroy the country themselves, or force its partition, rather than to yield on any issue . . .'.[1]

In addition, the Ketaeb's bombing of the markets may have aimed, as the same historian also noted, at pulling the whole national army into the conflict on their side. But Premier Karami held firmly to his prerogatives as Minister of Defence, and refused to sign the necessary orders.

The Ketaeb campaign against the markets prompted the arrival of the foreign minister from neighbouring Syria. Under his auspices, a twenty-man 'National Dialogue Committee' was convened, on which Jumblatt took his place along with Ketaeb leader Pierre Gemayyel and other established Muslim and Christian politicians. However, Jumblatt insisted the body discuss a political reform plan which his

LNM had proposed the previous August, while Gemayyel was equally insistent that the restoration of security must precede any talk of reform. So meetings of the committee quickly became deadlocked.

The Ketaeb then sought to bolster their position inside the Lebanese system by bringing into play what they saw as a sympathetic conservative current then sweeping most of the rest of the Arab world. In answer to a request from the Ketaeb, a conference of Arab foreign ministers was held in Cairo in mid October to discuss the Lebanese crisis . But Syria, Libya and the PLO all boycotted the meeting, and it was unable to take any tangible action at all.

Towards the end of October, the security situation in Lebanon took another turn for the worse. The Nasserists of Beirut and some of their Palestinian allies had apparently been emboldened by the failure of the conference in Cairo. Now they pushed an offensive in West Beirut which drove the Ketaeb out of the prosperous Qantari quarter and down to the soaring, ornate towers of the sea-front hotels.

Street-fighting in Beirut thenceforth became a three-dimensional matter, as Nasserist artillerymen in the thirty-two storey Murr tower traded mortar fire with their Ketaeb counterparts in the hotels. Soon, the hotels – once the very symbol of Beirut's modernity and economic well-being – were also taken by the Nasserists. Over the following weeks, the Nasserists, leftists and Palestinians were able to push the Ketaeb eastwards to the port and the downtown Martyrs' Square.

Those successive battles reduced the dense web of commercial buildings which lay in their path to a haunting maze of bullet-pocked, burnt and looted ruins. A swathe of destruction a kilometre broad came to engulf the entire former downtown commercial area. The 'Green Line' which separated the Maronite militias of East Beirut from their opponents in West Beirut, snaked down inside this swathe. And as the city's southern suburbs became more sharply polarized between the opposing factions with every week that passed, the Green Line was extended even further southwards.

Throughout November and early December, the fighting continued in Beirut and other parts of the country. It hardly even paused to mark the arrival of reconciliation missions from such longstanding allies of Lebanon as France and the Vatican.

On 6 December, Ketaeb Party leader Pierre Gemayyel made for the Syrian capital, Damascus. That same morning, the bodies of four slain Ketaeb activists were found on a hillside east of Beirut.

Without waiting even for Gemayyel's return from Damascus, militiamen from the Ketaeb and other Maronite groups went on the rampage in all the parts of Beirut under their control. In the port area and elsewhere, they rounded up and summarily killed any Muslim workers or passers-by they could lay their hands on. On that single 'Black Saturday', no fewer than seventy Muslims – and probably many, many more than that – were killed purely on the basis of the mandatory line in their ID cards denoting 'religious affiliation'.

As news of the killings spread throughout the country, all its confrontation points erupted once again.

By 15 December, the fighting inside Beirut had just about been brought under control. But that same day, the Ketaeb and their Maronite allies launched a new type of action with grave implications for the future of the country. At this time the areas controlled by the Maronite militias still housed many Muslim residents. (As too, many Christians still lived in the regions which the Nasserites and other LNM parties held.) Now, the Maronite militias started on the process which they called 'cleaning' the areas under their control: that is, expelling their remaining Muslim residents.

On 15 December, Maronite fighters entered the small Shi-ite suburb of Haret al-Ghawarina north of Beirut. Rounding up all its inhabitants, they then summarily expelled them into West Beirut. Two days later, the Maronite militias 'cleaned' a small settlement of semi-nomad Sunnis away from an area near the presidential palace at Baabda.

However, much larger concentrations of Muslims still remained under the overall control of the Maronite militias. East of the Beirut River was the vast Tel al-Zaatar refugee camp, and just below it was the smaller refugee camp of Jisr al-Basha. Also east of the river was the huge suburb of Nabaa, home to close on 100,000 Shi-ites. North-west of Nabaa, pinched between the river and the port, were the two Shi-ite-dominated shanty-towns of Qarantina and Maslakh. One by one, the Maronite militias now set about subduing and 'cleaning' these areas.

On 4 January 1976, the Maronite fighters imposed a siege around Tel al-Zaatar and Jisr al-Basha. This action posed a new dilemma for PLO Chairman Arafat. For ever since the formal cease-fire he had agreed to back in July, he had remained wary of getting drawn into a conflict in Lebanon which might drain the PLO's strength before the expected Middle East peace conference in Geneva. He had thus tried hard to keep the bulk of the PLO forces out of the fighting in Lebanon.

But not all the groups in the PLO coalition agreed with Arafat's strategy. In late 1974, four of the more radical Palestinian groups – all much smaller than Arafat's own Fateh group – fromed an opposition within the PLO which they called the 'Rejection Front'. Backed by Iraq, the Rejection Front was dedicated to preventing any negotiated settlement of the Palestinian problem.·

Most Rejection Front member groups supported a general radicalization of the Arab political scene – in Lebanon as elsewhere. Some Rejection Front units had thus continued to take part in the fighting in Lebanon alongside Jumblatt's LNM throughout 1975, even while Arafat had kept the much larger Fateh units largely out of the fray.

When the large Palestinian community in Tel al-Zaatar came under siege in early January 1976, the pressure mounted on Arafat to join the Rejection Front groups in the fighting in Beirut.

On 14 January, the Maronite militias seized control of the small Palestinian refugee camp at Dbayyeh, five miles north of Beirut. That camp had housed mainly Christian Palestianians. But even they were not exempt from the fanaticism of the Maronite fighters, who unceremoniously expelled them to West Beirut.

Now, the PLO and Fateh leaders could see what might lie ahead for Tel al-Zaatar and Jisr al-Basha. From mid January 1976 onwards, the forces of the mainstream PLO were thus drawn willy-nilly into the Lebanese conflict, despite a few further attempts by Arafat to disengage them.

With the Dbayyeh camp in their hands, the Maronite militias turned their attentions to the shanty-towns of Maslakh and Qarantina. The LNM and their Palestinian allies responded by besieging the Maronite town of Damour, on the coast road south of Beirut. Damour was an important base of political support for former President Chamoun, who lived nearby.

On 18 January, the Maronite fighters were finally able to subdue the two Muslim shanty-towns. Their residents were driven out to West Beirut; and as they left, their victors brought in large bulldozers to raze their slender hovels to the ground.

Premier Karami announced his resignation. But by now even such an event as this attracted little attention. All eyes were turned towards Damour, where the last resistance of the townsfolk was broken on 20 January. Some 500 people lost their lives in Damour (only slightly fewer than in Qarantina). But most Damour residents were evacuated in army helicopters to the Maronite-held port city of Jounieh, 10 miles north of Beirut.

The fierce battles and terrible displacements of late January 1976 had several important consequences. On 31 January, seven leading exponents of hard-line Maronitism met near Jounieh to found a joint front which later came to be known as simply 'the Lebanese Front'. Ex-President Camille Chamoun and the Ketaeb's Pierre Gemayyel were both among the founding members of the Front. The Front exerted its political control over the areas held by the Maronite militias from 1976 through to the middle 1980s, surviving several bouts of internal dissent.

At the other end of the spectrum, 21 January saw the first major wave of the defections from the national army into the Jumblattist camp. These defections were led by a Sunni Lieutenant called Ahmed al-Khatib. His main complaint was that the army command had sanctioned the use of army planes to launch air strikes against the LNM forces besieging Damour.

Khatib organized his supporters into a body called the Arab Army of Lebanon (AAL), which provided heavy artillery backing for the Jumblattists from then on. But the organized defection on which the AAL was based also signalled the beginning of a whole series of schisms in the army, in a pro-Maronitist as well as anti-Maronitist direction.

Rushing in between these two increasingly polarized sides, the events of late January also brought the Syrian foreign minister hurrying to Beirut to try to negotiate a political solution. Discreetly backing up his efforts from afar, Palestinian units loyal to Syria rather than to Arafat moved into north Lebanon on 19 and 20 January.

The Syrian Minister's efforts seemed blessed with speedy success. On 22 January, President Frangieh's office announced that all the parties to the fighting had reached a cease-fire agreement, to be supervised by a committee representing the Lebanese and Syrian governments and the PLO. The next day saw the reopening of Beirut's international airport, which had been closed since the week before. On 24 January, Premier Karami withdrew his resignation. With the cease-fire continuing to hold, two weeks later Frangieh and Karami together made an official visit to Damascus.

While in Damascus, President Frangieh discussed a comprehensive reform package for his country with his Syrian hosts. On 14 February, one week after his return to Lebanon, he made public the terms of a new 'Constitutional Document' which would update the terms of Lebanon's 1943 National Pact.

The Constitutional Decument made several concessions to Muslim demands for greater participation in the affairs of the Lebanese state. The seats in parliament would henceforth be divided equally between Christians and Muslims, rather than in the 6–5 ratio in the National Pact had established. New legislation would henceforth be issued only after agreement between the president and the premier, and would bear the signature of both, rather than just of the president.

But the new document also retained many of the provisions of the National Pact which were criticized by Jumblatt and the Muslim radicals. The presidency, premiership and speakership of the House remained divided between the Maronites, Sunnis and Shi-ites respectively. Nothing was said about changing the Maronites' domination of the army command. And the text of the Constitutional Document spelled out that none of the proposed reforms would go into effect until after the PLO units had moved back within the limits set by the 1969 Cairo agreement – which would leave the LNM weaker during the crucial stage of implementing the document's terms.

None of the major Lebanese politicians was wholly satisfied with the terms of the Constitutional Document. In the end, though, the strongest opposition to it came from Kamal Jumblatt. He called for re-convening the moribund National Dialogue Committee which had been set up the previous September, to discuss the parts of the document he considered unsatisfactory.

Discussions continued throughout the country on how to move ahead with the reconciliation process the Syrians had started. Then, on 11 March, the commander of the army's Beirut garrison occupied the government TV station in West Beirut and went on the air to demand President Frangieh's resignation! This was the nearest Lebanon had ever come to experiencing a coup throughout its thirty years of independence!

The insurrectionary officer was Brigadier Aziz al-Ahdab, a son of Lebanon's first Sunni prime minister. Ahdab had been closely associated with former President Shihab throughout much of his career. Ahdab retained many of his Shihabist connections, but by March 1976 he had also acquired new friends. For the security unit which accompanied him to the TV station was provided by the security chief of Arafat's Fateh!

Ahdab's move certainly did reflect the Palestinians' dissatisfaction with Frangieh. But it also expressed a feeling widespread among the Lebanese themselves that the major obstacle to national reconciliation was Frangieh's continued occupation of the presidency.

Ahdab received general support for this view from the Muslim and

LNM leaders – although some, including Jumblatt, expressed reservations about the unconstitutional way he had intervened. Ahdab's move also received some initial encouragement from a couple of the smaller extreme Maronitist organizations. However, the Ketaeb and the Chamounists were still easily the most powerful groups in the Maronite Lebanese Front, and they both rallied strongly behind Frangieh. They insisted that he be allowed to finish his term, which was anyway scheduled to end the following September.

The call for Frangieh's resignation speedily won the support of just over the two-thirds of the members of parliament which was the quorum required for a presidential election. But still, the tough old clansman from Zghorta hung on in the presidential palace above Beirut.

By 14 March, Jumblatt had apparently overcome the reservations he had expressed to Ahdab about the use of the military. He now openly called for a 'military solution' to the impasse with the president. The next day, units from the AAL joined units loyal to Ahdab in a move towards the presidential palace. But their path was blocked in the outskirts of Beirut by pro-Syrian Palestinian units.

Syria was now clearly signalling its determination to support Frangieh in office. It continued to do so until the day six months later when his Presidential term expired. But the Baathist government in Damascus did not support only the Lebanese president during that period – it also backed the Maronite Lebanese Front groups who were now Frangieh's allies. On occasion throughout the months which followed, the Syrians were even to join battle at the Lebanese Front militias' side, against the leftist forces loyal to Kamal Jumblatt and their Palestinian allies.

How was it that a government ruled by hard-line Arab nationalists of the Baath ('Renaissance') variety came to play this role? The Baathist ex-officer who had ruled Syria since 1970, Hafez al-Asad, was subsequently to explain that he had been motivated by a concern for Lebanon's national unity. His intervention on the side of Frangieh and the Lebanese Front had been necessary, he explained, in order to prevent the Lebanese Maronites from being reduced to such desperation that they might even turn to Israel for support. In fact, Asad was probably glad to win the loyalty and near-dependence of a weakened president in Lebanon. Developments throughout the region possibly made it seem worthwhile to him to incur the wrath of Jumblatt and the mainstream Palestinians in pursuit of such a prize.

In spring 1976, the Syrian president was still busy gathering negotiating chips for a resumption of the Geneva peace talks – and especially chips which could enhance Syria's situation relative to that of Egypt. When Egypt had signed a second bilateral disengagement agreement with Israel in September 1975, this had reinforced Asad's fear of further Egyptian treachery to the Arab cause.

By 1975, Asad had already moved far towards papering over previous differences with Jordan. If he could now line up a grateful Lebanese president in the pro-Syrian camp – so Asad probably thought – then Syria would be better placed to prevent any further Egyptian backsliding.

Anyway, the Syrian president had already had problems dealing with the independent-mindedness of Kamal Jumblatt, who was certainly never inclined to volunteer his services for the greater glory of the Baathists' pan-Arab cause.

On 23 March 1976, leftist militiamen and AAL forces started bombarding the presidential palace, where Frangieh was still holed up. Two days later, he fled its cool marble halls for a temporary lodging near Jounieh, in the heart of the area held by the Maronite militias. Two days after that, Kamal Jumblatt travelled to Damascus, where he met with President Asad in a last attempt to settle their differences.

Jumblatt pointed out to Asad that a broad majority of Lebanese citizens and parliamentarians supported the demand that Frangieh resign, and he refused to budge from this demand. But Asad was adamant that Frangieh should stay in office. After nine hours of talks with Asad, Jumblatt returned to Beirut with this most basic issue unresolved. It was then just a matter of time before Jumblatt's forces and Asad's tried to resolve this question on the battlefield.

The break between Jumblatt and Asad posed a difficult dilemma for the PLO leaders; for they considered their relations with both the Syrians and the LNM to be of prime importance. The substantial numbers of PLO fighters in Lebanon would not be able to avoid taking sides between these two parties if they should fall out. PLO Chairman Arafat, therefore, expended great efforts in trying to prevent a total split between Syria and the LNM, but to no avail.

The final break between Syria and the Lebanese leftists did not take long to play itself out. The Syrians already had several thousand troops loyal to them deployed, under the guise of various pro-Syrian

Palestinian organizations, in various parts of Lebanon. In early April, they started reinforcing these units.

On 5 April, pro-Syrian PLO units moved into Beirut airport, and into all the sea-ports through which the LNM had been receiving arms. On 9 April, further pro-Syrian PLO units moved openly across the border into Lebanon along the Damascus–Beirut road. Three days later, they advanced to the crest of the Mount Lebanon range at Dahr al-Baidar, whence they might perhaps expect a simple downhill run into Beirut itself.

President Frangieh joined the leaders of the Maronitist 'Lebanese Front' in openly supporting this Syrian intervention. But the Syrians were still trying to finesse a compromise solution to the question of Frangieh's remaining in office. On 10 April, pro-Syrian Lebanese deputies were among the ninety members of the Chamber who made their way to a makeshift parliament building right on the Green Line which now divided Beirut. The assembled parliamentarians had one item of business. They passed an extraordinary amendment to the constitution which would, in this case only, allow the holding of presidential elections six months before the ending of the president's term.

Frangieh delayed countersigning the Chamber's decree for another two weeks. But finally, he became convinced that it was useless to hold out any longer – and he was anyway assured that he could continue to serve out his term until the bitter end, even after the early elections. So on 24 April he promulgated the Chamber's decree. Attention then immediately swung back to the deputies to see whom they would elect to succeed him.

From the beginning, the election campaign was a continuation of the power-struggle between Syria and the LNM. Syria's candidate was the Governor of the Central Bank, Elias Sarkis. Sarkis had previously served long years as *chef de cabinet* for Presidents Shihab and Hélou, so he had an established reputation as a loyal Shihabist. In addition to the support he received openly from Syria, and from Syrian allies such as Premier Karami, Sarkis quickly also gained the support of the Ketaeb and many of their Lebanese Front allies.

The candidate supported by Jumblatt and the LNM was the veteran National Bloc leader, Raymond Eddé. Like Sarkis, Eddé was a Maronite. He had long been renowned for his opposition to outside intervention in Lebanon's affairs – from the Syrians, as well as from the Israelis and Palestinians. Eddé's respected position in the Lebanese political constellation was underlined in his widely-used nickname of 'the Dean'. He thus seemed a strong and appealing candidate for the leftists.

The decisive session of parliament was scheduled for 6 May. The Syrians threw a tight security cordon around the temporary Chamber, and went to great lengths to ensure the presence of at least the sixty-six deputies needed for an electoral quorum. But to no avail: Sarkis's supporters were able to muster the attendance of only sixty-three deputies that day.

Then finally, ex-President Chamoun, whose hard-core supporters in parliament numbered four, declared for Sarkis. On 8 May, another parliamentary session was hurriedly convened. In a last-minute attempt to deter the parliamentarians, some leftist artillery units loosed a few rounds towards the Chamber just as the session was about to begin. But the leftists failed. The added presence of Chamoun's bloc was enough to ensure that the quorum was exceeded. And there had never been any doubt that once it was, Sarkis could win a sufficient majority of the votes cast.

Within days of the election, Kamal Jumblatt had entered into direct talks with President-elect Sarkis. Sarkis proposed convening a round-table conference to bring all the fighting parties together. But Jumblatt and the Syrians were not to be so easily reconciled: Sarkis's mediation attempt failed.

Already, back in December 1975 and January 1976, the LNM militias had pushed northward from the traditional Druze mountain area of the Shouf into the mixed, Maronite–Druze area called the Upper Metn. In May 1976, they were in control of a salient stretching about 12 miles northwards into the Upper Metn from the main Beirut–Damascus road. Now, after Sarkis's election, they pushed a little further northward still, cutting off a secondary road which linked Beirut with Damascus by looping up through Faraya and Uyoun as-Semaan.

This resumption of the LNM's 'Mountain offensive' struck deep fear into the heart of the Maronite community. For with the Uyoun as-Semaan road cut off, the Maronites found their last direct link broken with their new friends in Damascus. And the whole of the coast, through which the Maronites might still hope to communicate with the outside world, lay within easy artillery-range of the leftist guns up in the mountains.

Up until that point many Maronites – perhaps even a majority – had questioned the aggressive tactics of the Ketaeb and the Chamounists. But now, they saw a direct threat to the survival of their community in its Mount Lebanon heartland. The national army offered no hope of protection; for by May, the schisms which had started back in January had reduced it to an impotent skeleton. With the sole exception of the committed leftists among them, practically the whole Maronite community now saw the Ketaeb and Chamounist militias as providing their only hope of salvation.

The Syrians, too, were determined to halt the LNM's offensive. They already had many units they considered loyal to themselves fighting within the ranks of the PLO and the LNM. But these were not strong enough to sway the decisions of the leadership in either of these groups, away from the confrontation on which Jumblatt now seemed set. So on the night of 31 May/1 June, 2000 Syrian troops crossed openly into the Akkar plain in northern Lebanon. The next day, 4000 more crossed into the Beqaa along the main Beirut–Damascus road.

In the Beqaa, the pro-Syrian elements inside the LNM were strong enough to prevent it from mounting any more than token resistance to the Syrian advance. But as the Syrian units fanned out westwards from the Beqaa, making for Beirut and Sidon, they came up against LNM concentrations which were much more loyal to Jumblatt.

As the Syrians advanced against the LNM position, the PLO leadership realized it would now have to make the hard decision it had avoided taking until now. The PLO units in Lebanon were the only forces the PLO leaders still retained under their own autonomous command. Should they be deployed in support of long-time PLO ally, Jumblatt? Or should they be used to support Syria, which at the pan-Arab level was still an important military and diplomatic prop for the PLO? There could be no middle path.

So harsh was this dilemma, that it came close to splitting Yasser Arafat's veteran Fateh leadership in the PLO. But the Fateh leaders on the ground in Lebanon were strong enough within the organization to force their decision on the rest. It was: to support Jumblatt against the Syrians. The whole PLO leadership in Lebanon thus cast its weight behind the LNM in the areas it was defending, and this strengthened the resistance to the Syrian advance.

On 7 June, when the Syrian columns reached the entrance to Sidon, and the southern outskirts of Beirut, the LNM and its PLO allies were able to stop their advance.

The Syrian column which had been advancing directly along the Beirut–Damascus road reached the ridge of Mount Lebanon, but was unable to advance any further than the town of Sofar, a couple of miles east of the ridge. The LNM remained in control of the mountain roads which snaked up between West Beirut and the Upper Metn salient, though some of these tracks passed right under vertical cliffs near Sofar which had Syrian guns nosing over their top.

In the south-western outskirts of Beirut, meanwhile, the LNM was able to surround a substantial group of pro-Syrian forces in the vicinity of their international airport. But the whole leftist-held enclave which included West Beirut plus the mountain salient was, in its turn, completely encircled by the Syrian and Maronitist militia units.

On 8 June, the Arab League convened an urgent meeting of Arab Foreign Ministers in Cairo, to discuss Lebanon. Not surprisingly, all the parties involved in the fighting hoped that this would provide a way out of the tangle they were in.

The Foreign Ministers called for an immediate cease-fire, and for the despatch of an Arab peace-keeping force which would replace the Syrian units. This force would be placed at the ultimate disposal of Lebanese President-elect Elias Sarkis, the ministers decided.

The Syrians painted many of the tanks they already had in Lebanon, including those trapped at the airport, in the white colours of the Arab peace-keeping force. Then on 24 June, they extricated their forces from the airport in this guise. With these hostages to fortune now withdrawn to safety, Syrian President Assad announced that his troops in Lebanon would no longer henceforth be at President-elect Sarkis's disposal, but rather at President Frangieh's.

By this stage, Frangieh was participating openly in the leadership of the Maronitist Lebanese Front. On June 16, he had expanded the official role of ex-President Chamoun, who was a leader of the Front as well as Minister of the Interior. Frangieh now gave him the foreign affairs portfolio as well, and named him deputy premier. These moves may have been purely formal, since the national government had long since ceased to function as such. But they were hotly protested by many Muslims, as they seemed to signify that Frangieh was 'kidnapping' the symbols of Lebanese legality, and holding them in the Maronitists' enclave.

As the Syrians regrouped their forces in order to resume their confrontation with the Jumblattists, the Front's fighting-groups also felt confident enough to go on the offensive. On 22 June, Chamounist militia units joined army defectors loyal to Frangieh in a series of attacks against the remaining Palestinian and Muslim population centres in East Beirut. Five days later, the more powerful Ketaeb militia joined these campaigns. And the day after that, the Front militias and Syrian forces launched a joint offensive in the mountains which re-opened the strategic Uyoun as-Semaan mountain road.

On 29 June, the Lebanese Front militias succeeded in storming the small Jisr al-Basha refugee camp in East Beirut. In all of East Beirut, only the Tel al-Zaatar refugee camp and the huge Shi-ite populated Nabaa quarter still resisted total Maronitist control. After six weeks of fierce fighting in East Beirut, the Front was finally able to take control of Nabaa on 6 August.

The leftists later claimed that Nabaa had only fallen because a local group loyal to the charismatic Shi-ite leader Imam Musa Sadr had betrayed the area's defenders. But this made little difference for most of Sadr's many followers in Nabaa. Along with the rest of Nabaa's 100,000 population they were expelled ignominiously to find what refuge they could in West Beirut, as the Front fighters ransacked the battle-scarred apartment buildings which had been their homes.

The Front militias now all gathered around Tel al-Zaatar. From the monastery of Mar Shayya above the refugee camp to the east, the militia commanders now planned the final assault on the camp.

By then, the camp's thousands of families had been living under siege for seven months already. And throughout the two months of the Front's active offensive, they had huddled into underground shelters, as their own militiamen had tried to defend the camp's ever-shrinking perimeter. The greatest need of the camp population was for water, which could be scooped up from broken pipes only at great risk from Front snipers. As tens of the babies in the camp started dying from dehydration, on 11 August the PLO leadership finally agreed to Front demands that Tel al-Zaatar be totally evacuated.

The young generation of Front fighters who now saw East Beirut nearly completely 'cleaned' of all Palestinian and Muslim presence were wild with excitement. They themselves had suffered quite high losses – estimated by some sources as high as 800 fighters killed – during the successive 'cleaning' operations. Most serious of all had been the death of the veteran commander of the Ketaeb militia, William Hawi.

Hawi was succeeded by a charismatic young military leader of a new generation, much closer in age to the youths in their teens and early 20s who had flocked to the defence of the Maronite community throughout 1976. When he became commander of the Ketaeb militia in July 1976, Pierre Gemayyel's younger son Bashir was only 28.

It was under the command of Bashir Gemayyel, and of Camille

Chamoun's younger son Dany, that the Front militias finally succeeded in 'cleaning' Tel al-Zaatar. As the women and children from the camp underwent the now familiar exodus to West Beirut on over-crowded trucks, the victorious Front fighters picked out all the men and youths they could spot, for summary execution. An estimated 1500 camp residents were killed that day, out of a total estimated at 2200 residents killed throughout the whole period of the siege.

Still elated by their victory, the Front militiamen proudly showed Western correspondents round the carnage in the camp. Then, after it had been picked clean by local looters, they brought in bulldozers to raze it to the ground.

Other fighting still continued around the perimeters of the two parts of the country where the LNM–PLO forces still held out. The first of these areas included Beirut, Sidon and the mountain salient; the other was the area around Tripoli in the north. The Front militias and the Syrians, between them, surrounded the landward sides and these enclaves. Meanwhile, the Israeli and Syrian navies, between them, blockaded them from the sea.

On 23 September, President Frangieh finally gave way to his successor. At a ceremony in the Beqaa town of Shtaura the full might of the Syrian army protected the sixty-seven Lebanese parliamentarians before whom Elias Sarkis now took his presidential oath. Notable absentees included Premier Karami, Kamal Jumblatt and failed presidential candidate Raymond Eddé – all of whom were presumably protesting Syria's current position.

With the Frangieh era at an end, the Syrians must have hoped they could rapidly extend their sway to the two enclaves still held by the LNM–PLO forces. On 28 September, they moved against the LNM–PLO positions in the mountain salient in the Upper Metn.

Inside the PLO, meanwhile, the dispute had continued to rage in the leadership, over whether backing Jumblatt against the Syrians had been the wisest move. Shortly after the fall of Tel al-Zaatar, the balance inside Fateh's Central Committee finally shifted, in favour of those who sought to *disengage* the PLO from its entanglement in Lebanon.

Thus, in late September, when the Syrians launched their offensive against the LNM–PLO mountain salient, the PLO forces there rapidly fell back to the Beirut–Damascus road at Bhamdoun in a 'fighting withdrawal'. And since the LNM militias were unable to hold the salient without them, they now had to fall back too.

On 13 October the Syrians tried to clear the way down to Beirut from the mountain town Bhamdoun, as well as pushing their way towards Sidon, further south. By now, the PLO leaders were committed to disengaging its forces from the conflict in Lebanon. But they still wanted to deny the Syrians any clear-cut victory in Lebanon. So PLO fighters continued to hold the Syrian army back in and near Bhamdoun, while Fateh's diplomatists persuaded Syria's financial backers in Saudi Arabia to put the brakes on Syria.

By 15 October the Syrians had still not broken through at Bhamdoun. That day, the Saudis announced that a mini-summit would convene the very next day in the Saudi capital, Riyadh, and would include the heads of state of Saudi Arabia, Kuwait, Egypt, Syria and Lebanon, along with the PLO's Arafat.

Saudi Arabia's ruling royal family had no direct interest in what was going on in Lebanon. But they and the PLO were both concerned lest the power-struggle between Egypt and Syria, which was one aspect of the fighting in Lebanon, should continue to polarize the Arab world. The Saudis were desperate to try to reconcile the Egyptians and Syrians so they might all resume the Middle East peace process together. And that required a halt to the fighting in Lebanon, without either a clear-cut Syrian or Egyptian victory.

The convening of the Riyadh mini-summit signalled the beginning of the end of the 1975–6 Lebanese civil war.

How could such a complex struggle as had been played out in Lebanon just come to a halt on the decree of some foreign heads of state meeting 900 miles away? This fact came as little surprise to most Lebanese. They had long been resigned to the extreme vulnerability of the system they had created to decisions taken by foreigners in far distant capitals.

What had become clear by the time the discussions started in Riyadh was that the PLO was prepared to withdraw its support from its local Lebanese ally. So, too, was Syria.

Part of the Syrians' original motive in helping the Maronite militias resist Jumblatt's advance had been to prevent them from turning to Israel for help. But by mid August of 1976 there was much compelling evidence – in the form of arms shipments, and reports of secret Israeli-Maronite contacts – that they had done so, anyway. By October, the Syrians were thus eager for a solution in Lebanon which could replace the rule of uncontrollable militias of both right and left with a return to law and order.

Thus it was that, when the Saudis issued their call for a mini-summit, both the Syrians and the PLO responded positively. And with Syria and the PLO disengaged, the various local parties on whose behalfs they had become drawn into the turmoil in Lebanon were too exhausted by the long months of fighting to continue on their own.

The decisions of the Riyadh mini-summit were ratified at a full Arab summit held later that month in the Egyptian capital, Cairo. They called for an immediate cease-fire in Lebanon to be followed by the deployment of an Arab force which should be placed under the orders of President Sarkis pending the rebuilding of the Lebanese army.

In contrast to the Arab force despatched to Lebanon the previous June, this new force would have a mandate actively to deter potential trouble-makers. It was thus named not a 'peace force', but the 'Arab Deterrent Force' (ADF). As had happened earlier with the formation of an Arab 'peace force', the Syrians immediately assigned most of the forces they already had in Lebanon to the new force. They formed 22,000 of the 30,000 troops it started out with. (The other ADF troops came from a spectrum of Arab countries. But they peeled away from the ADF over the years which followed, finally leaving it a purely Syrian force.)

The summit resolutions also reaffirmed the 1969 Cairo agreement between the PLO and the Lebanese government. They called for the immediate application of the Cairo agreement – that is, for the return of the PLO forces to the boundaries prescribed in the agreement. This was to be accomplished under the supervision of a committee representing Saudi Arabia, Kuwait, Egypt and Syria.

In short, the regime in Lebanon was to be a return to the *status quo* which had existed before the civil war – with the important difference that Syria could now hope to dominate the system through its participation in the ADF.

Between 10 and 21 November 1976, the ADF troops were deployed throughout the whole of Lebanon. On 8 December, President Sarkis named as his first premier Dr Selim al-Hoss, an economist who had worked closely with him in the country's banking system. The following day, Hoss announced the formation of an eight-man cabinet. All the new ministers had strong technocratic qualifications, some of them with a tinge of the Shihabist thinking which Sarkis found familiar from his own past. On 24 December, a parliamentary session attended by seventy-two deputies passed a unanimous vote of confidence for the new government, and granted it a six-month mandate to rule through special powers.

It was with this breath of support from the Lebanese parliament – as well as the backing of the Syrians in the ADF – that President Sarkis sought to heal the bitter wounds of the civil war, and to put Lebanon back together again.

The Lebanese civil war had passed through many phases. In April 1975, it was started by a confrontation between Maronites and Palestinians. The main bulk of the PLO's forces then disengaged. But the balance within the country was already so fragile, that a series of battles had already been sparked off between various Lebanese parties themselves.

Those battles continued throughout the summer of 1975. They pitted the Maronite militias against a wide variety of different Sunni, Shi-ite or leftist groups. What most of these groups had in common was their membership in the coalition led by the veteran Druze and leftist leader, Kamal Jumblatt.

In the months following September 1975, the hard-line Maronitists did all they could to draw the national army into the conflict on their side. But Premier Karami followed the distinguished precedent set by Fuad Shihab in 1952 and 1958, and was able to prevent this happening. (Later, when Maronite hard-liners in the army command were finally able to throw some army units into the fighting, the army did indeed fall apart.)

In the closing months of 1975, Jumblatt started advancing in earnest against the Maronite forces in their traditional mountain heartland. In doing this, he was making an all-out bid to dominate the whole Lebanese system.

Jumblatt's mountain offensive was launched in the name of the modern-sounding ideal of the secularization of the Lebanese system. If successful, it would have thrown aside the whole cumbersome system of inter-sectarian checks and balances which had been formalized in Lebanon in the National Pact of 1943. (It would also have cleared the way for Jumblatt himself to move into the presidential palace.)

In January 1976, the Maronite militias retaliated by launching their own new offensive in Beirut. These attacks forced the mainstream of the PLO to join the fighting on Jumblatt's side. That can only have strengthened the leftist leader's determination that the power-struggle in Lebanon should be solved on his terms.

It was at this stage that a switch in Syrian attitudes became clearly apparent.

For many years prior to the civil war, Syria's Baathist rulers had considered Jumblatt an ally inside Lebanon. But from the beginning of his offensive in the mountain, they had been backing away from the leftist leader's ambitions. There must have been many reasons for this switch. Among them were probably the Syrian leaders' own shift from their early Arab nationalist ideology towards a pragmatic form of *realpolitik*, their distaste for Jumblatt's continued, strident Arabism and their likely preference for as weak as possible a president in Lebanon, who might continue to be dependent on them.

In April 1976, acting in conjunction with the Maronitist militias, the Syrians started to prepare for an open showdown with Jumblatt. When the showdown came, two months later, it pitted the Syrians and the Maronite militias against the Jumblattists and their PLO allies.

This confrontation remained a stand-off. From June to September 1976, the Syrians and the Maronites were unable to break through into the two enclaves controlled by their opponents. But neither was Jumblatt able to continue his advance into the Maronite-dominated parts of the Mountain.

Was it ever possible that he could have succeeded? Probably not. True, he had probably been correct when he said, in early 1976, that the majority of the Lebanese people supported him, against Frangieh. But an important core of organized Maronites were determined to resist him. And Jumblatt, with the wealth of accumulated Mount Lebanon folklore soaked into his very being, should have realized that that would happen.

The Maronite hard-liners' resistance, moreover, was backed up by both of Lebanon's more powerful immediate neighbours, who shared a strong interest in not seeing Jumblatt dominate the Lebanese system. Again, the expertise in regional affairs the Druze leader had acquired over the years should have indicated to him that this would be the case.

If Syria had taken no steps to thwart Jumblatt's plans, Israel almost certainly would have. And in either case, there was little point in hoping – as Jumblatt apparently did – that the far-off Egyptians or Iraqis would do very much to help him.

Jumblatt's bid to dominate the system was thus doomed to failure. So history will never know whether a Jumblatt-dominated Lebanon would have seen the establishment of the modern, non-sectarian state he advocated; or something very different.

The National Pact system in Lebanon had survived Jumblatt's

challenge with its two major principles – the formalization of explicit quotas for inter-sect power-sharing; and the continuation of Maronite primacy within the system – intact. Some details of the Pact's provisions had been slightly altered in the February 1976 Constitutional Document. But the essential principles of the Pact had been reconfirmed therein. That much, Syria's intervention against Jumblatt had achieved.

What the Syrian intervention had not solved, however, was the chronic crisis of the traditional Sunni leadership who, after the Maronites, were the second principal parties to the National Pact. Even after Jumblatt's challenge to them had been beaten back, the Sunni leaders continued to feel themselves squeezed between opposing radicalisms.

On the one side, the radicalism of the hard-line Maronitists was to continue to grow over the years which followed 1976. And on the other side, the radicalism of Jumblatt was soon to make way for a new kind of radicalism, far more novel to long-time participants in the Lebanese system than Jumblatt had ever been. That new force was the sectarian radicalism of the country's long-neglected Shi-ite communities. The rise of Shi-ite radicalism would prove to be a major theme in the years following 1976.

At the internal level, the civil war of 1975-6 may have resulted in the reassertion of Lebanon's political *status quo ante*. But at the external level, the civil war had seen the emergence of a substantially new phenomenon: the first major, direct intervention by Israel.

As far back as 1967, the Jewish state had established itself as the foremost power in the East Mediterranean region. And in the years which followed, it had had an enormous effect within Lebanon, by virtue of the harsh retaliatory policies it pursued there towards the emerging PLO. But the Israelis had waited a further nine years after their victory of 1967, before they intervened *directly* in the Lebanese system.

Starting in mid 1976, that intervention took two major forms. The Israeli government gave military support to the Maronite militias fighting in and around the Lebanese capital. And it, meanwhile, found new ways of affecting the situation in south Lebanon, through the introduction of the 'good fence' policy there.

By the time the civil war ended, the Israelis had built up a string of commitments to their local allies in Lebanon – mainly the Maronite hard-liners. They had also become intrigued by the huge potential they had discovered inside Lebanon, for strengthening their own position in their continuing dispute with Syria.

From 1976 onwards, Lebanon came to live in the daily shadow of the sharp regional rivalry between Israel and Syria. At first, perhaps, many Lebanese had not worried about this too much. After all, their country had lived through periods of intense regional rivalry before. Between 1958 and 1967, for example, the East Mediterranean had been polarized primarily between Egypt and the USA. And throughout that earlier dispute, Lebanon had been able to survive and prosper. It had been ruled by a virtual condominium of the two powers which contested the domination of the region; and it had been able to profit from that situation.

This new dispute was different. Now, Lebanon was to become a raw fighting-pit, in which Israel and Syria would seek to bruise and bloody each other like two fighting-cocks. That, they certainly achieved. But in the process, they bloodied Lebanon much more.

It took some time to learn the rules in the new Israeli-Syrian confrontation in Lebanon. For example, it was certainly of note that Syria's successive moves during the 1975–6 civil war had aroused little official opposition from Israel. Even while Syria was preparing for the large-scale military offensive of June 1976, Israel's prestigious English-language daily, *The Jerusalem Post*, was already writing of the existence of 'tacit Syrian–American–Israeli collaboration' in Lebanon.[2] And from June to October 1976, the Syrians and the Israelis were both giving certain kinds of military support to the Maronitist fighters.

The Israelis' main concern seemed to be that Syrian troops should not exceed a limit in Lebanon they called a 'Red Line'. This limit was often referred to by Israeli government officials. But it had never been explicitly agreed to as such by the Syrians, and was rarely even openly acknowledged by them. Nevertheless, right down till 1981, the Syrians were always quick to step back from the Red Line if the Israelis warned them – usually through American intermediaries – that they were straying too near it.

The Syrians' task was made more complex by the fact that the exact path and nature of the Red Line were never officially defined. Instead, its Israeli authors could and did re-define it in the light of continuing developments.

The major consideration the Israelis seemed to follow in fixing the 'Red Line', from 1976 onwards, was that Syrian troops should not be deployed within about 25 miles of Lebanon's southern border with

Israel. Nor should the Syrian deployment on the ground in Lebanon do anything to interfere with the air superiority which the Israelis had already clearly established over Lebanese air-space. Finally, from 1976 onwards, the two regional powers seemed well able to apportion their respective zones of control in Lebanon's coastal waters.

As far back as 1974, the Israelis and Syrians had shown themselves able to reach a disengagement agreement along their own bilateral frontier in the Golan. Through the Red Line arrangements of 1976, they then extended this disengagement line *de facto* so that it passed right through the southern parts of strife-torn Lebanon and deep into the Mediterranean.

These arrangements left a large part of south Lebanon outside the Syrian zone of influence. In the months following the end of the civil war, that area was to become a virtual free-fire zone between the Israelis and the PLO, and the local supporters of both those parties. Throughout Elias Sarkis's presidency, the instability which continued in the south then increasingly came to undermine the stability of the central government itself.

For the moment, however, as 1976 came to a close, the Red Line arrangements still allowed the Syrians unequivocally to dominate the administration which Sarkis was setting up in Beirut. And at the Riyadh and Cairo summits, the other major players in the Concert of Arabia gave their tacit approval to this situation.

But Syria's predominance over the Lebanese system would not for long go unchallenged. And the new challenger – Israel – had already made its first moves.

Notes

1 Salibi (1976), pp. 126–7.
2 Quoted in *Fiches du monde arabe*, no. 1798 (21 January 1981).

Syrian soldier of the Arab peacekeeping force in Beirut, 1978

7 A troubled inter bellum (1977–82)

Some 30,000 residents of Lebanon had died during the 1975–6 civil war. An estimated quarter of a million required immediate relief, and 600,000 had been displaced from their homes. Capital losses caused by the war had totalled 7.5 billion Lebanese pounds – about 3 billion dollars.[1] The losses suffered by Lebanese manufacturers were particularly heavy: a total of 172 large manufacturing firms suffered direct losses totalling 244.6 million Lebanese pounds, which came to some 51.4 per cent of their aggregate authorized capital.[2]

From 1976 on, the Lebanese economy became even more heavily dependent than previously on its service sector, which had been relatively less hard-hit by the fighting than manufacturing, and on remittances from the many Lebanese who now migrated down to the oil states. These two sources of income, along with a continuing inflow of hefty political subsidies from various Arab states, were sufficient to keep the economy afloat, and the Lebanese pound relatively stable, right until the Israeli invasion of 1982. The functioning of the economy was, however, radically affected by the *de facto* partition to which the country was subject after 1976. With Beirut's former downtown centres reduced to a heap of rubble, new commercial centres grew up in both East and West Beirut – as well as in Jounieh, Sidon and other outlying regions.

The man who, as the Republic's new president, was in charge of putting the country back together again was Elias Sarkis. Sarkis broke the mould of 'big family' presidents much more thoroughly than Camille Chamoun had done, twenty-four years earlier. When he came into office, he was 52 years old, unmarried, a meticulous but grey technocrat whose experience had been gained in the nation-building Shihabist school.

Why was Sarkis unable to replicate, in the years after 1976, the stunning political achievements Shihab had registered after the civil war of 1958?

The history of Lebanon must, I think, be written in terms of men and women who made it, as well as of abstract historical 'forces'. True, in 1976, the Lebanon's regional environment was far harder to deal with than it had been in 1958. True, by 1976 deep historical and demographic processes were underway inside Lebanon which more fundamentally challenged the status quo than had been the case in 1958. Nevertheless, my judgement remains that Sarkis himself contributed substantially to the breakdown which occurred during and following his time in office.

A man from a modest, small-town Maronite background, in the end Sarkis proved that he lacked the compelling vision of the Lebanese nation, which had been one of his master's major motive forces. Even if Shihab himself had come into office in 1976, he could not have achieved as much then as he had done in the period after 1958. But he would not have failed as abjectly as Sarkis. At points where crucial decisions had to be made, one conjectures that Shihab would not, as Sarkis did, have displayed the weakness of personality which let him slide along with the option which may have appeared 'easiest' in the short run, but which in the long run proved most harmful to the country.

The 'easy' option which was being presented most forcefully to Sarkis throughout his rule was the Maronite sectarian, or 'Maronitist', option. A Shihab, one hopes, would have had a strong enough sense of, and power within, his nationwide constituency to turn it down. Sarkis did not.

The main proponent and author of the Maronitist option in the Sarkis era was Bashir Gemayyel, the young man who in July 1976 had become head of the Ketaeb Party's militia.

Bashir Gemayyel was born in 1947, second son of the Ketaeb Party founder and leader, Pierre Gemayyel. Bashir was never groomed for high political office: in accordance with a widespread tradition of Lebanese clan life, that honour had been reserved for his elder brother, Amin.

One had the distinct impression that Bashir passed most of his early, formative years in the shadow of his polished and successful brother. Bashir could never hope to compete with the witty urbanity and demi-mondaine good looks which Amin showed off to full effect after being elected to the parliament while still in his 20s. In their place, Bashir developed a down-to-earth approach to people, which later matured into the roly-poly good humour of a worn but favourite teddy bear.

That public image must have formed a useful defence for Bashir

Gemayyel over the years. Behind it, a personality was developing in which ruthlessness was the handmaiden of a voracious hunger for power.

Towards the end of August 1976, the coalition of hard-line Maronite politicians which called itself the 'Lebanese Front' had set up a joint military command to co-ordinate the activities of all the Maronite militias. Bashir Gemayyel had gained new strength when he was named head of the new body, which was named the 'Lebanese Forces' (LF). By virtue of this new position, he was then invited to join the Front's political leadership as well. Still only 28, he provided a startlingly youthful contrast to the other ageing figures at meetings of the Front leadership.

Throughout the summer of 1976, too, Bashir Gemayyel and the new generation of activists he represented inside the Ketaeb militia had worked hard to establish a network of social institutions inside the LF-held enclave. These included a consumer co-operative, subsidized clinics, and a bus service linking East Beirut to the mountain hinterland – as well as a much more sinister organization called the 'Section Ketaeb de Sécurité' (SKS).

The logo employed by the SKS had the two S's streaking down like thunderbolts, in conscious imitation of the way the German Nazis had presented their 'SS' storm-troopers in the 1930s. Even while the civil war was still raging, Bashir found the resources to outfit the SKS units in smart charcoal-grey uniforms. During the latter months of the war, motorized SKS teams fitted up with medium machine-guns fanned out to impose Ketaeb rule throughout the Maronite enclave, and to collect the heavy 'taxes' which the Ketaeb militia's leadership demanded from its residents.

Thus, in the heat of the war effort, was first established Bashir Gemayyel's 'state-within-a-state'. It continued to stand as an open challenge to the authority of the country's legal institutions right down to the mid 1980s.

In November 1976, the Syrian troops of the newly-constituted ADF rolled down the mountain to try to extend the Sarkis government's writ into East Beirut (as they were also doing inside rival West Beirut). Many ordinary citizens on both sides of the city welcomed the ADF, thinking they presaged an imminent end to the country's violence.

But Bashir Gemayyel and his allies were in no mood to give up the total social control they had established in the Maronite enclave with their Ketaeb militia (now merged almost totally into the LF), and their SKS. Bashir Gemayyel's men were nowhere near strong enough to prevent the ADF deployment. So for the moment, they stood sullenly by, planning their next move.

President Sarkis probably came into office hoping that he could eventually apply some kind of Shihabist solution to the internal political problems of Lebanon. The two major vehicles through which President Shihab had ruled in the late 1950s and the 1960s had been the Ketaeb and the Jumblattists (see Chapter 4). And at first sight, it may have seemed to Sarkis that these same two parties had both emerged from the fighting of 1975–6 much strengthened within their respective constituencies.

Welding these two nominally modernizing parties back into a Shihabist-style coalition may indeed have been Sarkis's eventual aim. But so long as he was totally reliant on the Syrians for his security he would have to tread carefully. For the Syrians were in no mood to favour the granting of a significant role in Lebanon to the Ketaeb – or, indeed, to Kamal Jumblatt, who had shown himself so independent of their will throughout 1976.

At the beginning, Sarkis played a politically cautious game. He, and the government he had formed under Premier Selim al-Hoss, addressed themselves first of all to the kind of basic infrastructural tasks which their former mentor Fuad Shihab would certainly have approved, and which were certainly required in the aftermath of the civil war.

Then in early February 1977, the government turned to the crucial question of re-constituting the national army. Those officers who felt unhappy serving under the new president were given a special dispensation to resign, with all their benefits intact. The rest were expected to report back for duty forthwith.

The Sarkis presidency thus seemed to be starting to gather some cautious momentum. But in the single month of March 1977, two separate developments occurred which, between them, signalled the impossibility of implementing any Shihabist political scheme in Lebanon.

The first of these events was the assassination of Kamal Jumblatt. The socialist aristocrat who headed the Druze community and Lebanon's leftist coalition was killed on 16 March in a mountain ambush near his Shouf home. Enraged Druze villagers went on the rampage in the Shouf, arbitrarily and brutally killing more than 140 Shouf Christians. But the circumstances of Jumblatt's killing pointed not to any Christian hand, but to the involvement of the Syrians, against whom Jumblatt had fought tenaciously throughout the last year of his life.

The elders of the Jumblatt clan did not take long to endorse the succession of Jumblatt's only son, Walid, then 27 years old, to the leadership of the clan. This automatically made him head of the federation of Jumblattist clans which was the predominant grouping within the Druze community.

Later, Walid Jumblatt also succeeded to the leadership of the Progressive Socialist Party (PSP), which his father had founded; and later still, to the leadership of the leftist LNM coalition.

But Walid Jumblatt lacked the breadth of political experience his father had acquired. Throughout the early years of his succession, the younger Jumblatt managed to consolidate his own base within the Druze community. But outside the ranks of the Druze, he lacked the personal charisma and the harsh ambition which had brought his father a nationwide following.

It was a transparent weakness of the unwieldy LNM coalition that no clear means had been established, apart from the age-old rule of family succession, for the transfer of its leadership. Kamal Jumblatt's killing proved conclusively the extent to which the support of this Druze aristocrat of ancient lineage had been central to the unwieldy 'leftist' edifice.

The LNM maintained the appearance of an organized existence until it finally stopped publishing its central newspaper in 1981. But the coalition which it represented was falling violently apart, torn alike by the extreme dependence many of its leaders had developed to the petrodollar wealth of far distant Arab 'nationalist' regimes, and by these regimes' uncaring manipulations.

Few had been better placed than Kamal Jumblatt, in his day, to understand and deal with the fractiousness of the progressive and Arab nationalist regimes. But with him gone, the contending factions and parties inside the LNM now had no single figure of national authority left to mediate their many disputes. The most sincere of those Lebanese individuals who had been inspired by Jumblatt's stated aim of a secular, democratic Lebanon, continued for some years to hold together the coalition he had established. But they were eventually swept aside by powerful new forces of Druze and Shi-ite sectarianism.

Kamal Jumblatt's killing in March 1977 dealt a weighty blow to President Sarkis's chances of finding a powerful interlocutor within the Muslim community who might enter a Shihabist-style coalition of modernizing nation-builders. Less than two weeks later, and 'Shihabist' plans Sarkis might have entertained received a further blow – this time from within the Maronite community.

On 28 March, as part of the plan to re-build the national army, Sarkis named a new army commander. He needed someone who would be totally loyal to himself, who was acceptable to the major Muslim leaders, and who had strong pro-Shihabist credentials. The man named was Brigadier Victor Khoury.

Khoury was not, however, acceptable to the Ketaeb militias. That night, a bomb blast rocked the sumptuous East Beirut apartment of Sarkis's Defence Minister. And the following day Bashir Gemayyel called for a strike in the LF enclave to protest the government's move.

Bashir Gemayyel's action that day marked a decisive turning point in the power-balance within the Maronite community. For his strike call was criticized openly by none other than his father, Pierre Gemayyel. But still he did not retract it.

The residents of the LF enclave (most of them, Maronites) now had to choose whether to follow Bashir's call for open defiance of the government, or his father's call for a more cautious approach. In the maze-like back-streets of East Beirut, Bashir's militiamen gave the residents little chance to choose. Threading their way carefully between the ADF units which dominated the capital, they forced most of East Beirut's traders to comply with the strike call.

By the end of the day, Bashir Gemayyel had registered a significant victory – not so much over the Sarkis administration, which continued its plans for the army regardless, as over his own father. He had established that he was no longer merely boss of the militia controlled by his father's party, but an effective political personality in his own right.

Bashir Gemayyel's challenge to his father that day marked a double break with the traditions of Lebanese family politics. First, for any Lebanese public figure openly to confront his father was at odds with the country's whole system of family allegiance. And he was the family's younger son!

Even after March 1977, Bashir still lacked any broad political credibility. He was still so young! A mere hothead! – that was what many still thought, hoping for the day his father would be able to control him once again. But Bashir already had a weighty political backer, who helped him to gain political credibility *on his own terms*, and without going back to apologize to his father. This was ex-President Camille Chamoun, who from 1976 onwards had encouraged Bashir's hard-line Maronitist attitudes.

The wily old Chamoun, as old as the century itself, had not mellowed with the years. Far from it; by the late 1970s his vigour and rancour seemed only to have increased since 1958, when his early Maronitism had brought the independent nation to its first civil war. The 'Tigers' militia which Chamoun's younger son Dany commanded, had never attained the level of technical expertise of Bashir's Ketaeb militia. So the elder Chamoun seemed happy, from 1976 to 1980, to throw his own broad political prestige behind Bashir Gemayyel's Maronitism.

Over the months which followed March 1977, Pierre and Bashir Gemayyel were playing a cat-and-mouse game for control of the Ketaeb cause. This game had a political impact, because Gemayyel the father was more generally co-operative towards the Sarkis regime than Gemayyel the younger son.

Many of Pierre Gemayyel's veteran allies in the political leadership of the Ketaeb Party still resisted the challenge posed by Bashir and the youngsters he commanded in the LF. Bashir countered by creating a whole new political infrastructure under the wing of the military apparatus he controlled. Then, over the years following 1977, he was gradually able to put key members of this infrastructure into leading positions inside the formal Ketaeb Party leadership itself. Seeing himself outflanked, Pierre Gemayyel finally reconciled himself to his younger son's ambition, and he came to endorse Bashir's hard-line political aims.

Thus it was that, during the early years of the Sarkis presidency, Bashir Gemayyel came to exert his authority over that of his father and the rest of the Lebanese Front leadership.

This process was still near its beginning on that day in late March 1977 when Bashir organized a strike in East Beirut against his father's wishes. But that event, like the collapse of the Jumblattist machine set in train by Jumblatt's killing earlier that month, boded ill for Sarkis's chances of re-building any Shihabist political coalition in Lebanon.

The first months of 1977 had seen the first augurs of the ills to come for the Lebanese system. Nevertheless, that period was generally a hopeful one for those parts of the country that had been ravaged in the 1975–6 civil war. (From the end of 1977 onwards, a wave of new births bore witness to the hopeful mood of those earlier months.)

By contrast, the sun-scorched hills, winding valleys and citrus groves of south Lebanon entered into a new phase of increased violence, with the start of the Sarkis presidency.

The early months of the 1975–6 civil war had been relatively peaceful ones for the people of south Lebanon. However, after the start of the large-scale Syrian intervention in Lebanon in June 1976, their situation rapidly deteriorated.

The Israelis never allowed the Syrians to deploy south of the 'Red Line' they drew, running inland from a point on the coast about midway between Sidon and Tyre. From June to October 1976, the area south of the Red Line formed a heavy bulge at the bottom of the enclave which the PLO-leftist coalition controlled.

Along with the rest of the leftist enclave, south Lebanon found itself hemmed in by hostile forces from June 1976 until the end of the civil war. To the east was Syria, to the south Israel, and to the west a coast whose ports were blockaded by the Israeli navy.

The villagers of the south were among those who suffered the most from the siege. Basic foodstuffs, fuel oil and medical supplies were scarce. The south's farmers and merchants were cut off from the traditional markets for their citrus and tobacco crops. And while the attention of the Palestinian and leftist leaders was focused on the battles further north, some of the more unruly followers were riding roughshod over the people of south Lebanon.

It was on 24 June 1976 that the Lebanese press first reported a new twist in this situation.

For more than a decade, the major contact most villagers in the south had had with their Israeli neighbours had been through the reprisal raids the Israelis mounted against the Palestinian refugees there. Those raids had caused heavy damage to the south's native residents as well.

Now, however, the Israelis appeared to be offering a hand of friendship to the southern villagers in their time of need. They opened two new gates in the electronic border fence, and allowed southerners through them to attend special mobile medical clinics, to stock up on basic supplies, and to earn some hard cash labouring on Israeli farms.

This 'good fence' policy rapidly paid dividends for the Israelis. The population of the south contained a large majority of Shi-ites, with much smaller groups of Maronites, other Christians and Sunni Muslims. Half a dozen of the Maronite villages, however, nestled up close against the Israeli border. And within the few months following the opening of the fence, most of them had sprouted their own home-grown Maronite militias – all armed by Israel.

It was left to a Greek Catholic Major in the Lebanese army to try to weld these local groups into a single coherent force. This was Saad Haddad, a tightly-coiled spring of a man who in mid 1976 commanded the army barracks at Qulei«a, a poor Maronite village a few miles north of Israel's northernmost point.

Even while the main drama of the 1975–6 civil war was coming to an end in the rest of the country, Haddad was preparing to go into action in the south. In October 1976, forces under his command pushed north-east from Quelei«a and easily stormed the barracks in the much larger town of Marjayoun. From there, his pro-Israeli fighters could dominate the major supply route linking Palestinian guerrilla bases in the foothills of Jebel al-Shaikh (Mount Hermon) with the coast.

Soon after Haddad had captured Marjayoun, the Syrian-dominated ADF was able to deploy throughout the rest of Lebanon. But the ADF was kept out of the south by the Israelis' continuing insistence on their Red Line limitations.

In January 1977, ADF units moved cautiously down to the environs of Nabatiyeh, six miles north-west of Marjayoun. The Israelis immediately protested through the Americans, and the Syrians pulled back to the Zahrani River. Nabatiyeh, like the rest of south Lebanon, was left as a free-fire zone, in which the Israelis and their allies could confront the PLO and their allies, without the interference of any legitimate local authorities.

The Israelis were not totally displeased at that outcome. Their premier, Yitzhak Rabin, wrote in his memoirs that, '. . . because the Syrians were prevented from moving south of the "red line", southern Lebanon became a haven for the (PLO) terrorists. We had foreseen such an eventuality *and preferred it to Syrian military control of the area bordering on our territory.*'[3]

This free-fire zone, moreover, was never separated from the continuing political drama in Beirut. Far from it. From the beginning, it had a powerful potential to act as a lever in developing events in the capital. The major internal and external actors in the Lebanese drama all seemed to understand this clearly. They hoped that, by changing the balance on the ground in the south, they might swing the political balance in Beirut.

By late July 1977, President Sarkis seemed to have reached a formula for a disengagement in the south. This formula was part of an agreement named the 'Shtaura agreement' – from the scenic Beqaa town, still a key centre of Syrian influence in Lebanon, in which it was concluded.

The Syrian government, the PLO and the Lebanese government were all parties to the Shtaura agreement. It called for reimposing the limits the 1969 Cairo agreement had set on the PLO's military presence in Lebanon. In south Lebanon, as elsewhere, PLO units were to return to the refugee camps, as the earlier agreement had stipulated. Meanwhile, the Lebanese militias of all shades should disengage, disarm and make way for the deployment of the legal Lebanese army in the south.

A few first steps were taken towards implementing the new agreement. But soon, any further progress became grounded on the shoals of an endless 'who-does-what-first' kind of argument. The Lebanese Front leaders argued that *their* militias could not disarm so long as the PLO had not fully satisfied its portions of the Cairo agreement. The leaders of the leftist and Muslim militias said *they* could not disarm so long as the Front's militias were still in operation. And the PLO leaders argued that *they* could not move back fully to the refugee camps before the Lebanese army was full deployed outside them.

All of these 'internal' parties were still scarred by the traumas they had suffered during the civil war. None was prepared to devote much effort to helping re-establish the one force which might, theoretically, one day stand neutral between them – the Lebanese national army. And President Sarkis was unable to hold out any national vision which might have persuaded them to do so.

The Shtaura agreement's sharpest critic of all was Major Haddad. The rebel southerner still clung on to his claim that he remained an officer in the legal Lebanese army. His claim was backed up forcefully by most of the Lebanese Front leaders. And it received important support within the army command, which continued to pay his men throughout the years which followed.

But the Muslim and leftist politicians had already seen the Sunni officer Ahmed al-Khatib, leader of the earlier Muslim secessionary movement, cashiered from army ranks in the first days of the Sarkis era. They argued that Khatib's infractions of army discipline had been no greater than Haddad's, and that Haddad should therefore be court-martialled. The question of Haddad's exact status in the army was to plague national politics right through until his death in late 1983. It was never an issue which President Sarkis wanted to address directly.

Throughout the latter months of 1977, Haddad's meagre units were being beefed up by the LF militiamen, who were shipped in from the LF enclave to the north through Israeli ports. As the clashes multiplied between the Haddad fighters and units of the PLO-leftist coalition, Israeli army regulars also, on occasion, crossed the border to back up Haddad. The south now found itself being used as a lever not only in the Lebanese political game, but also in the wider web of the overall Middle East conflict.

In January 1978, the uneasy southern front-line threatened to erupt yet again. Then, in the early morning of 11 March, eight commandos from Yasser Arafat's Palestinian guerrilla group, Fateh, infiltrated into northern Israel in rubber dinghies and hijacked a bus to Tel Aviv. During the shoot-out which followed, thirty-one Israelis and six of the guerrillas were killed.

That incident rocked the Israeli public. For Menachem Begin's toughly nationalistic Likud Bloc government had come into power only the preceding June, and it had promised to maintain previous Israeli governments' tough stance against PLO terrorism.

On 14 March, the Israeli army retaliated in force. While Israeli planes and warships hammered the bases and supply routes used by the PLO and their allies in south Lebanon, Israeli ground forces numbering some 25,000 pushed steadily northwards towards the Litani River. By 21 March, the Israelis had almost reached Hasbaya in south-east Lebanon, and had occupied all the area south of the Litani except for a slim coastal pocket reaching down to Tyre.

Total civilian casualties from Israel's March 1978 invasion were estimated by one Western source at 2000, while between 150 and 400 fighters of the PLO–leftist alliance (and twenty-four Israeli soldiers) also lost their lives.

Hundreds of thousands of southern villagers fled northwards to escape the fighting. Many then found they had no homes to return to. A UN commission which visited south Lebanon shortly after the fighting found that in 100 southern villages a total of 2500 houses had been completely destroyed, while twice that number were partially damaged.[5] Throughout south Lebanon, roads and bridges had been devastated in the fighting; many orchards had been ploughed up by tanks or burnt by phosphorus shells; wells, water-pipes and electric lines lay broken and unusable.

As late as 1983, one demographic researcher was reporting that a total of 141,000 Lebanese Shi-ites who had originally left their villages in south Lebanon during the March 1978 exodus were *still* living a hand-to-mouth existence in and around West Beirut.[6]

From the beginning of the crisis, the Lebanese government called urgently on the UN Security Council to try to check the Israeli advance. On 19 March, the Security Council adopted Resolution 425, which called for a cease-fire in Lebanon, and for the Israelis' immediate withdrawal. The resolution also called for the dispatch of a 6000-man UN force to replace the Israeli presence in south Lebanon: this force would be called UNIFIL (for UN Interim Forces in Lebanon).

It took a little time for the UN cease-fire to take effect. But by 28 March, the Israelis and the PLO had both agreed to respect it, and to ensure that their respective allies did as well.

The Israelis started their withdrawal two weeks later, and appeared to be dragging their feet about each successive stage of the pull-back. By 30 April, they had pulled out of 42 per cent of the occupied area, but international pressure continued for further withdrawal. On 13 June they effected one last pull-back. But only fourteen of the positions evacuated that day were handed over to UNIFIL.

The remainder, which formed a continuous 'security belt' between three and six miles wide along Israel's northern border, were handed over to the Israelis' long-time Lebanese ally, Major Haddad.

The Syrians had studiously avoided getting drawn into the fray during the 1978 invasion, even when their PLO and Lebanese leftist allies were taking a bad beating there. This fact was clearly noted in Beirut. The conclusion drawn by many was that Syria's power in Lebanon was no longer as all-pervasive as it had appeared at the end of 1976. With their invasion, the Israelis had challenged Syrian supremacy in Lebanon – and the Syrians had not reacted to defend it.

After March 1978, those Lebanese who most wanted to free their government from Syrian control felt emboldened to step up their efforts to this end. Bashir Gemayyel's LF militias were at the forefront of this movement. The months following March 1978 saw a steady succession of clashes between the Syrians and the LF in East Beirut.

First omens of the troubles the Syrians would face in East Beirut had come in early February 1978. Then, an argument between Lebanese army troops and Syrian ADF units had rapidly escalated into an open battle. The army troops had been joined, in that battle, by some groups of the Chamoun family militia. In an attempt to punish the Chamounists, the Syrians then shelled East Beirut, killing around 100 East Beirut residents in two days.

That incident had been shelved, through the time-honoured manoeuvre of setting up a joint investigation commission. But two months later, in mid April 1978, Syrian ADF units were once again drawn into a battle with the LF militias in East Beirut. The Lebanese government was still reeling from the effects of the Israeli invasion. Once again, the Syrians turned their heavy artillery against an East Beirut suburb, this time leaving a total of around sixty dead.

This second round of fighting led to an extremely significant victory for the LF militiamen. After it, the Syrians agreed to withdraw from some sectors of East Beirut, where they were replaced by ADF troops from conservative-ruled Sudan and monarchic Saudi Arabia.

By then, Camille Chamoun was openly calling for a total Syrian withdrawal from Lebanon. Then, after the April clashes, Bashir Gemayyel announced that the LF militias would henceforth look after the security of the areas under their control themselves, rather than leaving it to either the ADF or the Lebanese government security forces. 'Where there are police stations, of course we will support the police', Bashir explained at the time. 'Or they can support us, *but always under our authority.* Wherever we can enforce our authority, we will do it now.'[7]

In June 1978, Bashir Gemayyel turned his militia's attentions away from the Syrians, towards a different set of rivals. These were the Maronite mountain-men of northern Zghorta, supporters of Zghorta's most prominent son, ex-President Suleiman Frangieh.

Unlike Bashir Gemayyel, Frangieh had never forgotten the help the Syrians had given him back in the dark days of 1976. His appreciation of Syria went back, indeed, to 1957. For he had found a refuge there after the messy affair in which some opponents had been killed in a local church (see Chapter 5). In addition, Frangieh's son, Tony, a former telecommunications minister of some wide repute, was rumoured to have many interesting business deals underway with President Asad's strongman brother, Rifaat.

Throughout 1977 and early 1978, Frangieh had counselled his colleagues in the Lebanese Front against a break with Syria. But they had not heeded him, and in May 1978 he had stopped attending their meetings. A battle to control the northern part of Mount Lebanon then seemed to be brewing between the Frangiehs and their former allies in the Front.

At stake in that growing confrontation was far more than 'mere' territory, however. For the northern part of the Mountain was the original heartland of the Maronite sect in Lebanon. Whoever controlled it could claim with some authority to carry the full weight of the sect's traditions.

Bashir Gemayyel decided to gain the advantage of surprise in the confrontation in the north. Early on 13 June, he sent a group of 100 fighters up to the Frangiehs' summer quarters at Ihden. Striking just before dawn, they gunned down Tony Frangieh, his wife, their 3-year-old daughter and two family retainers – along with twenty-nine other sleep-heavy Ihden residents.

For Suleiman Frangieh and his family, this action was worse than simple murder – it was 'sacrilege'.[8] Immediately, the old Zhgorta clansman blamed Bashir Gemayyel for the raid, and he cut his last remaining links with the Lebanese Front. He now publicly accused the Front of working with Israel, and of aiming at the partition of Lebanon. By the end of August he had entered into a formal alliance with Walid Jumblatt and his own neighbour, the ex-Premier Rashid Karami; and he increased his public support for Syria and for the ADF.

Frangieh's defection from the Front took the historic Maronite heartland away from Front control, and clearly into Syria's orbit. In the weeks which followed the Ihden affair, Syrian ADF units cleared the last centres of Ketaeb military activity out of the regions to the north of Byblos. Members of the Zghorta militia applauded and aided their efforts.

Back inside the reduced LF enclave, most of the old-style political bosses, including Pierre Gemayyel, were nonplussed at Bashir's audacity. Killing the heir to an important political family was a significant break with Lebanese tradition, after all. Throughout Lebanese history, the leaders of the Lebanese factions had never known from one day to the next whether today's ally might turn into tomorrow's opponent, or vice versa. So their tradition was seldom try to kill other leaders, but to strike mainly at the 'little people' caught in between.

But Bashir got away with it. The fact that he maintained the momentum of his confrontation with the Syrians helped him to do so.

On 1 July, the Lebanese Front announced a one-day strike against the continued Syrian presence in the country. The strike sparked off a new round of LF–Syrian fighting throughout East Beirut.

Since the April clashes, those Syrians who remained in East Beirut had been 'redeployed' into a single tall tower-block which assured them strategic control of that half of the city. However, in the web of streets, twisting alleys and labyrinthine buildings which sprawled below the tower-block, there was little to impede the activities of the LF militias. Such units of the slowly re-forming Lebanese army as were stationed there busied themselves with traffic control and other auxiliary tasks, under the supervision of the militias. And the few Sudanese and Saudi ADF troops who had nominally replaced the Syrians on the ground, appeared too terrified to show themselves in public during any altercation. (Soon thereafter, the Sudanese withdrew from the ADF completely. They were followed by the Saudis in early 1979.)

As always in Lebanon, it was impossible to tell who pulled the first trigger in July 1978. But from 1 July to 7 July, East Beirut was again caught up in an inferno of fighting. The Syrians in the tower-block blindly rained a stream of rockets on to undefinable targets below, while Syrian artillery and tanks parked around the perimeter of East Beirut pumped round after round into the dense housing which faced them beyond the pocked and battle-scarred 'no-man's-land'.

By 7 July, President Sarkis could see no end in sight. His foreign minister had gone to Damascus to plead with the Syrians to stop the shelling, but to no avail. So now, Sarkis himself went on national television to announce his inttention to resign.

The Israelis also made a powerful argument to the Syrians that day. Until then, there had been much rhetoric from Israeli officials about the need to prevent a 'genocide' of Christians in Lebanon. On 7 July, they finally acted. A flight of Israeli war-planes screamed in low over West Beirut, breaking the sound barrier as they skimmed the tops of the highest buildings of the Corniche Mazraa area. As all the glass shattered in the streets below, motorists, suddenly blinded, smashed into each other and into stunned pedestrians.

The Israelis had proved potently to the Syrians that the Syrian tanks and guns ringing East Beirut were vulnerable. Within hours, those guns had fallen silent.

They stayed silent for about six weeks. However, the first week of October saw a renewal of the LF–Syrian fighting, on a new and more deadly scale. The International Red Cross later reported that 400 residents of the LF areas had been killed that week – most of them civilians, as usual – and 5000 East Beirut apartments had been destroyed. On 5 October, Israeli gunboats shelled West Beirut. Two days later, a cease-fire finally took hold.

The October fighting was occasioned in part by a political battle over renewal of the ADF mandate, which was due to run out later that month. On 15 October, foreign ministers from those Arab countries contributing men and money to the ADF gathered for a meeting in the historic mountain palace of Beiteddine in the Shouf. Syria obtained the mandate renewal it was seeking. But the price it paid was to agree to withdraw from that last East Beirut tower-block.

Bashir Gemayyel and his allies in the LF were more or less satisfied at that outcome. They had now effectively formalized their control of a 'no-go' area covering the whole of East Beirut. They continued to call for a total Syrian withdrawal from Lebanon. But some of the more honest LF spokesmen admitted that, for now, East Beirut and its mountain hinterland was all they were capable of controlling on their own. From the secure base they had won there, they now had time to plan how to extend their control over the rest of the country.

President Sarkis was, meanwhile, making only scant progress in his plans to reunite the country and revive its administration. Illegal ports dotted the entire coastline, with their militia patrons of every hue skimming off the customs dues which should have formed a major part of government revenues. (The largest of these illegal port operations was in the heart of the capital itself, where Bashir Gemayyel's men controlled the entire fifth basin of Beirut's well-appointed international harbour.)

The Ketaeb and Beirut's major Nasserist party, meanwhile, each ran its own illegal radio station, and both kept threatening to go on the air with party television stations. As the polarization between the two halves of the city became sharper, only the pretence of a central administration was left at all. Sometimes, government ministries in one half of the city would not even recognize paperwork generated by ministries 'on the other side'.

It should be noted, however, that despite the far-reaching political breakdowns of the Sarkis years, the country did manage to avoid total social and economic chaos in that period. This was due to several factors. The emigration of young Lebanese to the wealthy economies of the Gulf had been stimulated by the 1975–6 fighting: from there, they sent a steady stream of remittances back to their families over the years which followed. Additional 'external' revenue came from the many Arab governments of differing hues, whose contributions to local parties and militias formed an important growth sector in the economy. The PLO, too, maintained an entire economic structure in Lebanon which generally benefited local producers and traders. So much money was washing round the private sector, indeed, in those years that real estate prices rocketed to astronomical figures; the number of banks increased dramatically; and the banks even took to bailing the government out from its financial woes on a more or less regular basis.

After the crisis of early July 1978 passed, President Sarkis had revoked his resignation threat. But at the end of that month he faced another setback to his plans.

The UN Security Council had followed up the resolution through which it created UNIFIL with another, calling on Lebanon to deploy units from its army alongside UNIFIL as soon as possible. On 31 July 1978, Sarkis made a first attempt to do this. His plan called for a battalion of 650 Lebanese troops to be deployed within the UNIFIL zone. But the plan failed. Haddad's forces started shelling the army battalion just as it neared his zone.

Five weeks later, after a heated nationwide debate over the issue, the government finally got around to relieving Haddad of his commission. At the end of October, he was court-martialled for 'collaborating with the enemy', and the following January he was supposedly expelled from the army.

But still, the controversy over Haddad's status continued. In April 1979, the army command was finally able to deploy a few hundred troops in the UNIFIL zone, by sending them down the coast road through Tyre. Once again, Haddad's men shelled these troops. And once again, he was supposedly expelled from the army. But still, he remained a loyal member of the officer corps.

The success of the army's April deployment was certainly limited. But it gave President Sarkis and Premier Hoss the confidence they needed to proceed with the next phase of their political plan for the country. This involved Hoss's government of technocrats making way for a political government, which would tie the country's powerful political bosses into the business of re-asserting government power.

Hoss took the first step in this plan by resigning in mid May. But after six weeks of consultations, Sarkis was unable to find any viable Sunni politician to replace him. He thus turned back to Hoss, asking him to form as broadly political a government as he could.

This Hoss achieved in mid July. Of the twelve ministers in the government, two were close to the Lebanese Front, two to the Jumblattists, and two to Syria. (One of the Front members named to the government resigned before the government list came up for confirmation by parliament, and his seat was left vacant: this was the formerly Shihabist ex-president, Charles Hélou.)

When the parliamentary vote was taken in early August, the second Hoss government was accepted by fifty-four votes to nine, with thirty-two absentees. But this new government was never able to achieve anything more significant than its technocratic predecessor.

The main reason for the government's continuing paralysis was still the harsh conflict between the pressures being exerted on it by Syria, from one side, and Bashir Gemayyel, on the other. Then, in July 1980, Bashir increased his leverage over the government when he eliminated the Chamounist 'Tigers' militia from the Maronite enclave.

The operation in which Bashir's LF fighters achieved this was reminiscent of their sneak attack two years earlier against the Frangiehs in Ihden. In the early morning of 7 July 1980, they surrounded Tigers' bases throughout East Beirut and along the coastal road leading north. They timed their actual attack for 8 a.m., to allow Tigers commander Dany Chamoun to escape being caught – like Tony Frangieh – in the bloodshed. Immediately after he and his family had left their heavily-fortified beach-side compound, Bashir's men attacked it and all the other Tigers' centres simultaneously.

By evening it was all over. Camille Chamoun had long ago recognized that the Tigers were militarily far inferior to Bashir's men. Now they had been nearly wiped out. Only a few score survivors were able to regroup in the strongly pro-Chamoun suburb of Ain al-Rummaneh, south-east of Beirut city centre. There, Lebanese army units protected them from the further wrath of Bashir's LF.

The final casualty toll of this latest intra-Maronite violence lay somewhere between 100 and 150 dead. The casualties included well over forty of the Pakistani labourers who were employed in the illegal ports controlled by the Tigers, and many luckless Lebanese civilians.

The political effects of the 7 July battles were almost immediately clear. Bashir had once again demonstrated the ruthlessness which he could turn against former allies. His personal supremacy over the Maronite enclave now seemed unassailable. As the distinguished American correspondent Jonathan C. Randal described it: 'Right after the civil war Sarkis consulted with Sheikh Pierre (Gemayyel) and Camille Chamoun, then in 1978 with Bashir and Chamoun, *but after the "double seven" (7 July), Bashir alone drove to the Baabda palace when Sarkis sought to line up support in (the Maronite enclave).*'[9]

Camille Chamoun had long treated Bashir as a valued political stepson. He did not take long to forgive him. His younger son, Dany, was more directly aggrieved by the Tigers' many losses: he indicated his first reaction to the 'double seven'.by travelling up to Zghorta to consult with Suleiman Frangieh. But over the years which followed, he too slid back into support for Bashir, especially after it seemed that Bashir's winning streak could not be stopped.

The 'double seven' battles had rudely interrupted yet another delicate manoeuvre which Sarkis and Hoss were trying to make at the governmental level. One month earlier, Hoss had presented his resignation to Sarkis. Once again, he hoped to be able to make way for a more clearly 'political' government. At the time Sarkis, acting in obvious co-ordination with Hoss, had shelved the resignation request, pending the tortuous consultations which would be necessary for such a move.

By the time of the 'double seven' battles, these consultations still seemed no nearer fruition. Then, on 16 July, Sarkis took most Lebanese politicians (except perhaps Bashir Gemayyel) by surprise, when he suddenly accepted Hoss's still-operative resignation note.

Four days later, Sarkis asked veteran ex-Premier Taqieddine al-Sulh to form a government including people close to the fighting parties. But the cabinet list which Sulh produced met objections from all sides in Lebanon, as well as from Syria. So on 9 August he announced that he would give up his efforts.

It took Sarkis a further two and a half months to solve the cabinet crisis he had himself provoked. Finally, on 22 October – again without further warning – he named as head of government Shafiq Wazzan, the head of the country's Higher Islamic Council.

Wazzan, a genial but generally colourless personality, was the choice who was *unacceptable* to the fewest numbers of people in Lebanon – all that could be asked for at this stage. But he was still very clearly in the second or third echelon of the country's Sunni politicians. So the fact that his nomination was not seriously challenged by any first-echelon Sunni leaders indicated their own continuing crisis of self-confidence.

Within three days, Wazzan had put together a twenty-two man government which looked very like the second Hoss government which had preceded it. That is, it contained people who were close to, but not leading members of, all the major fighting parties. The fact that the Wazzan government managed to stay in office even after three of its four Shi-ite ministers tried to resign that November, merely underlined how marginal it was to the main flow of events in the country.

Days after Wazzan had formed his government, Bashir delivered the *coup de grâce* to the Tigers. His fighters brushed aside the Lebanese army units which were protecting the Tigers survivors in Ain al-Rummaneh, and went in for the final kill.

The army units in Ain al-Rummaneh had offered a notable lack of resistance to the Bashirists' advance in Ain al-Rummaneh. This fact yet further undermined Sarkis's efforts to portray the army he was re-building with much American help as a politically neutral, multi-confessional force. The government's hopes that the army might swiftly be able to deploy in real strength in the south, and eventually even replace the ADF throughout the country, were thus yet further delayed.

By March 1981, Bashir was prepared to go on the offensive on yet another front. Throughout that month, his militiamen were reinforcing their positions in and around Zahleh, the scenic Beqaa Valley town which was a major centre for the Greek Catholic community in Lebanon.

Like the rest of the Beqaa, Zahleh lay well within the zone of overall Syrian control. But its wily town leaders had won a special deal from the Syrians, by which this control could be exercised at the major entrances to the town but without the Syrians having to go inside it.

Towards the end of March, the Bashirists mounted a large-scale ambush of Syrian forces patrolling near the town. The Syrians – whose forces were still acting fully in accordance with the ADF's legal mandate – asked the Zahleh town leaders to hand over those responsible for the ambush. But the Bashirists refused to give themselves up, and formed a defensive line around the town to prevent the Syrians from coming in.

The Syrians then fell back to using the tactic which had proved unsuccessful in East Beirut in 1978: they started a massive ground bombardment of Zahleh. This caused scores of casualties among the townsfolk, and succeeded only in building up their resentment of its authors.

The fighting continued around Zahleh for ten more days. Saudi Arabia was finally able to mediate a shaky cease-fire there. But still, intermittent clashes flared around the town. Within weeks, they had propelled the unending Lebanese tragedy to the highest planes of world diplomacy.

The Syrians had lost several helicopters in the fighting around Zahleh, in addition to the tens of fighter-planes which they had lost elsewhere in Lebanon, to the Israeli air force, since 1978. Towards the end of April, they brought into the Beqaa, from Syria, some batteries of effective SAM-6 ground-to-air missiles. These should certainly protect their heli-borne troops in the Beqaa from any further losses.

Immediately, the Israelis protested that this move was an infraction of the longstanding – although always fluid – Red Line limits.[10] However, heavy cloud over the Beqaa prevented their air force from trying to attack the new SAMs immediately. And while the Israeli pilots waited for the cloud to clear, the US government moved quickly to try to defuse the developing Israeli-Syrian crisis, through diplomacy.

The US President, Ronald Reagan, sent veteran diplomatist Philip Habib to Lebanon, as his own special envoy, to try to negotiate the removal of the SAMs. In sending Habib, Reagan plunged the US more directly into developments in Lebanon than it had been at any stage since the 1958 civil war. Habib successfully staved off the direct Israeli attack on the SAMs which Reagan had feard. But he was less than successful in effecting the SAMs' withdrawal.

Two months into his task, the American envoy's attention became diverted elsewhere. In mid July, the simmering Israeli-Palestinian confrontation in south Lebanon escalated. Deadly Israeli air force bombing runs over Palestinian and other targets there became locked into a rising spiral of violence with damaging PLO rocket attacks on settlements in northern Israel. Then, on 19 July, the Israelis struck within West Beirut itself. Their planes swooped in and bombed targets inside the city for the first time since 1974. They left well over 200, Palestinians and poor Lebanese, dead. This new crisis in Beirut threatened to unravel all efforts Habib had already made in that delicate Israeli–Syrian affair. He returned to Beirut to deal with this crisis and by 24 July he had obtained the first cease-fire agreement ever reached between Israel and the PLO through US mediation. He was then able to return to the slow business of dealing with the SAMs. The SAMs were to remain the principal focus of Habib's activities until June 1982. But in the process, he found himself having to consider the whole issue of the power-balance within the central Lebanese government.

Habib well knew that September 1982 would see the end of

President Sarkis's somewhat undistinguished term in office. And the outcome of the presidential elections of 1982 would have a direct effect on the Israeli–Syrian balance in the country – and thus on the SAMs question which was Habib's primary responsibility there. Habib, and the weight of the US administration with him, thus became drawn increasingly deeper into the course of Lebanon's internal affairs.

Thus far, I have cast the history of the inter bellum period of Lebanon mainly in terms of the interactions between three major Lebanese players – Sarkis, Bashir Gemayyel, and Haddad – and the country's two powerful immediate neighbours. Towards the end of the period, however, it became clear that another Lebanese personality was starting powerfully to affect the Lebanese system. What was most surprising about this fourth major actor was that by the time his movement really started to swing events in Lebanon, Musa Sadr was already dead.

Musa Sadr had been born in the Shi-ite city of Qom, in Iran, in 1928, to a family with branches in Iran, Iraq and the south Lebanese region of Jebel Amil. His was a family which had produced many of the Shi-ite savants called «ulama' (see Chapter 1). Young Musa, too, followed this path. He became an «alim by pursuing studies in Qom and Tehran. Then, he worked in the religious establishment in Qom.

By the time he was 30, Sadr's abilities had brought him to the notice of the spiritual leader of the Shi-ites of Jebel Amil, who then designated him as his successor – a common enough form of succession in Shi-ite lore. Two years later, in 1960, that much older *alim* died. The youthful Sadr moved to Tyre, in south Lebanon, to take up his designated duties. Because of his position, as well as his family background, he was immediately given Lebanese nationality.

From the beginning, Sadr was a radicalizing force in Jebel Amil. He questioned the near-total domination of the Shi-ite community there by the few powerful landowning families, and argued that the region's «*ulama'* should have a far greater say in its affairs. The landowners tried to build up a case against the handsome, youthful «*alim,* on the extremely damaging charge of sexual immorality. He countered by appealing to the Shi-ites of the northern Beqaa to support him; which they did, in their tens of thousands.

In 1968, Sadr increased the power of the «*ulama'* considerably, by winning government recognition of a specifically Shi-ite religious establishment. Until then, family and inheritance matters inside the community had been dealt with by the Higher Islamic Council, which was dominated by the Sunni juridical establishment. Now, Sadr established the Higher Shi-ite Islamic Council (HSIC).

The HSIC contained representatives of many strands of the country's two major Shi-ite communities, in Jebel Amil and the Beqaa. But its highest committees were dominated by the «ulama. It thus proved an important new means through which the «ulama could challenge the landowning families for leadership of the community.

Sadr's concern for social justice was not limited to his own sect. From the beginning, he worked with the radical Greek Catholic Archbishop of Beirut, Gregoire Haddad, in a campaign to better the lot of the disadvantaged of all the different communities in Lebanon. He also campaigned for better protection for the villagers of the south, from the remorseless attacks which Israel mounted against them from the late 1960s on.

In 1974, Sadr used the enormous charismatic power he exerted over the Shi-ite villagers to form a new movement called 'The movement of the deprived'. The following year, he founded an armed organization, designed to boost the southern villages' defences against Israeli attacks. That movement was originally called *Afwaj al-Muqawama al-Lubnaniyya* ('Lebanese Resistance Battalions'). But it rapidly became known by its acronym, 'Amal', which is the Arabic for 'Hope'.

Throughout the twists and turns of the 1975–6 civil war, Sadr generally followed close to Syria's position. In doing this, he confused many of his followers, whose leftist inclinations would have led them to support Kamal Jumblatt's bid for power. In the immediate post-war years, it even looked for a while as though Sadr's star (which had risen so rapidly in the Lebanese galaxy!) was now on the wane.

But in August 1978, in a development which for many Shi-ites eerily recalled the much earlier disappearance of their sect's 'twelfth imam', Sadr disappeared.

He and a close aid had been in Libya that month, for discussions with the gadfly Libyan leader, Muammar Qadhafi. The Libyans later swore that the two travellers had left their country, on a plane bound for Rome. But they never arrived there. Sadr's followers in Lebanon were thrown into a state of shock.

Over the weeks which followed, the evidence began to mount that Sadr and his associate had never boarded that plane to Rome. The Libyans only said they had. With ever increasing strength, the evidence began to point to the conclusion that their government hosts had abducted, and possibly even killed, them while they were still in Libya.

Sadr's disappearance galvanized nearly the entire Lebanese Shi-ite community. Until then, his leadership had been questioned by many Shi-ites of a more left-wing inclination. But now, these Shi-ite leftists began to realize that Qadhafi – hero of much of the Arab left! – had stripped their community of the most powerful symbol of its cultural and social renaissance. The tide of Shi-ite opinion shifted rapidly against the left, back towards identification with the sect's deepest roots, and with Amal.

For many years the remaining organizers of Amal, and the HSIC, refused to take the last formal step of naming a successor to Sadr – which would give final recognition to the fact of his liquidation. The first 'deputy leader' elected to head Amal pending Sadr's return was a parliamentarian from the Beqaa called Hussein al-Husseini. In 1981, he was replaced by a Jebel Amil lawyer called Nabih Berri. The man elected 'deputy leader' of the HSIC, meanwhile, was a member of a family with a long tradition of producing «*ulama*': Muhammed Mehdi Shamseddine.

Throughout 1969, Amal's growth was also stimulated by the rise of the Shi-ite movement led by Ayatollah Ruhollah Khomeini, in Iran. The Shi-ites of Jebel Amil had always felt themselves closely linked to their co-believers in Iran. Indeed, 450 years earlier, the Iranians had taken their first steps in Shi-ite learning under the tutelage of teachers from Jebel Amil (see Chapter 1).

In more recent times, the first military trainer of Amal, Mustafa Shamran, had been, like Sadr, of joint Iranian Lebanese heritage: he went on to become the first defence minister in the revolutionary regime in Tehran. And Sadr himself, while in Qom in the 1950s, had worked with another «*alim* whose prestige was rising there at that time – Khomeini!

In January 1979, Khomeini swept to power in Iran's tempestuous Islamic revolution. His victory gave a new sense of pride to Shi-ites everywhere, including those in Lebanon. When he then issued ringing declarations that his movement represented all the world's dispossessed, they struck an especially resonant chord among his co-believers in Lebanon. For they had suffered a string of violent communal uprootings since the early 1970s, in south Lebanon and in and around Beirut.

Throughout the years from 1978 to 1982, the Shi-ite slums of south-west Beirut continued – along with their Maronite counterparts in south-east Beirut – to bear the main brunt of the fighting which periodically rocked the capital. Meanwhile, the Shi-ite villagers of south Lebanon were the major victims of the deadly game of cat-and-mouse which Major Haddad and his Israeli backers were playing against the PLO and their local leftist allies.

In spring 1978, the UN and the Lebanese government had intended that the UNIFIL forces which deployed in south Lebanon should, at the very least, insulate the villages of that area from the confrontation between Israel and the PLO.

But UNIFIL was never able to seal its lines completely against the infiltrations of either side. UNIFIL reports from that period spoke of numerous violations by both parties. Moreover, in a whole strip of terrain in the south-east of the country there was no UNIFIL buffer at all. Instead, Haddad's forces in Marjayoun faced the PLO and leftist fighters in the Shi-ite market town of Nabatiyeh directly across the gorge of the Litani river.

Normal life was scarcely possible in south Lebanon throughout those years. On numerous occasions, Haddad turned his guns on Shi-ite villages neighbouring his zone, and threatened to fire on the village and its UNIFIL protectors unless the villagers paid ransom, provided hostages to serve his forces, or allowed him to set up checkpoints in the village. Sometimes the local UNIFIL commanders found they could provide protection against such intimidation. Sometimes, they could not; and Haddad was able gradually to increase the area under his control, at the expense of UNIFIL.

The Shi-ites living in the zones of PLO and leftist control were little better off. The PLO had developed a whole network of institutions in south Lebanon over the years, building up their own virtual 'state within a state' there. The Lebanese state was unable to offer even the most basic services to its own citizens, who were thus thrown on the mercies of the PLO for many basic needs. A southerner who wanted his telephone repaired, who needed hospital treatment, or who wanted to import goods through the port of Tyre, would find his local PLO commander a much better channel to go through than any Lebanese government official.

Over the years, this dependence on their PLO 'guests' gave birth, among many southern villagers, to a smouldering resentment against the PLO. And the PLO's leftist allies were unable to mediate relations with the southern villagers very effectively because they themselves had become riddled with corruption and riven by burning inter-Arab differences.

For over a decade, the Shi-ite population of Jebel Amil had given remarkable support to the PLO in its fight against Israel. They had continued to do so, despite the severity of Isreali 'retaliations' against local PLO collaborators. But towards the end of the 1970s (at the same time that many Shi-ites were anyway turning away from the Lebanese left), the tide of feeling in Jebel Amil started to turn against the PLO.

The first major indication of this swing came not in the south but in Beirut. On 12 March 1980, open clashes broke out in a Beirut suburb between the Amal militia and units of the PLO–leftist alliance. Intensive contacts between PLO and Shi-ite leaders succeeded in bringing those clashes under control. But further battles continued to flare up between them in the Beirut suburbs and in the south.

In September 1980, the Baath Party regime in Iraq invaded Iran, in an abortive attempt to topple the ayatollahs' regime there. Over the years which followed, the vast military machines of the two states became locked into a punishing war of attrition.

From the beginning of the war, Khomeini demanded that the PLO leaders announce their support for the 'Islamic' – that is, Iranian – side. When they refused to do this, their relations with the Lebanese Shi-ites only became further soured.

Musa Sadr's Shi-ite movement, Amal, grew rapidly in the years which followed his disappearance. But as 1981 turned into 1982, it had yet to move to centre stage in the continuing Lebanese drama. That position was still occupied by the Maronitist movement led by Bashir Gemayyel.

In 1982, the inter-sect system in Lebanon was still reeling from the after-waves of the shock it had received fifteen years earlier, in the regional upset of 1967. The first effect of that shock had been to render the Shihabist recipe for social peace unworkable. It was, meanwhile, seriously undermining the ability of the traditional Sunni leaderships to uphold their end of the 1943 National Pact arrangement.

From 1943 until the late 1960s, the National Pact had proved a successful anchor for the inter-sect balance in the country. But after 1967, this balance was set adrift. In the dozen years following 1970, it was to swing wildly.

The first major challenge to the Pact had come from the bid Kamal Jumblatt launched to control the whole country, in 1975–6. His challenge had been beaten back, but only at the cost of the strengthening of the Maronite-exclusivist forces represented by Bashir Gemayyel's LF.

The second major challenge to the National Pact was then that which, throughout the inter bellum years, Gemayyel himself was preparing to launch. As he viewed the situation in Lebanon at the beginning of 1982, Gemayyel must have felt satisfied that all the pieces were falling into place for the takeover of the entire country which had been his dream since 1976.

Those of us who were analysing Bashir's options in the late 1970s still wondered how he could hope to attain this dream. Even if he brought the population within the LF areas to maximum military mobilization, his forces would still clearly be inferior to the task of taking the rest of Lebanon by force. Some kind of an alliance with other Lebanese parties would seem to be prescribed. But as he had already graphically shown in his dealings with his erstwhile allies, Bashir Gemayyel never willingly opted for any dilution of his personal power.

But the LF commander did have another option. It was to try to take over Lebanon politically, through the presidential elections, while his Israeli friends would do the military dirty work, clearing his foes from south Lebanon and West Beirut on his behalf.

Ever since he had routed the Chamounist militia in mid 1980, Bashir's control of the LF enclave had remained unchallenged. At some time between then and early 1982, even President Sarkis himself finally succumbed to his own small-town Maronitism. He, too, now became convinced that Bashir was the Maronites' only salvation; and thus, that he should be the next president. (The US mediator, Philip Habib, later reported that, by early 1982, he too had come to concur with that view.)[11]

Sarkis's whole presidency had been dominated by the power-struggle between the Syrians and the extreme Maronitists, led by Bashir Gemayyel. But the aggressive policies pursued by both Israel and Bashir Gemayyel had tipped the power-balance in the country against the Syrians. This left Bashir's the loudest single voice heard in the presidential palace in Baabda.

As for the Israelis' role in Bashir's plan – well, another Israeli invasion of the south had been keenly expected in Lebanon since early 1981. The Shi-ite majority in that area were turning against the PLO, and some of them were even starting to co-operate openly with Major Haddad. The PLO's remaining allies on the Lebanese left were weak, and rent by myriad factions. The PLO's first rank of major external allies, in the Arab world, were also weak and divided. They seemed unlikely to mount any major international campaign to save the PLO forces if attacked in Lebanon.

At the beginning of 1982, only a single obstacle remained in the way of the co-ordinated Israeli–LF pincer-movement against the PLO which had long been predicted in Beirut. This was the final act of the peace process between Israel and Egypt, which was due to be played out on 26 April 1982. On that date, Israel would withdraw from the final part of the Egyptian land in Sinai it had occupied since 1967.

Israel's governmental backers in Washington were deeply committed to the successful implementation of the Israeli-Egyptian agreement, which had been mediated by a previous US administration. The Americans feared that any major Israeli action in Lebanon would provoke a furore of anti-Israeli feeling in Egypt, which might force the new Egyptian president, Hosni Mubarak, to back away from his commitments under the peace process.

On 26 April, the last phase of the Israel–Egypt process was completed without a hitch.

Six weeks later, a Palestinian gunman killed the Israeli ambassador in far-off London.

Three days after that, on 6 June 1982, Israel invaded Lebanon. Bashir Gemayyel's dream was coming true.

Notes

1   Quoted in Khalidi (1979), pp. 104–5.
2   *Fiches du monde arabe*, no. 1644 (23 July 1980).
3   Rabin (1979), p. 280 (my emphasis).
4   Khalidi (1979), p. 128; and *Fiches du monde arabe*, no. 946 (3 May 1978).
5   Khalidi (1979), p. 128.
6   Salim Nasr, 'Conflit libanais et restructuration de l'espace urbain de Beyrouth', in T. Mettral (ed.), *Politiques urbaines au Machreq et au Maghreb* (Lyons, France: Presses Universitaires de Lyons 1984).
7   Interview with Bashir Gemayyel, as reported in my despatch to the *Christian Science Monitor* (18 April 1978).
8   For a lively account of the Ihden affair and the reaction of the various parties to it, see Randal (1983), pp. 118–25.
9   ibid., p. 138 (my emphasis).
10   Zeev Schiff and Ehud Ya'ari write that the Israeli army's chief of

intelligence suspected that the flare-up in Zahleh was 'essentially a Phalange plot to draw Israel into a clash with Syria' (Schiff and Ya'ari 1984, p. 33).

11 Habib's comments to me in Atlanta, Georgia, November 1983.

8   The battles of Beirut
(1982–4)

On Sunday 6 June 1982 Israel's long-awaited invasion of Lebanon began. 250 tanks and scores of thousands of infantrymen rolled through UNIFIL's lines towards Tyre, Nabatiyeh and the southern Beqaa. Israeli amphibious units landed at several sites along south Lebanon's Mediterranean coast, while helicopter-borne troops landed at strategic inland points to provide cover for the advance of the tank columns.

In March 1978, the Israelis had advanced into south Lebanon by pushing a solid front up northwards to the Litani. This time, their attack plan was considerably more complex. It called for a leap-frogging advance which would break the PLO and leftist forces' communications at numerous points in south Lebanon. Only after they had pushed their front line well up towards Beirut would the Israelis finally finish 'pacifying' the total area in their southern rear.

In June 1982, there was a clear expectation among the Israeli commanders that many more south Lebanese villages than in 1978 would welcome – or at least, not actively oppose – the Israelis' arrival. This made the 'leapfrog' strategy much more feasible in 1982 than it would have been in 1978.

At the strategic level, Israel's control over the air-space to the west of the Mount Lebanon range had been demonstrated repeatedly since at least July 1978. There remained, of course, a huge gap between that overall strategic position and detailed control of developments on the ground in western Lebanon. It was this gap which the massive invasion of June 1982 was designed to bridge.

On 8 June, the Syrians and Israelis engaged in an enormous air-battle over Beirut. The Israelis emerged from that battle with their control of the city's air-space absolutely incontestable. The next day, the Israeli air force pursued its offensive against the Syrians to the sites of the controversial SAM-6s, in the Beqaa Valley. Ninety-two Israeli planes took part in the raid against the SAMs. They reportedly destroyed seventeen SAM batteries completely.

On those two days, the Syrian leaders faced the possibility of an all-out war with Israel which they did not feel ready to win. Rather than provoke such a confrontation, they decided to leave Beirut and the rest of western Lebanon to its fate, while reinforcing their own strategic defences in the Beqaa.

The boss of the Maronitist militias in Lebanon, Bashir Gemayyel, had long been opposed to the Syrian troops' presence in his country. On the day they pulled out of the capital, he called for the formation of a Lebanese 'government of national unity'.

By 13 June, the Israelis had arrived at the presidential palace at Baabda, on the hills directly overlooking Beirut. There they were in direct contact with Bashir Gemayyel's 'Lebanese Forces' in East Beirut. The PLO and their allies inside West Beirut were now encircled.

At the beginning of this new Lebanese crisis, the American presidential envoy, Philip Habib, had returned to Lebanon to try to deal with it. On 14 June, in co-ordination with Habib, President Elias Sarkis announced the formation of a 'National Salvation Committee' (NSC). Headed by Sarkis, the NSC also included Bashir Gemayyel; the Sunni premier, Shafiq Wazzan; the Greek Orthodox foreign minister, Fouad Boutros; Druz and socialist leader Walid Jumblatt; the head of the Shi-ite Amal movement, Nabih Berri; and a veteran Greek Catholic politician called Nasri Maalouf.

The NSC's stated task was to find a formula through which the Lebanese army could take the place of the beleagured PLO fighters in West Beirut. At first, Jumblatt refused to take part in its proceedings on this basis. But on 20 June, after conferring with Habib, he finally agreed to do so. So did Berri, who had stated he would do whatever the younger Druze leader did.

At the NSC, Jumblatt at first put forward a plan of the PLO leaders' devising, which would have involved an Israeli pull-back and guarantees for the PLO's safety, in return for the army's deployment. Three days later, Habib told the NSC that both Israel and the US rejected this proposal.

Walid Jumblatt had apparently been personally devastated by the Israelis' advance into his family's traditional fiefdom in the Shouf. In 1982, he was still only 33 years old. A delicate but changeable personality, he had entered political life only five years earlier – and then, only through the family-imposed necessity of succeeding his slain father, rather than through any volition of his own.

In the years between 1977 and 1982, many people had written off Walid's ability ever to replace his charismatic and strong-willed father. But this, Walid had never wanted to do. His father's eclectically left-wing interests had never interested him much. But what he had gained – perhaps more from other members of the extended family than from Kamal Bey himself – had been an abiding interest in the history and affairs of the Druze.

The younger Jumblatt was never particularly religious in his outlook. (Neither, come to that, were Bashir Gemayyel or his associates in the Maronitist camp.) But he could drive through the Shouf, and point out the exact spot at which such-and-such a family had betrayed the Jumblatt cause to the Yazbekis 200 or more years before. It was also widely noted that, soon after he became head of the Progressive Socialist Party his father had founded, he would address the Party faithful with the typically Druze avocation, 'Ya bani Ma«rouf'.

In the immediate aftermath of Israel's 1982 invasion, Jumblatt seemed more erratic than ever. On 25 June, he washed his hands of the NSC's negotiations. He baldly declared that his allies in the PLO leadership probably needed to be replaced; while at the same time he announced his resignation from the NSC, describing it as 'a grave-digger for the Lebanese and Palestinian peoples'. (Amal leader Berri then said he would suspend his membership in the NSC, too.) Four days later, in another apparent reversal, Jumblatt declared that Lebanon would be 'closed for ever' to PLO activity.

While these political dramas had been played out, the Israelis had kept up a near-constant barrage of air, sea and artillery fire against West Beirut, and had tightened their ring of steel around that last major PLO stronghold.

On 2 July, Israel's burly and aggressive Defence Minister Ariel Sharon, was staging a press conference in East Beirut. He stressed his country's determination to expel the PLO totally from the other half of the city.

Two days later, Israeli officers supervised the cutting-off of West Beirut's water and electricity. West Beirut – cosmopolitan birthplace of so many cultural, intellectual and political trends throughout the preceding century – now had to live through what Tel al-Zaatar had lived through six years earlier, the horrors of a devastating total siege.

The 600,000 people who remained trapped inside the Israeli vice were already living (or dying) through continual, heavy bombardments. Now, they were to be squeezed by the rigours of a near-total siege. (In a barely noticed act of protest at this, on 4 July Premier

Wazzan announced the suspension of all negotiations with Habib.)

It was from the desperation of these circumstances that, according to the accounts of those who survived the siege, a new spirit of resistance was born. Gone was the factionalism which had rent West Beirut's heterodox (and highly-armed) society for the past five years. In its place grew the elation of holding back the Middle East's most formidable military machine, using only the hand-held, street-fighting technology, which was the true metier of all Beirut's militias.

The PLO, leftist and Muslim fighters in West Beirut were able to establish a defence perimeter around their area sturdy enough to halt the Israeli tank columns. This forced the Israelis to fight house-to-house if they wanted to continue any further.

At the start of the war, the Israelis had publicly defined their aim as the clearing of a 40-kilometre-deep security zone inside south Lebanon. However, they had advanced considerably beyond this zone. The Israeli government was facing a mounting chorus of questions back home, over the purpose of continuing the fighting around Beirut. It was thus unwilling to incur the high degree of casualties which a steady house-to-house advance into West Beirut would entail.

Nor were the Israelis' local LF allies willing to take on this job. Bashir Gemayyel's major war aim, after all, was to win election as president of all Lebanon. He did not want his men too closely associated with the Israelis' actions against the capital.

One significant obstacle to the Israelis' advance into West Beirut was that thrown up by the Shi-ite residents of the area's crowded south-western suburbs. In Jebel Amil, further south, many Shi-ite villagers had quietly welcomed the Israeli army into their area. They hoped that its arrival would signal a way out of the cycle of Israeli-Palestinian violence which had plagued their region for over a decade. But the Shi-ite community of south Beirut marched to a different tune.

The south Beirut Shi-ites were overwhelmingly only first- or second-generation immigrants to city life. They had forged new community bonds there, largely removed from the sway of the feudal landowners who had dominated their south Lebanese or Beqaa Valley home villages. In recent years they had experienced some tension in their relations with their PLO or leftist neighbours. But still, they saw the primary threat to the lives they had made for themselves in the suburbs as coming from the Maronitist militias.

Many thousands of south Beirut Shi-ites had been among those forcibly expelled from previous homes in East Beirut, by the Maronitist militias, back in 1976. And ever since then, sporadic clashes had continued across the 'Green Line' which snaked its way through the suburbs.

Thus, in summer 1982, even while some branches of Amal in south Lebanon were collaborating with the Israelis, the Amal militia in south-west Beirut formed the backbone of their area's defence *against* the Israelis.

On 24 July, Bashir Gemayyel announced his candidacy in the forthcoming presidential elections. From then on, it was clear that the prize in the fighting around Beirut was nothing less than the powerful position of Lebanon's head of state. Two days later, the Israelis again tightened the screws around West Beirut, now adding medical supplies to the list of articles they would not allow to enter.

Premier Wazzan had, meanwhile, resumed his job as messenger in the complex string of negotiations from the Israelis, to the Americans, through him, to PLO Chairman Arafat, and back again.

It was on 3 July that Arafat first handed a written pledge to Wazzan, stating that the PLO did intend to withdraw from Beirut, provided it could win the guarantees it felt it needed to allow it to do so. Proposals and counter-proposals then chased each other up and down the negotiating string, as the principals at either end hammered out the finer details. For the ruthless Ariel Sharon, the bombardments and siege conditions maintained against the overwhelmingly civilian population of West Beirut were powerful levers in these negotiations.

By early August, it had been agreed that a Multi-National Force (MNF) would supervise the departure of the PLO fighters from Beirut. In this force – which was most decidedly *not* put together under United Nations auspices – American and French units would be joined by such other Western nations as the US could persuade to take part. On 7 August, the first officers of the proposed force came in through the Israeli-held Beirut airport, to start preparing for the force's deployment.

The final details of the PLO's departure were not worked out until 18 August. They were spelt out in an agreement which called for a cease-fire in place, and for the deployment of MNF troops to protect the departure of the PLO fighters. The agreement also included formal guarantees for the safety of Palestinian civilians left behind in Beirut.

Three days later, the PLO's fighters started to leave Beirut. By the time their evacuation was completed on 1 September, there was no effective PLO armed presence left in the Lebanese capital. The mainly Muslim population of West Beirut was left to its own fate.

West Beirut's Muslim politicians, led by veteran ex-premier Saeb Salam, had laboured mightily throughout the PLO evacuation negotiations. Their first concern was to end the travails through which their city was passing. But they had also tried to assure the safety of their own community subsequent to the PLO's withdrawal.

This latter aim, they tried to achieve through a combination of two principal strategies. First, they tried to secure effective guarantees that the Israelis would advance no further, once the PLO had withdrawn. And second, they searched desperately for an intra-Lebanese political entente which would secure West Beirut against any threat the LF militias might pose.

The first of these aims they thought had been realized in the unequivocal terms of the 18 August agreement. But after 18 August, there was little time left to realize the second, for the presidential elections were scheduled for the very next day!

August 18 was a terribly busy day for the Muslim politicians. They had no time to find anyone to run against the sole contender in the presidential elections, Bashir Gemayyel. So instead, they called for a boycott of the elections until a candidate of national union could be found.

That same day, leftist militiamen in tanks rolled towards the site, right on the Green Line running through the city, which the Lebanese Parliament had occupied since 1976. They lobbed a few tank-rounds towards the temporary Chamber there. The Speaker of the House then announced that the electoral session would be postponed until 23 August. And it would be held in the Fayyadiyeh barracks, which overlooked Beirut from well within the zone of Israeli military control.

As election day dawned, Bashir Gemayyel's opponents had still not found any alternative candidate. But they were still banking on calculations that he could not obtain the two-thirds quorum required for parliament to elect a president.

Salam and his allies in West Beirut tried to persuade deputies from throughout the country to boycott the electoral session. But they were countered by the joint efforts of Bashir's militias, the Israelis and outgoing President Sarkis. The Israelis cut all communications in and out of West Beirut, while their troops and Bashir's militiamen brought as many deputies as possible to Fayyadiyeh under virtual armed guard. Meanwhile, Sarkis sent army helicopters to fly in three deputies stranded in Cyprus.

Shortly after 1 p.m., the quorum was finally reached. And as in the case of Sarkis's election back in 1976, there had never been much doubt that once it was obtained, the provision of sweeteners to those attending could ensure the candidate's successful election.

In that earlier election, Sarkis had secured his victory behind an umbrella of Syrian tanks. This time it was Israeli tanks which ringed the electoral session of the Parliament. One of the first of the visitors who crowded to congratulate Lebanon's 34-year-old president-elect was the commander of the Israeli troops in the area.

Bashir Gemayyel was due to be inaugurated as President of Lebanon on 23 September. Nine days before that, he was attending a high-level Ketaeb Party meeting in East Beirut, when a massive bomb levelled the building where it was being held. Bashir, and a score of other high party functionaries, were all killed in the blast. (The prime suspect was picked up by the Ketaeb soon after. He was a young Maronite living above the party offices, who had been linked to a pro-Syrian faction of the PPS.)

For many of the Israeli commanders, Bashir's killing meant the shattering of their dream. They had courted him heavily ever since he had taken over the Ketaeb militia in 1976. They had encouraged his political ambitions – probably right back to the time he had first openly challenged his father's authority in 1977. They considered him very much 'their boy' inside the Lebanese game.

In the last weeks before Bashir was killed, there had been some signs of differences arising between him and his principal Israeli 'handler' – Defence Minister Ariel Sharon. Informed Israeli sources spoke of sharp disputes between the two over Bashir's refusal to take part in the Israeli offensive against West Beirut.

After his death, there remained an intriguing question about the ambitious LF commander. If he had lived to become president, would he have exchanged his previous narrow Maronitism for a truly pan-Lebanese policy? American envoy Philip Habib for a long time remained convinced that he would have. Habib had also been encouraged by signs that Bashir would shed his dependence on the Israelis for stronger links with the US, after becoming president.

No one will ever know how Bashir would have acted as president. But the way his lieutenants and followers did indeed act in his absence was shown all too clearly in the days after he was killed.

The MNF units which had deployed in West Beirut to protect the PLO evacuation had seen the last evacuees leave on 1 September. The US contingent in the MNF then declared its job finished; and on 10 September it left Beirut – twelve days before the MNF's original mandate had been due to expire. It was followed by the French contingent.

A thin smattering of Lebanese army troops was all that was left in West Beirut, together with the local Muslim and leftist militias who had fought alongside the PLO. The militias had been considerably weakened by the PLO's departure, and most of them had already promised to co-operate with the army. But the militias remained un-pacified; and substantial quantities of arms still remained in militia caches throughout West Beirut.

The night after Bashir Gemayyel's killing, the Israelis moved into West Beirut in clear contravention of the 18 August agreement. The next day they met with some of the surviving LF leaders to plan the entry of LF units into the Palestinian refugee camps in West Beirut's Sabra and Shatila districts.

At six o'clock that evening, the operation started. Israeli units already surrounded the two camps, nearly all of whose former defenders had left with the evacuation. Now, the Israeli commanders sent the LF into their huddled alleyways and cinder-block shelters. By the time the LF were withdrawn some forty hours later, many hundreds of camp residents lay slaughtered in the area which had long been their only home.

The massacres at Sabra and Shatila shocked the whole world. In Israel itself, 400,000 people took to the streets to call for a public inquiry. (In February 1983, that inquiry produced a report which called for the resignation of Defence Minister Sharon. He and several high-ranking army officers then resigned their posts.)

Inside Lebanon, the revelation of what had happened in the camps sent a sharp chill of fear through the rest of West Beirut's population. The people of West Beirut were desperate for any solution which might prevent the Israelis from bringing the LF into their areas too. After all, the victims in the refugee camps had not been only Palestinians. Around one-quarter of them were lower-class Lebanese Muslims who had moved into the camps over the years. Their Lebanese identity cards had not saved them from the slaughter.

Two days after Bashir Gemayyel's killing, the Ketaeb had nominated his elder brother Amin as the Party's new presidential candidate.

From the beginning, Amin Gemayyel's candidacy received wide

support from Lebanon's Muslim politicians. Almost right across the political spectrum, they considered him the only hope to save them from the horrors of the LF.

Amin Gemayyel was generally thought to be significantly less extreme in his Maronitism than Bashir. Since his youth, he had been groomed as prime heir to his father's political position. After entering parliament in 1972, he had cut a dapper and generally friendly figure in the Chamber. Then, during the 1975–6 civil war, he kept up important contacts with the Muslim, leftist and PLO leaders. On several occasions since 1975, his intervention had even resulted in the release of prisoners or hostages captured by his fiery younger brother's militiamen.

In September 1982, the Muslim politicians were calculating that Amin was the candidate best placed to protect their communities from the LF. They realized that the Israeli invasion had already significantly tipped the sectarian balance on which their country had rested since 1943.

The Muslim communities had been traumatized by the Israeli invasion of south Lebanon, and by the long weeks of the brutal siege of West Beirut. They had been weakened by the departure of their former PLO allies. And their own, home-grown defences had been stripped away in the rigorous 'pacification' measures undertaken by the Israelis in south Lebanon, and in West Beirut.

In mid September 1982, the Israeli army was seizing control of the Muslim militias' arms caches in West Beirut: at the same time that in East Beirut it was negotiating for the transfer of additional arms *to* the Maronitist militias.

The leaders of the Muslim sects fully comprehended their own vulnerability. They could see no quick way to tip the inter-sect balance back in their favour. So they opted instead to throw themselves completely on the mercy of Amin Gemayyel to save them from further Sabras and Shatilas.

The Muslim leaders were further encouraged to take this step when they learnt that he would not be standing alone between the Lebanese Muslims and the LF's sectarian zeal. He would have at his disposal a significant force of neutral Western troops, which could back up his authority over the hard-liners of the LF.

In the US, as elsewhere, the refugee camp massacres had met with a shocked response. American policy-makers realized that the killings had been possible only because the Israeli government had violated the undertakings it had given, that Israeli forces would not enter West

Beirut after the evacuation of the PLO. Those undertakings had formed a central underpinning of the guarantees provided to the PLO leaders in the 18 August agreement signed by US envoy Philip Habib.

The Americans felt that the credibility of their guarantees was at issue after the massacres. So they pressed heavily on the Israelis to pull out of West Beirut as quickly as possible. They, meanwhile, hurriedly planned for the re-establishment and redeployment of the MNF, which would take the place of the departing Israelis.

On 20 September, the remaining skeleton of the Lebanese cabinet formally requested the return of the MNF. The next day, the Lebanese Parliament convened for another presidential election. Unlike his brother's candidacy, Amin Gemayyel's was contested – by Raymond Eddé, and by ex-President Camille Chamoun. The eighty deputies who attended the session nevertheless produced seventy-seven votes for Amin Gemayyel, along with three blank ballots. He was, thus, duly elected.

On 22 September, the Israelis started to pull out of West Beirut. The next day, Amin Gemayyel's inauguration as the seventh president of independent Lebanon went ahead exactly according to the timetable decreed by the constitution.

On 29 September, the Israelis finished their withdrawal to the lines they had held before Bashir Gemayyel's killing. Within hours, Beirut airport was receiving units of the US Marines, who were to be the largest contingent within the re-formed MNF.

1500 American troops took control of the airport and the area around it. Italian troops meanwhile deployed in the area of the refugee camps, while French troops fanned out throughout West Beirut's Hamra district. A token British unit later arrived, to provide logistic support to the MNF. Amin Gemayyel, who had never previously commanded many troops on his own account, now controlled a force made strong by virtue of its powerful diplomatic symbolism.

Within days of taking office, President Gemayyel asked the outgoing premier, Shafiq al-Wazzan, to stay on in office. On 7 October Wazzan announced the formation of a ten-member government of apolitical technocrats. But Gemayyel had not even waited this long, before he sent the ragtag Lebanese army into action, to 'pacify' West Beirut.

Army roadblocks fanned throughout that part of the city, checking the identity papers of all who passed. Many hundreds of people picked up at these roadblocks and in house-to-house searches were packed into open trucks and taken away to hastily organized detention centres. Many of the detainees had been picked up at seeming random. Conditions in the detention centres were crowded and chaotic. Some detainees later reported that they had been packed scores to a room, and kept without food for several days.

Most of the Lebanese detainees were released over the weeks and months which followed; and the non-Lebanese were deported. But many scores of those arrested by the army in the early weeks of Gemayyel's rule – Lebanese as well as foreigners – never re-appeared. Their families feared they had been handed over to the LF, and executed.

The army also busied itself removing illegal housing in the south-western suburbs of the capital. The families evicted from the demolished structures were mainly Shi-ites; many of them had been among the groups expelled from East Beirut back in 1976. Now, they protested the fact that the army was forcing them out of their homes once again – while it was leaving quite alone the Christian families still illegally occupying their former homes in East Beirut.

On 11 October, 5000 residents of the mainly Shi-ite coastal suburb of Ouzai staged a demonstration against the demolitions. Throughout the following week, the confrontation sharpened between the Ouzai residents and the army: on 16 October, an open clash left three dead, and a number of other demonstrators wounded. The army was able to reinforce its position in Ouzai, but the mood of the residents remained surly.

In early December, Gemayyel made a series of appointments to key official positions. His new appointments as army commander and head of internal security had both been closely associated with Bashir Gemayyel. A purge of Shihabists was set in motion throughout the state bureaucracy.

By the end of December, the leaders of the Muslim communities were clearly worried that Gemayyel was turning the Lebanese state and army into an extension of the Ketaeb. So, when the Muslim feast of Adha came round at the end of that month, the Sunni, Shi-ite and Druze religious leaders attended a joint celebration of the feast, to serve as a united, public affirmation of Lebanese Muslim identity.

Throughout the latter half of 1982, the Druze had come to play a special role in the growing Muslim resistance to the LF. This was because the Druze in Beirut's mountain hinterland were the only

Lebanese group which was still actively fighting against the LF at that time.

Tension had built up between the LF and the Druze in the Mountain within the first weeks after Israel's entry into Lebanon. The Israelis had found it easy to move into the Druze-dominated mountain area of the Shouf. Then, soon after they had linked up with the LF enclave near Beirut, they allowed some LF units to move in to help them control the Shouf. This, the LF did with a vengance. From many of the villages they entered ugly rumours were soon emanating of massacres and humiliations endured at their hands.

The LF's entry into the Shouf severely dented the inter-sect coexistence which had marked Shouf life throughout most of the preceding years. (Even during the 1975–6 civil war, many Shouf Christians had continued to support Druze leader Kamal Jumblatt.)

The Druze saw the LF's arrival in their sect's ancient heartland as threatening the very survival of their community. Before June 1982 was over, the first open clashes had erupted between the LF and Walid Jumblatt's Druze-based PSP militia. The Israelis were disturbed by the hornets' nest they had stirred up. On 2 July they issued an order outlawing the carrying of arms in the Shouf.

That order was obsolete before the ink had dried on it: the history of all the imperial armies who had traversed the East Mediterranean proved that no outsider could ever control the daily life of the Lebanese Mountain.

The Israelis proved themselves quick learners in the realities of mountain life. Besides, they were also subject to some pressure from their own small Druze community at home.

Within weeks of the first eruption of battles in the Shouf the Israelis moved some distance away from outright support of the LF there. Soon, they were adopting a stance of neutrality in the area, in public; while behind the scenes they quickly established links with people close to Jumblatt.

By the end of 1982 it was clear that the Israelis were arming both sides in the Shouf confrontation. But their own troops were still caught in the cross-fire, and started taking increasingly heavy losses there.

The Druze, unlike the Israelis and most of the LF fighters, were operating on their home turf in the Shouf, between villages where every home could provide a potential refuge. Small wonder that they generally found they could hold their own in the battles there. And from the Shouf, throughout the latter half of 1982, they held up a banner of inspiration to all the Lebanese Muslims who were chafing under the pro-Ketaeb partisanship of Gemayyel's rule.

President Gemayyel had come into office with a strong personal record of maintaining links with the Muslim politicians even when that was unpopular inside his own party. Throughout the early months of his rule, veteran Muslim leaders such as ex-Premier Saeb Salam continually warned him against turning his back on the Muslims' many grievances, and against giving the Ketaeb free rein of the entire state apparatus.

But still, Gemayyel took few steps which indicated any desire for a genuine national reconciliation. Why?

It is true that, even as president, Gemayyel was still subject to a constant pressure from the loyalists of his slain brother who controlled the powerful LF militia. In the early weeks of the Gemmayel presidency, the young man who had succeeded the slain Bashir Gemayyel as commander of the LF, Fadi Frem, was exultantly crowing that 'this time there *is* a victor and a vanquished in Lebanon'.

However, the strong support offered to President Gemayyel by the Western countries, as indicated by their presence in the MNF, could have assured him valuable protection against the LF's extremism – if national reconciliation had indeed been his and the Americans' common goal. But Philip Habib, special envoy of the country which was the mainstay of the MNF, had his own ideas as to what needed to be done in Lebanon.

Habib argued forcefully to Gemayyel that the withdrawal of the Israeli and Syrian armies from Lebanon should *precede* any intra-Lebanese reconciliation. A genuine political settlement between the Lebanese would be hard to obtain, Habib argued, so long as the Israelis and Syrians remained on Lebanese soil. Repeatedly, he promised that American diplomacy would be able to persuade those two countries to pull out of Lebanon before the end of 1982. Internal political efforts could thus be shelved until that had been attained, he strongly implied.

Gemayyel took Habib's advice. It must have seemed the easiest thing to do, since it meant he could postpone the day when he himself would have to grapple with the Gordian knot of internal reconciliation. Meanwhile, he could leave it largely to the Americans to sort out the Israelis and the Syrians. If Gemayyel had had any qualms about following Habib's advice, then the Americans never heard them: in all its dealings with US officials the Gemayyel government seemed pathetically eager to follow whatever words of guidance the US side might utter.

So, Lebanon's internal political problems were left to fester while Habib and his team went to work on the Israeli and Syrian withdrawals. The trouble was that developments throughout the whole Middle Eastern theatre had led both these two neighbouring governments to the conclusion that stalling on the withdrawal from Lebanon would be the best policy.

Habib's strategy was first to try to negotiate an agreement on the Israeli troop withdrawal. He hoped that after this was achieved, Gemayyel could then take the lead in negotiating a Syrian withdrawal.

But Habib's ability to broker a quick Israeli withdrawal from Lebanon was unwittingly undercut by his own boss back in Washington, US President Reagan. For back in September 1982, Reagan had unveiled a Middle East peace plan, which called for a diminution of Israeli control over the West Bank of the Jordan, occupied since 1967. But he later explained that the US would not start implementing the plan until *after* the Lebanese-Israeli negotiations had been concluded.

Israeli Prime Minister Menachem Begin was totally opposed to opening any discussions concerning the West Bank. So he now had every incentive to try to drag out the Lebanon negotiations as long as possible.[1] Habib's end-of-1982 deadline came and went, and still there was no sign of any imminent Israeli withdrawal.

Then, in mid April 1983, the negotiations between Jordan and the PLO which were an important prelude to the Reagan peace plan were abruptly broken off. The threat which Begin had seen the plan as posing to his dreams of controlling the West Bank had receded. Now he could start looking at his troops' position in Lebanon on its own merits, rather than in relation to the diplomacy of the Reagan plan.

What he saw must have been disturbing. The Israelis had lost a total of about 350 dead throughout their first four months in Lebanon in 1982. Then, between October and February, they had lost a further 100. Their stay in Lebanon was proving very much more costly than its occupation of any other Arab territories had ever been.

The vast majority of the actions against the Israeli troops in Lebanon were being undertaken not by members of the Palestinian population which still eked out a terrified existence there, but by the Lebanese themselves. The Shi-ite majority in south Lebanon had accorded the Israelis a quiet welcome when they had first arrived there in June 1982. But by early 1983 they were starting to join the Druze of the Shouf in actively fighting Israel's continued presence.

The trend of opinion among the Lebanese of the south was summed up by the Mayor of Sydon, when he said of the Israelis, 'They invaded us to hunt Palestinians *and have stayed to occupy our land.*'[2]

Almost any action the Israelis took to punish the Lebanese of the south seemed only to increase their resistance to the occupation. On 18 March 1983, for example, Israeli officials arrested a prominent Shi-ite cleric in the Jebel Amil village of Jibsheet, who had been urging resistance to the occupation in his popular Friday sermons. The protests against his arrest grew quickly into open confrontations between Israeli troops and unarmed demonstrators. On 23 March, the Israelis decided it was not worth holding on to the preacher, and he was released.

The continuing Israeli casualties inside Lebanon were fuelling a mounting campaign in Israel in favour of withdrawal. So, once the linkage between the pull-back from Lebanon and the Reagan peace plan no longer mattered, it did not take Menachem Begin long to conclude a withdrawal agreement with Amin Gemayyel.

At the end of April, US officials engaged in a last burst of diplomacy which saw Secretary of State George Shultz making a two-week shuttle between Beirut and Jerusalem. On 17 May, the Israeli and Lebanese governments signed the first formal agreement between the two states since the Armistice agreement of 1949.

The 17 May agreement formally terminated the state of war which had existed between Israel and Lebanon since 1948. Each party was declared to be entitled to maintain a liaison office within the territory of the other party, 'if it so desires'. A Joint Liaison Committee was established in which the US was also to be represented to oversee the development of 'normal relations' between Israel and Lebanon.

The agreement also established the existence of a special security region covering all of Lebanon south of the Awali river and stretching inland to link up with the Israeli-occupied Golan Heights. Joint Israeli-Lebanese supervisory teams would inspect the security measures both within the security region, and throughout the rest of the country.

In the text of the agreement, the Israelis undertook to withdraw from Lebanon 'within eight to twelve weeks of the entry into force of the present agreement'. However, in a secret side agreement reached the same day between the US and the Israelis, the Americans expressed their understanding that the Israeli withdrawal would only take place after the Syrians had also agreed to withdraw from Lebanon.

This, the Syrians then calmly but obdurately refused to do. President Hafez al-Asad objected to the special privileges the Israelis would enjoy throughout Lebanon under the agreement. He said these privileges jeopardized the security of Syria itself. So he announced Syria's unequivocal opposition to the 17 May agreement.

The Israelis went ahead and opened a liaison office inside the Maronite-dominated area north of Beirut. But the rest of the 17 May agreement remained a dead letter. Israeli and Syrian forces remained where they had been in the south and east of Lebanon.

The Americans had misread the Syrian position badly. The apparent ease with which the Israeli air force had destroyed the Syrian missile bases in the Beqaa in June 1982, had tempted many US officials into an outpouring of exultation over 'the victory of American arms' and 'the humiliation of the Syrians'. So in May 1983, the Americans still thought it would be easy – with some help from Syria's financial backers in staunchly pro-Western Saudi Arabia – to persuade the Syrians to do as they wanted.

But the strength of the US officials' rhetoric seemingly blinded them to what the Syrians had actually been up to between June 1982 and May 1983. The Syrians and their Soviet allies had not just been sitting still since the destruction of the Beqaa batteries: the months which followed saw a substantial Soviet restocking, and even up-grading, of Syria's arsenals.

Secretary Shultz had seemed unaware of all this as he shuttled between Jerusalem and Beirut. And though he was willing to make the Israeli withdrawal totally contingent on the Syrian withdrawal, he had not even bothered to visit the Syrian capital before concluding the Lebanese-Israeli agreement. He then seemed genuinely hurt when the Syrians blocked the implementation of his plan.

For Amin Gemayyel, the Syrians' blocking of the 17 May agreement put him in a double bind. He had delayed any moves towards internal reconciliation until Lebanon's two powerful neighbours had withdrawn their troops from the country. But now he ended up without the troop withdrawals, and without any internal reconciliation either. Meanwhile, the terms of the agreement itself, with its implied acceptance of Israeli-imposed limits on Lebanese sovereignty, further prejudiced his chances of increasing the support he could expect from the Lebanese Muslims.

It is entirely possible that, if the 17 May agreement had been part of an overall strategy which resulted in the speedy withdrawal of Israeli and Syrian troops from Lebanon, then most Lebanese Muslims might have swallowed the distaste they felt for it, and accepted it. In mid June, for example, Gemayyel was able to win a parliamentary vote ratifying the agreement by sixty-four votes to two.

The fact that the withdrawal process never got off the ground meant the Syrians found it easy to build up a head of opposition to the agreement inside the Lebanese body politic. In mid July, Walid Jumblatt, the leading politician of Sunni Tripoli, Rashid Karami, and ex-President Suleiman Frangieh joined together under Syrian auspices to form a body called the National Salvation Front, whose declared aim was the abrogation of the agreement with Israel.

More important than these public political manoeuvrings was the support the Syrians were giving to the resurgence of the militias under Jumblatt's and Berri's command.

Jumblatt's Druze fighters in the Shouf had never been fully subdued by the Israelis. Their commanders had continued to receive military supplies from the Syrian forces in the nearby Beqaa. These supplies continued to flow into the Shouf even after it became plain, in late 1982, that the Druze were also receiving some help from the Israelis.

The Shi-ite communities in south Lebanon, on the other hand, had been disarmed and 'pacified' by the Israelis; and the Shi-ites of the Beirut suburbs had been 'pacified' by the Lebanese army. So it took the commanders of the Shi-ite 'Amal' militia in both those areas a little to re-establish their military operations after the traumas of summer 1982.

Once the Amal commanders had achieved this, they found a ready source of military supplies in Syria. They were easily able to establish supply-routes leading from the zone of Syrian control in the Beqaa, through Israeli lines, into the south-western suburbs of Beirut. (Amal was also able to smuggle lesser quantities of arms from the Beqaa to the growing anti-Israeli movement inside south Lebanon.)

In July 1983, a first serious clash erupted between the army and Amal in West Beirut. The army had tried to move some Shi-ite squatters from a district near the Green Line. The squatters resisted; and the Amal militiamen helped them to prevent the army's advance.

That battle lasted two days. It was limited to a small area and did not result in a clear victory for either side. But it was a portent of things to come in West Beirut – most especially since it led to the reported defection of a number of Shi-ite troops from the army unit involved.

Ever since early 1977, the US had been pursuing vigorous efforts to help re-vamp the Lebanese army, but such tentative progress as they had achieved by summer 1982 was undercut again by the strains of the Israeli invasion. Thus, when Amin Gemayyel came to power in September 1982, he did not have much of a national army at all. So the US, as part of its attempt to bolster President Gemayyel's position, had agreed to try again.

The early months of Gemayyel's term saw the army command restructuring the officer corps through encouraging selective resignations – just as had happened six years previously, at the beginning of Elias Sarkis's presidency. Under Sarkis, the army commander had been close to the Shihabists. In contrast, Gemayyel's new army commander, Ibrahim Tannous, was a veteran Ketaeb ally, and his re-modelling of the officer corps slanted heavily towards the Ketaeb. American officers who worked with the Tannous command were later to recall that his officer corps seemed to collaborate closely with the LF, and that Muslim officers were seldom included in the most important planning meetings.

However, every army also needs soldiers. In the case of Tannous's army the rank-and-file troops were raised from a general call-up which took in its first batch of 18-year-olds in mid April 1983. The outlying parts of the country, with their large Muslim majorities, were still under Israeli and Syrian occupation, so the draft could not be fully implemented there. But the general demographic trend, even just in the 'Greater Beirut' area was reflected in the fact that some 60 per cent of Tannous's draftees were Muslims – most of them from the Shi-ite community.

By the end of July, the army command became aware it would soon have to face a tough new challenge.

At that stage, it was clear to all the parties to the 17 May agreement that the Syrians would not swiftly be triggering the dual withdrawal process. But internal pressure was still mounting on the Begin government to cut down Israeli losses in Lebanon. Israeli officials thus started talking about making a partial pull-back, from the Shouf region, without waiting for any parallel Syrian withdrawal.

Until then, the Gemayyel government and the Americans had been pressing for a quick Israeli withdrawal from Lebanon. But when the Israelis proposed their unilateral pull-back from the Shouf, the question was immediately raised as to what force could replace them in that strife torn region.

There was some initial suggestion that the MNF might extend its control there. But none of the nations contributing to the MNF wanted to become caught in the same uncomfortable role the Israelis were leaving in the Shouf. So it was decided that the Lebanese army should try to control the area after the Israelis had left.

Deployment of the army in the Shouf would have the added advantage of increasing the area under the central government's nominal control, and thus also the general prestige of the Gemayyel regime. However, neither Gemayyel nor the Americans wanted to send the army into the Shouf before a political settlement had been reached between the LF and the Druze. They feared that to do so might risk another splintering of the supreme national force.

While Gemayyel pondered how to solve this problem, the army was faced with another major test. On 28 August, which was the fifth anniversary of the disappearance of Musa Sadr, Amal militiamen burst into the principal government television station in West Beirut. The tension which had been simmering between Amal and the army units in West Beirut for many months erupted into full-scale fighting. For the first time, the US Marines at the airport became drawn marginally into this round of the fighting.

The next day, more than 10,000 army troops moved in to cordon off Beirut's south-western suburbs from the rest of the city. Once again, the Marines were caught up in the fighting, which resulted in their first fatalities since the MNF's deployment the year before.

As the battles continued in West Beirut, Druze leader Jumblatt pledged his mountain militia's 'all-out support' for the Shi-ites.

The army was gathering its strength for a counter-attack against Amal; and on 31 August this started. Army tank columns advanced towards suspected Amal centres throughout West Beirut, with all guns blazing. The protests of the area's shocked residents were met with the imposition of a strict dusk-to-dawn curfew.

The army's August push into the heart of West Beirut had antagonized many of the area's residents. But it had failed in its aim of stifling the re-emergence of the local militias there. In tacit recognition of this fact, the army command was soon forced to enter into negotiations with the leaders of Amal. These talks resulted in vast stretches of the south-western suburbs – some of them abutting right on to the US Marines' base in the airport – being established as 'no-go' areas for the army, under *de facto* Amal control.

On 3 September, the Israelis abruptly withdrew from the Shouf, despite pressure from the Americans and President Gemayyel to wait until some kind of political settlement could be found for the area. The battles that erupted as the Israelis left recalled the conflict which had been played out between the Druze and the Maronites in the Mountain in 1861. The Druze in the Shouf had come under threat from the Maronite extremists of the LF for fifteen months already. Now, they felt they were fighting for their lives. As in 1861, the Druze families now hunkered down in the villages, while their menfolk were joined by co-religionists from both Hawran (in Syria) and Galilee (in Israel). They were coming to help in a battle for survival in which they knew no mercy would be shown by either side.

The Druze may not, by 1983, have been the most numerous community in the Shouf, but they proved they were still far and away the toughest. The historic clan distinctions which had divided their community were forgotten. Yazbekis and Jumblattis alike rallied round the Jumblatti-led Druze militia as it moved against the LF throughout the area.

On 4 September, some Lebanese army units made a feeble attempt to fill the vacuum the Israelis had left in the Shouf. But they only made it to Aley. The Druze then accused them of openly siding with the LF in the Mountain, and were able to prevent them from advancing any further. The Druze were soon able to push them back from Aley to a small town on the ridge overlooking Beirut, called Souq al-Gharb. Then, the Druze resumed their momentum against the LF.

In the battles of September 1983, the sectarianism which had been stirred up by the LF's original entry into the Shouf fifteen months earlier, finally ran riot. As the Druze fighters advanced, their ferocity was fuelled by the putrefying evidence they found of massacres which the LF had committed against their people throughout the preceding months. In many instances, they now retaliated in kind.

Streams of terrified Christian villagers poured into the Israeli-held zone, and into East Beirut. Some 20,000 of those who could not make it to those havens gathered in the historic Shouf capital of Dair al-Qamar, where they were surrounded by the Druze. The remnants of the 3000 LF who had been in the Shouf since June 1982 quickly realized that their original high hopes of controlling the area were shattered. They too slunk into Deir al-Qamar.

The major battle which remained was that for control of Souq al-Gharb. If the Druze had been able to break through the army's lines there, Gemayyel and his American backers feared they might then link up with the Amal-held areas in south-west Beirut to form an insurrectionary belt around half the capital.

On 7 September, the fighting in the Mountain overflowed into the capital itself: American troop positions came under fire, and three French soldiers in the MNF were killed by artillery fire. The next day, the US navy sought to retaliate. One of the dozen ships lying off the Lebanese coast opened up with its 5-inch guns against suspected Druze positions in the Mountain.

The Druze forces were, meanwhile, building up their pressure against the army in Souq al-Gharb. On 19 September, they managed to capture some of the town's outskirts in fierce hand-to-hand fighting. This time, the US navy responded with the fiercest naval bombardment it had undertaken since the Vietnam War, firing more that 350 5-inch shells into Druze positions around Souq al-Gharb, and forcing the Druze to fall back from the town.

Throughout that week the battles escalated. The Lebanese army brought in the Lebanese air force's ageing fleet of Hawker Hunters to strafe the Druze positions. The US continued its naval bombardment, and the French sent a wing of ultra-modern jets in to bomb the Druze in the Mountain.

The Druze then tried to add to the pressure on the army's position in Souq al-Gharb by asking the Muslim militias in Beirut to open a second front against the army's rear.

Back in 1958, the Sunni militias under Saeb Salam had failed to respond to a similar version of this appeal, then launched by the elder Kamal Jumblatt. In September 1983, the Shi-ite fighters of Amal acted differently. On 23 September, the clashes between Amal and the army in West Beirut started escalating rapidly towards the full-scale insurrection Gemayyel and the Americans had feared.

Two days later, as the Lebanese army battled for its life, the extensive American flotilla already lying off the Lebanese coast was joined by the battleship 'New Jersey', which boasted of huge 16-inch guns. All direct and indirect parties to the battle of Souq al-Gharb now realized that in any additional escalation the stakes would be extremely high.

Throughout the preceding weeks, the Lebanese government had been involved in indirect talks with the Syrians about the Shouf. On the evening of the 'New Jersey's' arrival, the Lebanese and Syrian governments announced that they had now reached agreement on a cease-fire in West Beirut and the Shouf.

That cease-fire went into effect at dawn the next morning. It was supervised by a joint security committee containing members from the Lebanese army, Amal, the LF and the Druze PSP militia.

The 23 September agreement also stipulated that Gemayyel and all the major political leaders in Lebanon should open talks aimed at national reconciliation, in the presence of Saudi and Syrian observers. The promise of these talks held out a hope of political reform to Amal and the Druze: to open the way for such reform, Premier Wazzan submitted his resignation on 26 September.

For their part, supporters of the LF viewed the prospect of political reform with unabashed horror. They realized that the military and political balance had dipped sharply against their interests since the heady days of August 1982. The LF had lost some of their most experienced units in the debacle in the Shouf. Rubbing salt in this wound was the fact that the debacle had come about as a direct result of the Israelis' abandonment of the LF there. Bitter LF supporters were forced to conclude that the support from Israel on which they had based so many of their earlier calculations, would henceforth be extremely limited.

The Maronitist hard-liners thus realized that any political settlement reached in September 1983 would severely reduce the privileges their community had enjoyed in the Lebanese system until then. They tried to stall, to put off the holding of the talks until they could tip the strategic balance in the country back in their own direction. The only hope they saw of achieving this was now to draw the US further into the conflict on their side.

For its part, the US administration was badly divided on how to deal with the situation in Lebanon. One substantial party argued that any lessening of US support for the Lebanese army would be a setback for American credibility around the world. This argument was countered from within the US military establishment, which warned against being drawn into a punishing and probably unwinnable civil war in Lebanon.

The indecision in Washington meant that for some weeks Gemayyel felt himself under little American pressure to go ahead with the promised reconciliation talks. So he largely complied with the wishes of the Maronite hard-liners, and consistently played down the importance of the promised talks. Finally, on 19 October, he announced their indefinite postponement.

Four days later, a new factor suddenly jolted the US into pushing hastily for the talks to start. Early that morning, two men believed to be linked to an extremist Shi-ite group drove trucks loaded with explosives into the barracks of both the US and the French MNF contingents. The US barracks, near the airport, collapsed in its entirety, killing 241 of the Marines who had been sleeping inside, and wounding many others. The French meanwhile lost fifty-seven dead in the collapse of their outpost nearer the heart of West Beirut.

The bombing of the Marines' compound prompted the Reagan administration to restore the concept of 'strategic co-operation' with Israel, which had been broken off in an earlier protest against Israel's annexation of the Syrian Golan Heights. However, the bombing also prompted the Americans to turn for the first time to the question of reaching an intra-Lebanese reconciliation – though US officials warned that this should *not* be achieved at the expense of the Israeli-Lebanese agreement of 17 May.

President Gemayyel got the American message. On 31 October, he opened the first session of the Lebanese reconciliation talks in Geneva; the only site in which all those taking part felt safe. With him there were Pierre Gemayyel and Camille Chamoun, from the Maronitist Lebanese Front; Walid Jumblatt, Rashid Karami and Suleiman Frangieh, from the pro-Syrian group; Nabih Berri of Amal; and Saeb Salam and Adil Osseiran representing respectively the Sunni and Shi-ite 'old guards'. Present at the talks with observer status were high-level US, Israeli and Syrian representatives.

Almost immediately, the conference became deadlocked over the issue of the 17 May agreement with Israel. The US and Israeli observers were putting heavy pressure on Gemayyel, from behind the scenes, to prevent the abrogation of the accord. The Syrians were pressing equally hard, in conjunction with their allies of the National Salvation Front, that it be put aside.

Unable to paste over differences on this issue, on 4 November the conferees decided on an interim solution. They would suspend their work, to give Gemayyel time to consult with the governments contributing to the MNF.

At that stage, Gemayyel promised that the conference would resume its work two weeks later. But soon thereafter, close presidential aides were deriding the whole idea of national reconciliation, as unnecessary. Meanwhile, in his visits to the MNF contributors, Gemayyel desperately asked them to up-grade their support for his army.

By the beginning of December he was in Washington, for talks with President Reagan. Just after he had left the American capital, the US navy sent a flight of war-planes in to bomb Syrian positions in the Beqaa. But if that was an attempt to demonstrate that the US retained some 'muscle' in Lebanon, it failed miserably. Two of the planes were shot down. One of the pilots concerned was killed; the other was taken prisoner by the Syrians.[3]

Still, Gemayyel stalled on re-convening the Geneva talks. And meanwhile, the cease-fire reached on 23 September was eroding badly in both the Shouf and the Beirut suburbs.

In the middle of January, Walid Jumblatt finally declared that he had lost his patience with Gemayyel. He accused the president of blatant pro-LF partisanship, and, on 22 January, called for his resignation. Soon after that, however, the ever-volatile Druze leader changed his mind. He explained that he sought the resignation merely of the government, and not, for the moment, that of the president himself.

It was at this stage that the commanders of the French MNF contingent were making plans for a re-ordering of their troops' deployment in West Beirut. At the beginning of February, the French troops pulled out of positions along the line which divided the troubled southern suburbs of Shiyyah and Ain al-Rummaneh.

As the French withdrew, Lebanese army units moved in to try and replace them. But Amal saw this as an unwarranted army encroachment into a strategic area which had long formed part of the 'turf' of the Shi-ites of Shiyyah, and so resisted the army move.

General Tannous chose to take a tough stand on the Shiyyah issue. He rapidly built up the army's strength along the lines facing the Shi-ite neighbourhoods. Then, they loosed a heavy barrage of tank and artillery fire into the heavily-peopled apartment buildings there.

Under the pressure of this bombardment, on 4 February Amal leader Nabih Berri called on the Muslim members of the Wazzan government to resign. And he asked Muslim soldiers to refuse to take part in the shelling of civilian areas.

Berri had taken over the leadership of Amal only in 1980. A member of the second-largest family in the large Jebel Amil village of Tibneen, he had trained as a lawyer. He was thus typical of the whole generation of Shi-ite professionals who were the organizational core of Amal.

By 1983, he was 46 years old – certainly still young enough to qualify as one of the younger generation of national leaders. But he had already accumulated much political acumen. His political views were actually not at all extreme. (He still, in 1983, hung on to his US

immigrant's 'Green Card'.) But he was an effective head for Amal –
generally well able to keep its many disparate strands operating in
harmony, and possessed of a respected degree of personal charisma.

At this stage, Berri was still not directly calling on the Muslims in
the army to desert. But over the next few hours this is just what they
did – in numbers so overwhelming that by 6 February the authority of
the army had collapsed completely in all of West Beirut.

Jubilant militiamen of Amal and a handful of other, much smaller
West Beirut militias were now in uncontested control of their half of
the city. They found themselves responsible *de facto* for the security
of its public buildings, its many embassies – and the perimeter of the
US Marines encampment at the airport.

On 7 February, President Reagan made a surprise announcement
to the effect that he had now ordered the Marines to withdraw from
Lebanon, back to the nearby US navy ships.

That announcement was coupled with the issuing of new rules of
engagement, which allowed the naval commanders off Lebanon to
order sea or air bombardments against *any* forces attacking the
Greater Beirut area. (Over the days which followed, they used this
power quite liberally, sending hundreds of shells from the 'New
Jersey' and other ships into Druze-held parts of the Shouf.)

Immediately after Reagan's announcement the British said that
their token force would be withdrawn forthwith. The Italians also
said they would pull their MNF troops out. And though the French
did not immediately announce any plans for withdrawal, the French
president declared a public preference that they be replaced with a
UN force.

Over the days which followed 7 February, that part of the army
which remained loyal to President Gemayyel re-grouped alongside
the LF in East Beirut to prevent any Amal advance into areas of LF
control. The troops who had defected to Amal were meanwhile
hurriedly re-organized under the command of the army's sixth
brigade, which thenceforth operated in West Beirut in close co-
ordination with the Amal leadership.

The following week, the Druze in the Mountain resumed their push
against those army units which still remained around the edges of the
Shouf. The army was able to hang on to its heavily-fortified position
in Souq al-Gharb. but everywhere else throughout the Shouf, and
right down to the coast road from Khaldeh to Damour, the army was
totally routed by the Druze.

By 15 February the Druze had joined up completely with the

Amal-dominated areas of Beirut. Gemayyel was faced by a solid oppositionist block stretching from the Beirut Green Line down to the Israeli front-line on the Awali River. His army had been rent into two nearly equal parts. The Israelis had turned their back on him. And the MNF which had been his last hope of salvation was vanishing into thin air! Only Syria could now keep his presidency intact.

At the end of February, Amin Gemayyel made his first presidential visit to Damascus, to discuss the terms under which President Assad's regime there would save him.

In 1982, Bashir Gemmayel and his Maronitist movement posed a threat to the inter-sect system in Lebanon no less serious – and possibly far more serious – than that which Kamal Jumblatt had launched six years later.

Kamal Jumblatt's earlier movement had directly challenged two key aspects of the National Pact system through which Lebanon had been ruled since 1943. These were: the quota system for jobs in the state administration; and the Maronite ascendancy, as enshrined in that quota system.

But Jumblatt's aims could still be construed as being in accordance with the spirit of Lebanon's formal constitution, as promulgated in 1926. The constitution, after all, had spelt it out that the quota system would be necessary *only provisionally*; and that the basis of the system would remain the equality of all Lebanese citizens, of whatever sect or community.

It was this latter guiding principle of the 1926 constitution which Bashir Gemayyel's movement attacked head on.

Of course, it is possible to suppose that the movement *may* have acted differently if its leader had not – even as final victory appeared within reach – been slain. But he was. And the movement he left behind proved to be a sectarian, exclusivist movement which attacked the very fundamentals of inter-sect collaboration in Lebanon. And I – unlike Philip Habib – find it hard to imagine that, with the leader, the movement would have been very different.

The story of the twenty-one months which followed Israel's June 1982 entry into Lebanon was the story of how the LF's challenge to the Lebanese system reached its zenith– and was then, in its turn, defeated.

For several years, the LF militants had hoped that, if they could first get control of the Shouf, they could link up with their Israeli-supported counterparts in the south and declare their *de facto* control of the whole country. Their Muslim opponents in Beirut and the south would be surrounded, and the Muslims of the Beqaa and the north leaderless and vulnerable. New Muslim leaderships would emerge which would work with the LF, accepting its total control of the system. Thus would 'Lebanon' be saved. (I first heard LF people discussing this plan back in 1978.)

This plan was built on a flawed premise. For the whole history of the inter-sect entity called Lebanon had been built on the idea that no sect within it would allow others totally to dominate it. The Maronites, of all people, should have remembered this, from their own recent experience in fending off Jumblatt's offensive in 1975–6.

But the LF Maronites ignored that lesson. In 1982–3, they rode gleefully into the Shouf, thinking they could 'easily' dominate the Druze community there. In Jebel Amil, they and Haddad's ragtag army rode shotgun on the Israeli convoys, thinking the Israelis could 'easily' protect their ambitions there. In the capital, they thought that their control of the army command could 'easily' help them to control the troublesome Muslims of West Beirut. They thought their moment had come.

But it never did arrive. The Druze rapidly found the means to defend their Shouf heartland. The Shi-ites of Jebel Amil and West Beirut were not long following the Druze lead. The age-old necessity of coexistence was reasserting itself, by force, in the Lebanese arena.

What was happening in Lebanon from 1982 to 1984 was a third violent swing of the political pendulum, coming after the previous swings propelled by, respectively, Kamal Jumblatt and Bashir Gemayyel's LF. This time, it was the new coalition dominated by the Shi-ites of Amal which was the prime moving force. The Shi-ite-led coalition was able to beat back the threat which the Maronitists had posed to the Muslim communities, and to the inter-sect system itself.

The new swing of the pendulum probably saved the inter-sect system in Lebanon. But in doing so, it too, like Jumblatt's movement before it, challenged many particular aspects of the edifice which had been built up on the foundations of the Lebanese inter-sect principle over the preceding 150 years.

By the mid 1980s, it was still not evident how many features of that edifice would endure over the decades which were to follow. Could a unitary political system, such as that envisaged in the national Pact, survive? Or were the forces of sectarianism now so deeply entrenched that only a radical de-centralization would prove possible? What was clear was that much had already irrevocably changed since the apparently high point Lebanon seemed to have reached two decades before.

Notes

1   See William B. Quandt's article 'Reagan's Lebanon policy: trial and error', *Middle East Journal* (Washington, DC), *38* no. 2 (Spring 1984), pp. 237–54.
2   Augustus R. Norton, 'Making enemies in south Lebanon: Harakat Amal, the IDF, and south Lebanon', in *Middle East Insight* (Washington, DC), *3* no. 3 (Jan./Feb. 1984), p. 19. This was the second of two informative articles by Norton on trends inside the Shi-ite community between the late 1970s and 1983: the first was published in the preceding issue of the same publication.
3   The pilot was released a month later, following a trip to Damascus by black US presidential candidate Jesse Jackson.

9 Conclusions: the inter-sect system enters its fifth century

Much had changed in Lebanon between 1975 and 1985. Yet much, also, remained unchanged by all the turmoil there in that decade. So what, ultimately, would prove to be enduring in the future development of the place, and what merely transitory?

In the preceding chapters, I have traced, in particular, the fate of the political edifice which was erected, from 1920 onwards, on the ancient foundations of Lebanese inter-sectarianism. If we were to look at the country's development purely in terms of that edifice, then we would probably have to conclude that the period from 1920 until 1985 constituted a single, clear cycle of political growth followed by near-total decay.

What, after all, remained by the mid 1980s of the borders of 1920, the constitution of 1926, the National Pact of 1943, or the practice of Shihabism? Little enough, except for the desperate clinging of most Lebanese to the *idea* of their national borders, and to some *formalities* of their constitution.

However, there is another level at which we can examine the history of Lebanon, other than through the development of its 'modern-style' political institutions. We can look at the gradual, long-term shifts of power between the various groups within its inter-sect system.

At this level, we can look at the period from 1920 to 1985 as one which started with two substantial new groups (the Sunnis and the Shi-ites) being brought into the Maronite-dominated system. The Maronites continued to occupy the prime place in the system for the next fifty years after 1920. But gradually, one of the new groups within it (the Shi-ites) grew strong enough to challenge their ascendancy.

By the mid 1980s, it looked as though the Maronites and Shi-ites were locked into a prolonged struggle for the powerful first place within the inter-sect system. And, in my view, most indicators seemed to suggest that the Shi-ites would eventually emerge the stronger group.

In this perspective, the years following 1975 can be seen not simply as a period of decay (of the existing institutions), but rather, as the start of the transition period wherein the primacy within the system would pass from the Maronites to the Shi-ites.

Ever since the inception of the inter-sect system in Mount Lebanon, in the late sixteenth century, one sect within the system had been the 'first among equals' within it. As the system had developed, it became clear that there were definite limits on the power this leading sect could exercise: its position was always one of primacy, rather than domination or control. But provided these limitations on its power were always clearly recognized, the prime sect could impose its vision and interest on the whole system to a greater degree than any other sect could.

In earlier centuries, the struggle for primacy revolved principally around the institution of the princedom – though the prince always also had to win the consent of the powerful Mountain lords. In modern times, it has revolved principally around the twin institutions of the presidency and the army command.

One important point about looking at Lebanon in terms of the inter-sect balance, and the inter-sect struggle for primacy, is that a transfer of primacy from one sect to another such as seems to be happening today *is not new*. It has happened before. The Maronites themselves only emerged clearly into first place within the system after wresting that position from the Druze back in the mid nineteenth century.

That earlier transfer of primacy was certainly not accomplished easily. It was accomplished only after a period of acute civil instability, which lasted thirty-six years or more. It was accompanied by the rise of new radical social movements, and by the direct intervention of numerous outside powers.

And, of course, during that earlier transfer of primacy, many existing political institutions – including the Druze-based lordly system itself – were destroyed.

But what of Lebanon's regional environment? Did that not also play an important role in sparking the problems Lebanon lived through from 1967 on? I think it did. For the Lebanese rapidly found they could not isolate themselves from the chronic Palestinian-Israeli crisis which arose out of the 1967 war. But neither could they find any effective means to deal with this crisis, because the viability of the Lebanese system had depended since the Second World War on the maintenance of a weak, delicately-balanced government in Beirut.

The Lebanese were thus condemned to live with the escalating cycles of Palestinian-Israeli violence, and with an intense polarization over the Palestinian issue which cut right through their own body politic. As chronicled in Chapter 5, it was this polarization that crucially undermined the position of the Sunni Muslim leaders, who had been the second main pillar of the state since independence.

The weakening of the traditional Sunni leaders left the Lebanese system, as it had operated since 1943, seriously off balance. The way was then open for successive swings of the pendulum of discontent – from first Kamal Jumblatt, then Bashir Gemayyel, then Amal – which undermined ever more of the country's political institutions.

One argument often heard in Lebanon (and especially from Maronites) is that the whole instability the country lived through from 1967 to the mid 1980s was a result *only* of these regional factors. But I do not think this is a sufficient description of what was happening. In particular, it does not begin to describe the changes the inter-sect balance in the country was going through in that period.

By the mid 1980s, the Shi-ites had emerged clearly as major challengers to the Maronite ascendancy. How was the Shi-ite renaissance related to Lebanon's regional environment? In my view, scarcely at all.

The resurgence which the Shi-ite community experienced from the 1960s on was rooted far more deeply in the internal processes of what happens to a sect brought into the inter-sect system, than it was in any regional factors. President Fuad Shihab's roads and schools, and the invigorating effect of Lebanese liberalism, did far more to feed the Shi-ite renaissance than the actions of the Israelis, Palestinians or Iranians ever did. (Just as, in earlier centuries, the new opportunities presented by the inter-sect system had spurred a remarkable renaissance within the Maronite community.)

In this view, the Shi-ites would have had their renaissance anyway, almost regardless of what the Palestinians and Israelis did in Lebanon. They would have grown strong anyway, regardless of these and other regional factors.

Regional factors may have had a great effect on the particular *way* the Shi-ite challenge to the Maronite ascendancy occurred, and on its *timing*. But they did not affect the *fact* that it occurred. Had the regional situation been different, in my view, the Shi-ite challenge to the Maronites might have occurred earlier than it did, or it might have occurred later. But most probably, *it would still have occurred.*

Before we look at the regional environment Lebanon found itself in half-way through the 1980s, let us look at what had happened inside each of the country's major religious groups by then.

The Shi-ites

When the two Shi-ite communities of Jebel Amil and the northern Beqaa were brought into the Lebanese system in 1920, they were very separate societies. And they lagged far behind the Maronites, and most Druzes, in terms of their economic infrastructure, and their social and political development.

At first, much of Shi-ite public opinion resented the integration of these areas into Greater Lebanon, and their separation from the Syrian hinterland. This centrifugal trend continued to be strong in Shi-ite society for several decades after 1920. But in that period, the sect still came under the near-total domination of a handful of landowning families (in Jebel Amil), and tribal leaders (in the Beqaa). The French were able to win the loyalty of most of these community leaders for the administration in Beirut, through the judicious distribution of patronage.

The established families maintained their domination over Shi-ite society until 1958. Then, in the civil war of that year, they saw many of their followers swing violently away from them, towards the pan-Arab radicalism of the Nasserists.

Few of those old-style Shi-ite leaders saw any clear solution to the international crisis which racked their sect at that time. But Fuad Shihab did. His policy, once he became president, was to try to solve the many social problems which he thought dangerously increased the appeal of radical ideals in the Shi-ite areas. By bringing the Shi-ites up towards the levels of development of their Maronite and Druze compatriots, he sought truly to integrate them into the Lebanese system.

Shihab was only partially successful in realizing his overall economic plan for the country, but he was resoundingly successful in spurring the social development of its rural areas.

Previously, the most enterprising Shi-ite youths had often found their ambition checked by the conservatism of their sect's traditional leaders. Many of them had ended up emigrating, to West Africa and elsewhere, so that they could get ahead. After Shihab had finished his work, however, a Shi-ite youth could go to a nearby government school, pursue his or her studies at the new national university in

Beirut, and return to his village to work as a teacher or lawyer. The whole process would cost the youth's family very little. And the local landowner was powerless to stop the process of social change thus set in motion.

Not all the newly-mobilized Shi-ites returned to their villages. The migration of Shi-ite families to the suburbs of Beirut became a flood from the late 1950s onwards. By the early 1980s one-third of the whole Shi-ite population was found there.

The large-scale Shi-ite migration to Beirut accelerated the process of social change within the sect. In addition, in the city, Shi-ites from Jebel Amil and the Beqaa mingled for the first time; and they went through many of the same traumatic experiences there together. Urbanization thus helped to weave the interests of what were now three distinct areas of Shi-ite settlement – in Jebel Amil, the Beqaa and Beirut – into something like a single, national Shi-ite constituency.

The Shi-ites' true integration into the Lebanese system, as spurred by the Shihabists, set the stage for the rise of new radical movements, which threw out a strong challenge to the sect's traditional leadership, as well as to the Maronite ascendancy. (There were many parallels here with what had happened in Maronite society in the early decades of the nineteenth century.)

The first form the new Shi-ite radicalism took was broadly leftist in tone. As Kamal Jumblatt's leftist coalition gathered momentum in the country from 1968 to 1975, a majority of the members of its constituent groups were probably Shi-ites. Shi-ites fought and died in disproportionately large numbers during Jumblatt's bid for power in 1975–6. So strong was the tide of Shi-ite opposition to old-style sect leaders such as Kamal al-Asaad and Kazem al-Khalil, that they were forced to seek protection in the Lebanese Front enclave in those years!

After 1976, Jumblatt's movement was beaten back, and started to fall apart. Its particular mix of radical ideals – which revolved principally around non-sectarianism and pan-Arabism – had become unfashionable. The old-style Shi-ite leaders tried feebly to stage a comeback in their own community.

However, the causes of Shi-ite radicalism still persisted, and were as acute as ever. A majority of Shi-ites still blamed most of their problems on the Maronite extremists behind whose guns the traditionalists still sheltered. The break-up of Jumblatt's movement was thus followed, not by the return of the Shi-ite *ancien régime*, but by the growth of another form of radicalism, the Shi-ite sectarianism of Amal.

Amal's growth in this period was also spurred by Musa Sadr's disappearance in Libya, and by the victory of the Shi-ite revolution in Iran. But most of the causes of its gains were still purely Lebanese.

Amal was uniquely placed to spearhead the next phase of the Shi-ite renaissance. For it utilized the full energies of the 'new classes' of Shi-ite business-people and professionals, in a community-building effort which was free of the potentially divisive influence of imported leftist ideology. Amal had no need to import any ideologies, for the «ulama' tradition in which it was rooted already contained many important strands of social radicalism.

It was on the basis of Amal's new, specifically Shi-ite appeal that Shi-ite doctors, now running relatively successful practices in Beirut, would do volunteer work in Amal's rural clinics. The owners of Shi-ite banks in Beirut – a group which had not even existed in Beirut before 1977! – secured loans for Amal's rehabilitation and development projects. And many of the movement's expenses were met by the Shi-ite emigrants of an earlier generation, who had their own long grudges against their sect's old-style leaders.

There was thus a whole social, political, cultural and economic renaissance within their society which – in addition to their raw numbers – was propelling the Shi-ites towards the ascendancy in the inter-sect system by the mid 1980s.

Was the Shi-ite sectarian movement a merely transitory phenomenon, to be dissipated as easily as the earlier tide of Shi-ite leftism had been? I do not think so. For by the mid 1980s, it already seemed clear that there was a significant 'Shi-ite question' to be resolved within the Lebanese system. And if Nabih Berri's leadership of Amal could not resolve it, then there were plenty of other, more radical groups within the sect who would be eager to have a try.

By the mid 1980s, the Amal leadership had proved itself effective in many respects. (This fact received implicit recognition from some, at least, of the old-style Shi-ite leaders. For they now apparently judged that if they were to retain any political base at all, they would have to work within the movement's orbit.)

One of the Amal leadership's most difficult tasks was to knit together the widely varying interests of all the different groups of Shi-ites. In the first years of Amin Gemayyel's presidency, for example, the three different areas of Shi-ite settlement each had to deal with different rulers.

Since its inception, Amal had dealt with the diversity of its constituency by developing a loose, nearly collegial leadership style. Individual members of the leadership group could deal with opponents or allies from one side, without being either embarrassed or hamstrung by what their colleagues might be saying to another side. But all along, there remained enough core agreement between them on Amal's long-term goals, that short-term disagreements rarely impeded their activities for long.

Another, linked, respect in which the Amal leadership proved itself astute was in the sophistication of its dealings with local and outside allies. Like Sadr before him, Nabih Berri went out of his way to cultivate a broad range of relationships with leaders from other sects. And after his militiamen stormed West Beirut in February 1984, he took some important steps to try to protect the area's non-Shi-ite residents from the rising tide of Shi-ite fundamentalism.

In its dealings with Israel and Syria, Amal felt itself little capable of adopting a neutral stance between the two neighbours who still occupied vast portions of Lebanon in mid 1984. The religious and sectarian interests of the Shi-ites forced them strongly to oppose the occupation which the Jewish state maintained in Jebel Amil, with the help of Maronite extremists. Compared with this, the occupation which the Alawite rulers of Syria maintained in the Beqaa was definitely a lesser evil.

Despite this anti-Israeli skew in its position, the Amal leadership was careful to avoid the kind of wholesale reliance on Syria which would have been implied in, for example, membership in the National Salvation Front in 1983. And the Amal leadership remained in indirect contact with the Israelis in south Lebanon, even while it fought them.

Ever since the day in 1975 when it had received its original name of *Lebanese* Resistance Battalions, the mainstream of Amal had clearly signalled its intention of remaining Lebanese, rather than becoming Syrian or anything else. Through its actions in the first half of the 1980s, the movement's leadership showed itself determined to stay that way.

The Maronites

What of the Maronites, meanwhile? How was their community affected by the growing threat to its primacy within the system?

To a certain extent, the story of what happened to the Maronites in the four decades after independence parallels the story of modern Lebanon itself. For it is a story in which seemingly sturdy modern-style institutions were suddenly swamped, and nearly destroyed, in the rushing resurgence of the atavisms of a long-gone age.

The vision on which the modern state in Lebanon had been based was that of a liberal, merchant republic, built around the busy port of Beirut. That vision had informed the Christian banker who in 1926 had drafted the country's formal constitution. And it had informed the National Pact, whereby leaders of the Maronite and Sunni merchant communities in Beirut had divided most of the power in the country between them.

In the first years of independence, these arrangements seemed to be working phenomenally well. Vast amounts of money flowed through the banks of Beirut. Whole new classes of Beirutis, including many Maronites, became enriched beyond the wildest dreams their grand-fathers could ever have entertained. There were some small dis-agreements over, for example, just how President Khoury's friends had become so rich, so quick. But the firm commitment to *laissez-faire,* and to a weak central government, continued to bring an overall prosperity to the Lebanese merchant republic.

However, it was not a system which could withstand much internal or external strain. In 1958, the eruption of pro-Nasserist sympathies within the country brought it to a crisis. The merchant republic was only able to save itself by making significant concessions to the very different interests of the rural regions outside Beirut. These conces-sions were represented in the low-key statism of President Shihab.

The new strains which were placed on the system after 1967 were far more acute than those of 1958. The Maronite leaders were faced with the rise of a leftist movement which challenged both their sect's privileged position within the merchant republic, and many basic premises of the merchant republic itself.

Their first reaction was to withdraw back to their own sectarian roots. Up to 1967, most Maronite leaders, including the proponents of the merchant republic, had continued to try to win the best deal possible out of the ruling Shihabists. After 1967, they started working to undermine the Shihabist form of inter-sect compromise. This was true, most importantly, of the Ketaeb Party leader, Pierre Gemayyel. But a similar swing against Shihabism was taken by many others within the sect.

In 1970, the Shihabists fell from power. But the swing against the kind of social compact they had represented had already hardened, within the Maronite community, into a discernible swing against any kind of concessions to the other sects.

Pierre Gemayyel's son, Bashir, epitomized that swing. Each weekend, in the early 1970s, he and hundreds of other youths would leave Beirut's Maronite suburbs for the Mountain, to train with the Ketaeb militia. At the metaphorical level, many more Maronites were also retreating from the Beirut of inter-sect liberalism, back to the Mountain, with its ancient ideologies of their sect's survival.

The movement which Bashir Gemayyel came to head was not an exact replica of any of the age-old Maronite ideologies of the Mountain. It was always heavily coloured by the raw, inter-sect jealousies of the Beirut suburbs. The traditional Maronite society of the Mountain, after all, had had its own rough and ready form of give and take; it had its own longstanding feuds, which often readily criss-crossed inter-sect boundaries.

The Maronitism of Bashir Gemayyel was much harsher and less tolerant than this. It was Maronitism seen through the prism of the recently urbanized lower middle class. It was a monolithic view of Maronite society, parodied from the textbooks of West European fascists.

Bashir Gemayyel threw out a fundamental challenge to those Maronite leaders who had fostered the liberalism of the merchant republic. One of his first major Maronite targets was Raymond Eddé, a staunch liberal, and member of a prominent landowning and banking family. In 1976, Bashir's fighters forced him out of his home-base in Byblos. (Later, the Syrians forced him to flee the country completely.) Bashir's subsequent actions, against the Frangiehs and then the Chamounist militia, showed how narrowly he drew the bounds of disagreement among Maronites.

Did Bashir Gemayyel's movement aim at any genuine social radicalism? He and his supporters claimed that it did. They used to rail against the 'big families' whose squabbling and corruption had brought the country to the brink of ruin; and they vowed to replace them with a new, more moral order. (These kinds of ideas echoed many of those first voiced by leaders of the Maronite 'General Uprising' movement, 150 years earlier.)

There were always some in the Maronite community who thought that the Gemayyels really aimed at replacing the many 'big families' with the rule of just one 'big family' – their own. But these voices of criticism were muted, so long as they saw the Ketaeb militia taking effective action against the Palestinians (in 1976), and then the

Syrians (in 1977 and 1978). And they remained muted while Bashir Gemayyel seemed to be on a winning streak, from 1978 to 1982.

By 1982, a whole new political generation had matured inside the LF enclave, which was absolutely opposed to any form of compromise with the Muslims. These young Maronites had never rubbed shoulders with any Muslims during their formative years, as previous generations had. They knew so little about their Muslim compatriots! They knew nothing of the massive and momentous changes within the Shi-ite community. They knew only what the LF-controlled media in East Beirut wanted them to know.

The LF generation of Maronites thought it would be easy to dominate all the Muslims, to turn the clock back to a mythical earlier era when Maronites had not had to reach compromises with anybody.

There had never been such an era, of course. But the LF generation had been so pumped up with the aggressive spirit of Israeli backers such as Ariel Sharon that they thought they could dominate not just their sect, but also the whole of Lebanon.

Throughout 1983 and the first months of 1984 they were rapidly disabused of this notion. But it remained to be seen what kind of leadership would arise from the ashes of their wasted ambitions. Would the Maronite consensus continue to cling to the sectarian exclusivism which had ruled their enclave since 1975? Would the liberal proponents of the merchant republic be able to make some kind of a comeback? Or would community leaders throughout the sect be able to find some other, middle way?

These questions were still vitally important in the mid 1980s, since the Maronites still retained control of the most important levers in the Lebanese administration. Thus – until the Maronites should relinquish these levers to another group – the future of the whole country would continue to depend heavily on developments within this community.

The Sunnis (and the other 'minorities')

The system which found expression in the 1943 National Pact, gave the Sunnis second place only to the Maronites in the Lebanese system. High hopes were thereby invested in the contribution they might make to the country's future.

Then, in 1958, and again in the late 1960s and early 1970s, the Sunnis were thought to constitute the main threat to the status quo in the country. The previous high hopes had given way, for many

Maronites, to a generalized *fear* that the Sunnis might overthrow the system completely. But still, whether through hope or fear, they were considered of central importance to the country's destiny.

But neither the hopes nor the fears vested in the Sunni community were ever fully realized. By the mid 1980s, the Sunnis had been relegated to the margins of what was happening in the country, as the Maronites tangled with the Shi-ites and Druze over its future. Why had the Sunnis' role shrunk so dramatically?

I think three issues, taken together, help to explain what happened. The first of these is the question of the differing interests and histories of the Mountain and the city in Lebanon. The second is the distinction between *sects* and *minorities*, as mentioned in Chapter 1. And the third is the Lebanese Sunnis' position with respect to the Arab world.

I have already described the Lebanon of the National Pact as, 'a merchant republic, built around the busy port of Beirut'. The Maronite liberals were one group which profited from that system; and which were weakened when it was weakened. The powerful Sunni trading families of Beirut were another.

The 'merchant republic' formula in Lebanon had long historical antecedents, going back to the development of the country's ports in the early nineteenth century. However, it had always been a problematic notion. For Beirut was no Hong Kong. It had a mountain hinterland which always deeply affected the politics of the city; and which, now, was tied into the same political system as that ruling the city. Beirut's mountain hinterland was no easily-pacified backwater! It was always unruly, ungovernable by orthodox means, riven with factions – and close! The Shouf and the Metn, two of the areas which had been crucibles of the inter-sect system in the Mountain, loomed right over Beirut itself, dominating its all-important access to the interior.

The Ottomans had recognized some of the problems involved in tying the rapidly-developing commercial centre of Beirut too closely with the Mountain. Since the days of the Shihab princes, Beirut had deliberately kept separate from the special regime which evolved in the Mountain. In the nineteenth century, the continuing fact of this separation contributed much to the fifty-five-year-long success of the *mutasarrifiyya* formula.

In post-independence Lebanon, the fragility of the merchant republic formula first became evident in the troubles of 1958, which can be considered, in part at least, as an uprising of the hinterland against its domination by Beirut. For a while, the Shihabists were able to patch up a compromise between the interests of the city and the Mountain.

Then, in the instability of the years following 1967, one of the major casualties turned out to be the merchant republic itself. As described above, after 1967 the Maronite community swung away from the liberalism of the merchant republic. New forces were then unleashed in the country – Palestinian, leftist, Maronitist – which were all deeply hostile to it.

The Ketaeb militia's burning of Beirut's downtown markets in 1975 was certainly an apt symbol of those days. So, too, were the massive burglaries which the Palestinians carried out on downtown banks, and the Ketaeb on the port's overflowing Free Zone.

Over the nine years which followed 1975, the port of Beirut was unable to regain anything of its former eminence as an international entrepôt. The oil terminals of Tripoli and Sidon were closed on a seemingly long-term basis by the constant fighting. The international corporations which had previously made Beirut their region-wide headquarters moved to Athens, Amman, the Gulf or even London.

As the physical and political underpinnings of the merchant republic were dismantled, the first casualties were the great trading families which had dominated it in its heyday. Now, they were shoved brutally to the furthest margins of the country's politics. Their previous place centre stage was taken by a combination of the age-old forces of the Mountain, with the thrusting new forces of the outer Beirut suburbs.

The Sunnis, who had no great strength in either the Mountain or the outer suburbs could not but be weakened in the process. Their position as overwhelmingly big-city people was linked, too, to their position as a *minority* group, rather than a *sect*. In Chapter 1, I had referred this useful distinction, made by the Lebanese anthropologist Fuad Khuri. His view was that, especially in the Middle East, there is a discernible difference between a *minority*, as defined in the classic European sense, and a *sect*, which he described as compactly residing in some easily defensible heartland.

According to this distinction, Lebanese society contains three *sects* (the Maronites, Shi-ites and Druze), and a number of minorities, of which the Sunni community is the largest. The minorities could generally, according to Khuri, be expected to behave differently from the sects. Like classic minorities in Europe, they would focus their efforts on questions of civil rights at the national level, while sect leaders would focus on defending their prerogatives in their own heartlands.

This analysis suggests that minorities can make a great contribution to national politics during liberal eras – as the Sunnis, Greek Catholics and Greek Orthodox all had done in Lebanon. But in periods when sectarianism is dominant, the contribution of leaders from the minorities would be diverse, dissipated, and largely ineffective. The minority leaders could, typically, be expected to work hard to effect a reconciliation between the warring sects. But the success of their efforts would rest primarily on the decisions of the leaders of the sects themselves, to reconcile.

The Sunnis' position as a *minority*, in the era of heightened sectarianism from 1967 onwards, thus also contributed to the weakening of their political role.

One final factor needs to be mentioned: the traditionally close links the Lebanese Sunnis enjoyed with the Sunni majority elsewhere in the Arab world.

The defeat of 1967 was a disaster for nearly all the Sunnis of the Arab East. Its after-effects lingered on until the mid 1980s, little alleviated by a brief rise in Arab hopes during the war of 1973.

After the deaths of President Nasser in 1970, and Saudi Arabia's King Faisal in 1975, there was no charismatic leader left anywhere in the Arab world who could focus the ambitions of Lebanon's Sunnis as each of those men had done to a certain degree. Even after 1975, some Lebanese Sunnis continued to ally themselves with their co-believers in the PLO leadership, in the hopes that that might strengthen their position. But after the PLO's expulsion from Lebanon in 1982–3, that last external prop was removed.

There were thus many reasons for the demise of the Sunnis from the elevated position they had been granted within the system in 1943. The decline of the merchant republic and the rise of sectarianism both acted to push them, along with all the other minorities, into a back seat in the Lebanese theatre, by the mid 1980s. And, in the case of the Sunnis, the weakening of the Arab world further aggravated that tendency.

The Sunnis still probably occupied second place in Lebanon's population stakes. But the main action in the country over the following years would most likely not be theirs, but would be that occurring between the country's three major sects.

The Druze

The Sunnis' loss was, generally speaking, the Druze' gain. The resurgence of the Mountain at the expense of the city, the rise of sectarianism – both these important factors strengthened the Druze' role in the system from 1975 onwards.

But what had happened inside the sect meanwhile? And what kind of role could the Druze expect to play in the Lebanon of the future?

In the twentieth century, as in past centuries, the sect's internal politics continued to revolve mainly around its feudal-style leading personalities. From independence until 1977, the sect's affairs had been dominated by one man, Kamal Jumblatt. The 'Jumblatti' faction in the sect's traditional politics was thus strengthened throughout those years.

When Kamal Jumblatt was killed, the personal and political qualities of his son and heir, Walid, were still uncertain. The Arslan family and their Yazbeki followers thus tried to make a comeback against the still-entrenched power of the Jumblattis. They were subtly aided, from afar, by the LF leadership, which set up an embryo Druze militia in co-operation with Majid Arslan's willowy only son, Faisal.

But in the tempestuous summer of 1982, the LF fighters stormed into the Druze heartland in the Shouf. Their anti-Druze activities left those Yazbekis who had been considering an alliance with them terrified and dumbfounded. Faisal Aslan, in particular, was badly discredited within the sect. When his aged father died the following year, he left a virtual vacuum in the leadership of the Yazbeki faction, which could not be easily filled.

Walid Jumblatt, meanwhile, recovered quickly from the paralysis he evinced in mid June 1982, to start organizing the Druze resistance to the LF's encroachment. He, and the Druze warriors who fought in every village in the Shouf, met with startling and rapid success.

The Druze resistance in the Shouf was aided by the subtle diplomacy Jumblatt pursued with regard to Lebanon's two heavyweight neighbours. He acquired most of the arms the Druze fighters needed from the Syrians, and paid for them with much overt political loyalty. Meanwhile, however, some of his close aids were interceding with the Israelis, asking them to lessen their backing for the LF in the area.

Walid Jumblatt generally kept these contacts with the Israelis 'deniable', since he did not want to be seen either by the Syrians or within his own constituency as openly working with them. But when the Israelis (for their own reasons) responded positively to the Druze requests, the efficacy of Jumblatt's subtle blend of policies was proven.

His status, and that of the whole leadership of the Jumblatt faction, was hugely enhanced by the events of 1982–4. By 1984, some members of long-time Yazbeki families were earnestly averring that, 'There is no such thing as Yazbeki or Jumblatt any more. We are all just Druze. And, yes, Walid Jumblatt is our leader.'

So what kind of role could the Jumblatt-dominated leadership of the Druze expect to play from the mid 1980s on? In my view, a very important role.

In an era in which sectarianism looked as though it would continue to be strong in the country, their strength would be much greater than their raw population figures might indicate.

The geographic location of the Druze' Shouf heartland was also important. Since the Shouf lay midway along the Mountain between the Maronite heartland and the major Shi-ite heartland, the consent of the Druze would continue to be an essential condition for the survival of the inter-sect system in the Mountain. (The Shi-ites of Jebel Amil, or the Maronites of the Northern Mountain reaches, might each separately entertain hopes of seceding; and a truncated inter-sect system might still survive. But if the Druze should try to secede, the glue would fall out of the middle of the system itself.)

In addition, the Druze heartland was still one of the areas dominating Beirut. So the views of the Druze would necessarily carry some weight in determining the future relationship between the Mountain and the city.

One further factor might increase the importance of the Druze towards the end of the twentieth century. This stemmed from the particular history the sect had gone through in earlier centuries. For they were the sect which had incubated the inter-sect system in the first place. And they were the sole previous example of a sect which had moved from first to second place within the system successfully.

That transition was certainly not easy for the Druze. But by 1861, they had found themselves a second place in the system which they considered both realistic and acceptable. By 1943, they had slipped to a fourth place which many inside the sect (but not, it seems, Kamal Jumblatt) still thought they could live with. Their identity and interests *as a sect* had by no means been submerged by all these changes.

How had the Druze found themselves an honourable position

within the system even after the ascendancy had passed away from them? This was a question any Maronites interested in the survival of the inter-sect system might well be asking 150 years later.

The Druze could offer a further, more up-to-date lesson to the Maronites, as well. For the resistance they mounted to the LF in 1982–4 showed that even a small sect, far from the first place in the system, could in the end defend itself from complete domination by a stronger sect.

That was an age-old lesson established throughout the past millennium by virtue of Lebanon's mountain topography. The Maronites, who seemed fated to move away from the first place in the system towards the end of the twentieth century, might well take note.

One prediction can always be made with absolute certainty about future developments in Lebanon: they will not occur in a regional vacuum! In the 1980s and 1990s, as throughout its history, the country will continue to be seriously affected by the broader currents sweeping through its East Mediterranean region.

Will these currents make it impossible for the Lebanese to reach any internal reconciliation?

From independence down to 1967, the major polarity in the region around Lebanon was that between successive Western powers, and the ill-tuned Concert of Arabia. The 1967 war changed all that, weakening the Concert of Arabia, and replacing the US with Israel as the major non-Arab power in the region.

Over the years which followed 1967, the major external polarization affecting Lebanon came to be that between its two powerful neighbours, Israel and Syria. (In terms of this dispute, the PLO can be considered as generally included in Syria's camp. But, as the residents of Tripoli understood only too painfully in 1983, there were many subsidiary conflicts between Syria and the PLO, as well.)

The conflict between Israel and Syria/PLO was harsher and more direct than the earlier competition between the West and the Concert of Arabia. It raged across Lebanon with a ferocity unknown in the period prior to 1967. In the years following 1967, scores of Lebanese villages were destroyed because of Israel and Syria's rivalry (in addition to those destroyed by basically local disputes).

The people of Lebanon suffered from the actions of Israel and Syria/PLO in those years. And there was no immediate end in sight to the intense rivalry between these axes. Nevertheless, I do not think that these bleak regional facts, in and of themselves, ruled out the possibility of the Lebanese sects reaching a viable agreement over their country's future. A number of factors, taken together, make this estimation possible.

First, by 1984 it was clear to all these outsiders that what they might actually expect to *achieve* inside the Lebanese politic fell far short of what they might at times *desire*.

The Syrians were the first of this group to have their ambitions in Lebanon curtailed. When the Syrian army entered the country in 1976, it was much stronger, on paper, than any other forces there. At first, Syrian leaders seemed to think that this would enable them easily to dominate the country's political system. But only from Bashir Gemayyel's movement in East Beirut.

In Tripoli, in the years from 1976 on, local groups of Sunni fundamentalists bitterly opposed the new power they saw Syria's presence as injecting into the local Alawite community. In the Shouf, followers of the slain Kamal Jumblatt continued to blame the Syrians for his demise. In West Beirut, local families criticized the spread of gambling joints and sleazy bars under their auspices. Almost everywhere they operated, local people found the Syrian ADF troops rude, bullying, and often abusive.

When the Israelis thwarted Syria's ambitions in Lebanon in 1982, many Lebanese from these areas breathed a sigh of relief – although they soon came to consider Israel's presence just as oppressive, or much more so. But the Syrians had already, well before 1982, dramatically cut back their presence in western Lebanon, tacitly recognizing that they were little welcome there.

After February 1984, the Syrians returned to a position of relative power in Lebanon. However, their ambitions were now much more limited than they had been in 1976. In 1976, they had sought to sponsor political reform in Lebanon through their own grand scheme, the 'Constitutional Document'. In 1984, they did not seem much interested in seeking any long-term settlement to the country's festering internal problems.

There was one respect in which Syria's actions inside Lebanon appeared to be consistent from 1976 right through to 1984. This was the opposition Syria evinced to the emergence of any single, strongly-based local force in Lebanon. Syria tried to curtail Amal's power in 1984, as it had sought to contain Jumblatt's movement in 1976, and the LF from 1977 to 1983.

By 1984, Syria's aims with respect to internal Lebanese questions had shrunk to this, merely to maintaining the fragility of the intra-Lebanese balance. That way, Syria could still hope to optimize its influence as an arbiter among the closely-balanced internal groups.

The Israelis took far longer than the Syrians to start learning about the realities of internal Lebanese politics. When Defence Minister Sharon took the Israeli army towards Beirut in 1982, he thought it would be a simple matter to install 'their boy', Bashir Gemayyel, as president of Lebanon, and have him do exactly as they bid.

But the Israelis, to their credit, realized this would not be the case almost as soon as their troops reached the perimeters of Beirut. They learnt that even Bashir Gemayyel would not do just as they asked. They also learnt that he had, in effect, sold them a bill of goods regarding his movement's ability to control the whole of the country. They learnt that the security of the Israeli troops in Lebanon depended not on their relations with Gemayyel, but with a whole range of Lebanese groups of whose very presence Sharon had previously seemed unaware.

Once the process started, the Israelis learned fast, pushed by the fact that the openness of their society made their government more vulnerable to the question of troop losses inside Lebanon than the Syrians ever were. Disappointed with Bashir's LF, they quickly established relations with the Druze and the Shi-ites. The previous dream of installing a vigorous, openly pro-Israeli government in Beirut was now replaced with much more limited hopes, that they could reach the tacit 'understandings' with local forces in south Lebanon which would enable their troops to withdraw.

Why could the Israelis not have reached such 'understandings' back in 1968? Why did they know so little about Lebanon's internal make-up that, from 1976 on, they had bought Bashir Gemayyel's whole, vastly exaggerated estimation of the LF's strength?

I think this must have been because successive Israeli governments were unable to look at Lebanese issues on their own merits, but did so through the uncertain prism of their obsession with the Palestinian question from 1967 on.

It was this obsession which, from 1968 to 1976, had led the Israelis to blast away at the Palestinians inside south Lebanon, almost regardless of the consequences on the indigenous population. The same obsession later led Begin and Sharon to adopt Bashir Gemayyel as their major Lebanese ally, regardless of the narrowness of his support inside the country – but purely because of the depth of his opposition to the PLO.

It is entirely possible that the Israelis could have reached sufficient 'understandings' with community leaders in south Lebanon to assure the safety of Israel's northern villages from PLO incursions back in the late 1960s. But they did not try very hard to do so. Instead, they became drawn right into the cycles of violence which engulfed Lebanon from then on.

In the process, they built up a considerable fund of ill-will among Lebanon's largest and most vigorous community, the Shi-ites, who were also their closest neighbours in Lebanon. This ill-will was further perpetuated by the length of the Israelis' stay in south Lebanon from June 1982 onwards, and by their use of Maronitist fighters to maintain that presence.

Thus, even with their political ambitions significantly scaled down in Lebanon, the Israelis still looked as though they would encounter further problems realizing them.

By 1984 the Palestinians, too, had had their previous ambitions in Lebanon severely curtailed. Ever since the PLO had started pursuing its 'state-within-a-state' policy in Lebanon, in about 1970, this approach had been the subject of a bitter debate inside its highest leadership. Then, in 1982 and 1983, the Israelis and the Syrians both made it clear they would tolerate no such policy. And a majority of Lebanese, including previous PLO supporters in the Druze and Shi-ite sects, also showed that they would deal with the PLO on their own strict terms, or not at all.

By the middle of 1985, those Palestinian communities which remained in Lebanon were so preoccupied with the pressing needs of their own survival that they looked unable to intervene in Lebanese politics for several years to follow. Only a few, small Palestinian groups still seemed able to intervene, from behind Syria's lines in Lebanon. But they were more firmly under Syrian control than ever. The possibility of the PLO mounting any significant, independent intervention inside Lebanon thus seemed to be nearly totally absent.

Would the Americans, or any other outside power, play much of a role inside Lebanon in the years following 1984? I do not think so. For the USA had learnt some harsh lessons of its own between 1982 and early 1984. But the country would probably figure in official American thinking much more as a potential sparking point for a regional conflagration, than it would as a repository of many strategic or democratic virtues in its own right.

The USA could thus be expected to remain, for some years, in the back seat with regard to Lebanese affairs to which it had moved after

February 1984. It could not expect to exert very much more influence in Lebanon than did the USSR. The Soviets had taken a back seat to their Syrian friends inside Lebanon ever since 1976, when the Syrians had ignored their advice not to send their troops into Lebanon.

But the USA still had strong links with Israel, as the USSR did with Syria. These links would ensure that the two superpowers would continue to be felt, as a distant presence, within the Lebanese drama. Both, after all, would seem to have an interest in ensuring that they would not be drawn into an all-out confrontation by some problem which started with a local dispute between Lebanon's tiny sects.

However, neither the USA's relations with Israel, nor the USSR's with Syria, much resembled a classic patron–client relationship. Instead, the Syrian tail seemed often able to wag the Soviet dog; and the Israelis to wag the Americans. Therefore, the superpowers could not generally be expected closely to control the actions of their respective clients inside Lebanon, so long as their own superpower interests were not threatened.

Lebanon, Israel and Syria would thus be left largely on their own, to deal with what the percipient Israeli writer Zeev Schiff has called the 'Lebanese bear hug'.[1]

Did this make the aim of intra-Lebanese reconciliation any less attainable? I think not. For Israel and Syria had already shown themselves capable of reaching agreement over Lebanese issues, in the years following 1976. The Red Line agreement of 1976 was successful in avoiding a direct clash between Israel and Syria, in Lebanon, right through until 1981. And then, it broke down only after the Israeli attacks on Syria's helicopters in the Beqaa forced the Syrians to bring in the SAM missiles.

In the mid 1980s, a new agreement, or understanding, between Israel and Syria still seemed possible in Lebanon. Through such an understanding, each of these outside parties might (explicitly or, more probably implicitly) recognize the security concerns of the other side inside Lebanon. In addition, for such an agreement to be stable, Israel would have to resign itself to the Syrians being able to exert greater pressure on the government in Beirut than it could ever do.

Of course, the fact that an agreement might be possible between Israel and Syria did not mean that such an agreement *would be concluded*. And even if these two parties were able to reach agreement, this would not mean that social harmony would instantly be restored to Lebanon. It just meant that these regional factors, in and of themselves, could not be viewed as insuperable obstacles to inter-Lebanese entente.

The inter-sect system of rule has had a long and colourful history in Lebanon. Built on the basis of sects whose identities remained unchanged after the eleventh century, it first emerged during the reign of Fakhr al-Din II, who was prince of Mount Lebanon from 1585 to 1635. So, as the system enters its fifth century, what can we say about the stage it is passing through today?

We saw in Chapter 2 that the inter-sect system was incubated in the particular circumstances provided by the Druze-dominated lordly network in Mount Lebanon. The inter-sectarian ideal evolved in the period when Fakhr al-Din II's territorial ambitions led him to increase the numbers of Maronites (and other non-Druze) under his control. He needed to win their loyalty. So he gave them new civil rights which were denied them by the surrounding Ottomans.

For two centuries, the Druze lords continued to dominate the system. But the Maronite community gained in vigour under the inter-sect regime. Finally, between 1825 and 1861, the Maronites were able to use the vigour they had gained, and their status of civil equality, to lever themselves into the leading position within the system.

By 1920, the Maronites were still in the ascendancy. And a majority of them apparently welcomed the move the French made that year, to extend the area governed by the inter-sect regime. This increased the numbers of Shi-ites (and other non-Maronites) within the inter-sect system. The Maronite-dominated regime needed to win their loyalty. So they were given new civil rights denied them by the surrounding Syrians.

The Maronites continued to dominate the enlarged inter-sect system. But the Shi-ite community gained in vigour within it. Finally, from 1975 onwards, the Shi-ites were able to use their new vigour, and their status of civil equality. . . .

Elsewhere, history might not repeat itself. But in Lebanon it does. Not endlessly, certainly, nor mindlessly; but with a definite nagging persistence. What other country would have produced a figure such as Rashid Karami, who reappeared trying to form a 'reconciliation cabinet' after nearly every major civil crisis from 1958 to 1984?

Can we definitely conclude, then, that the Shi-ites are now in the midst of the same progress towards the ascendancy that the Maronites underwent 150 years ago? I think we can. But many conditions have yet to be met before the transfer of primacy between the two is complete. And until then, we will probably see a continuation of the swings between short relapse and terrible remission which have marked the Lebanese condition since 1975. (Always remembering, that it took thirty-six years for the Maronites to take over from the Druze.)

For the transfer of primacy to be complete, first, the Maronites must become able to *accept* that the first place within the system no longer belongs to them. That will be no easier for them to do than it was for the Druze, 150 years ago.

Already, the LF and other Maronites have proposed drastic steps to try to stave off such a distasteful moment. They have tried reducing the dimension of the Muslim threat through sheer terror. That did not work. They proposed an 'ingathering' of Middle Eastern Christians, to bolster up the Christian proportion of Lebanon's population. That did not work. (Indeed, one contrary effect of the LF's militancy was to drive up the rates of out-migration of all the country's Christian communities.) They proposed the establishment of a sect-based 'canton' system, without in any way explaining how this could succeed where the nineteenth century's *qa'immaqamiyya* system had so notably failed.

The age-old verities of the inter-sect system seemed to suggest that, eventually, the Maronite community would find a way to coexist with a future Shi-ite ascendancy.

For their part, the Shi-ites still had much to learn about how to operate a finely tuned system such as Lebanon's. The sect had yet fully to define its aims, both for itself and for the Lebanese system as a whole. And its leadership system had yet to establish itself as sufficiently stabilized to be able to exercise primacy within the whole system.

Do the Shi-ites want to establish a fully-fledged Islamic republic in Lebanon? Amal leader Nabih Berri has repeatedly said he does not want to. But many Maronites still think he does; or that, even if that is not his aim, still he might be pushed towards it by militants within his movement. What kind of relations would the Shi-ite ascendancy seek with Iran, with Syria, with Israel, with the West? These were all questions of burning importance to other members of the inter-sect system.

Two important internal issues had also to be addressed by the future leaders of Lebanon. The first of these was the question of the relationship between the Mountain and the city.

By the mid 1980s, Beirut was no longer the towering commercial centre it had been in the heyday of the National Pact's merchant future: its extreme vulnerability to the unyielding politics of the Mountain had been exposed too deeply for that. And in the 1980s, unlike in 1861, there seemed little possibility of trying to separate it from the Mountain.

The city could no longer expect to dominate the whole country. And neither could the process of urbanization which had brought nearly half the national population to its environs easily be reversed. The shape of the future of Lebanon would therefore hinge on what kind of balance might be found in relations between the Beirut suburbs and the Mountain.

The Maronites and the Shi-ites were the two sects which straddled that divide. They would both have a huge contribution to make in addressing this crucial social issue.

The other major issue awaiting the Lebanon of the future would be the question of Lebanese democracy.

Back in the optimistic period of the early 1960s, many analysts had considered that democracy was well on its way to taking root in Lebanon. The persistence of the ancient *za«im* system was seen as a mere wrinkle on the face of an otherwise rosy, democratic picture.

By the middle of the 1980s, however, the converse of this seemed more true. The *za«im* system had emerged generally strengthened from the chaos of the late 1970s. Now it seemed that democracy was the mere surface wrinkle, which might or might not be smoothed away from the country's much deeper-rooted *za«im* system.

Does this mean that democracy is doomed to disappear from the Lebanon of the future? I do not think so, for a number of reasons.

First, while it is true the *za«im* system was strengthened by the events of 1975–84, it is also true that Lebanon's democratic institutions survived the traumas of that period. They still represented, however imperfectly, something aproaching the will of the Lebanese majority, and the stubborn clinging of that majority to the outward forms of the Lebanese ideal.

Second, if we are to assume that the Lebanon of the future will see a transfer of primacy from the Maronites to the Shi-ites, then this very process might strengthen the hold of democracy in the country.

For the Maronite ascendancy had grown increasingly fearful, in its last years, of any free expression of the will of the non-Maronite *demos*; while a Shi-ite ascendancy should have little to fear from demography. Moreover, the Shi-ites had already shown, throughout their own sect's modern renaissance, considerable use of democratic ideals, and considerable use of democratic practice. The sect's own most ancient traditions also endorsed many aspects of a generally political stance.

There thus remains some reason to hope that, even after the rise of a new Shi-ite ascendancy, democracy might survive and strike further roots in Lebanon.

But will the future of Lebanon all happen in precisely the way that I have outlined above? Can the inter-sect system itself still be expected to survive? What if the Maronites or another group opt to leave the system completely? What if there is another Middle East war, or the Iranians score a major victory in the Gulf? Would not such developments as these all mark the end of the inter-sect system?

Not necessarily. For the inter-sect system has proved itself a remarkably hardy plant in Lebanon. It has survived major internal and external upheavals. And even when it seemed to have been submerged – as, for example, during each of the present century's world wars, or during the upheavals of the early nineteenth century – in the end, it always rapidly reasserted itself afterwards.

In my view, none of the dire contingencies mentioned above, except one, would leave much lasting mark on the system. The Maronites might try to secede for a while. But I think they would return to the system soon enough, once the non-viability of secession had been demonstrated. Another Middle East war might come and go. But short of its potential to draw the whole world into a nuclear holocaust, I do not see that it would leave much lasting effect on the inter-sect system in Lebanon.

The only contingency which might leave a lasting mark would be a major military victory for Iranian revolutionaries. For that might let loose upon the entire Middle East a significantly new and revolutionary force with direct links to a core-member of Lebanon's sect-system.

Just as a victorious Nasser had inflamed Lebanese Sunnis in the 1950s, so might a victory for the Iranian ayatollahs inflame the Lebanese Shi-ites in the late 1980s.

The Sunnis, being a minority, had ultimately been proved to be marginal to the development of Lebanon's inter-sect system; and the system had deflected the pro-Nasser threat of the 1950s. But the Shi-ites, being a sect, and moving towards the ascendancy, would be central to the future of the system in the 1980s. So a vigorous pro-ayatollah movement, in the event of a major Iranian victory on the battlefield, might bring a powerful new regional reality to the heart of the Lebanese system.

In mid 1985, however, an Iranian victory still seemed only a remote possibility. And though many Lebanese Shi-ites followed Iran's military fortunes closely, most members of the community were still much more intimately concerned with their own situation than they were with what happened to the Iranians. They still drew much more of their strength from their own traditions, in Jebel Amil and the Beqaa, than they did from distant Tehran.

The Shi-ites – and the rest of the Lebanese – were going through a difficult transition period in the 1980s. It was a period which underlined once again many of the oldest truths of the inter-sect system in Lebanon: that the Mountain, as always, remained the place of refuge for all sects, from outsiders and from each other; that no single sect could totally dominate the system; that no sect need fear for its survival provided its heartland was safe.

But it was a period, too, in which many of the prevailing ideas about Lebanon probably needed to be revised.

Since the early nineteenth century, Lebanon had been presented, in the West, primarily as a homeland for the area's Christians. By the 1980s, this was clearly no longer the whole truth. Lebanon still was the homeland of its Christian communities, certainly. But, as Albert Hourani has pointed out, it was equally the homeland of its Shi-ite, Druze, Sunni and other communities. And each of these groups also had their own rich vision of the country's purpose.[2]

Prior to 1975, Lebanon had also been seen by outsiders primarily in terms of the commercial fortunes of its capital, Beirut. After 1975, the fortunes of Beirut sagged; and many outsiders asked, 'What has become of Lebanon?', when what they meant was 'What has happened to the Beirut we used to know?'

The answer to that question is a searing one for the many of us who once enjoyed the cosmopolitan atmosphere and cultural openness of the city. That Beirut – the Beirut of restaurants, the stunning art shows, the whole spectrum of publishing ventures – will probably not return in any recognizable form. Always fragile, it has now been overshadowed by the more vigorous forces of the suburbs and the Mountain.

But the country still has, in my view, viable prospects somewhere in the future. What that future will be, will emerge from within the country itself, from the developments at the heart of its ancient inter-sect system.

Notes

1   Zeev Schiff, 'Dealing with Syria', in *Foreign Policy* (Washington, DC), no. 55 (summer 1984), p. 112.
2   Albert Hourani, in his key-note speech to the Ninth Annual Symposium of the Georgetown University Center for Contemporary Arab Studies (April 1984).

Select bibliography

Books

Alamuddin, Nura S., and Paul D. Starr (1980), *Crucial bonds: Marriage among the Druze,* Delmar, NY: Caravan Books

Antoun, R. and Ilya F. Harik (eds.) (1972), *Rural politics and social changes in the Middle East,* Bloomington, Indiana: Indiana University Press

Barakat, Halim (1977), *Lebanon in strife: Student preludes to the civil war,* Austin: University of Texas Press

Betts, Robert Brenton (1975), *Christians in the Arab East: A political study,* Athens: Lycabettus Press

Binder, Leonard (ed.) (1966), *Politics in Lebanon,* New York: John Wiley and Sons

Chamie, Joseph (1981), *Religion and Fertility,* Cambridge: Cambridge University Press

Chamoun, Camille (1963), *Crise au moyen orient,* Paris: Gallimard

Chevallier, Dominique (1971), *La société du mont Liban a l'époque de la révolution industrielle en Europe,* Paris: Librairie orientaliste Paul Geuthner

Churchill, Charles H. (reprinted 1973), *The Druze and the Maronites under the Turkish rule from 1840 to 1860,* New York: Cambridge University Press

Cobban, Helena (1984), *The Palestinian Liberation Organisation: People, power and politics,* Cambridge and New York: Cambridge University Press

Courbage, Y. and Philippe Fargues, in Arabic (1973 and 1974), *al-Wad« al-sukkani fi lubnan, al-juz'ayn al-awwal wal-thani* ('The population situation in Lebanon, Parts I and II'), Beirut: Lebanese University Publications

Deeb, Marius (1980), *The Lebanese civil war,* New York: Praeger

Entelis, John P. (1974), *Pluralism and party transformation in Lebanon: al-Kata'ib 1936–1970,* Leiden: Brill

Fuller, Anne H. (1966), *Buarij: Portrait of a Lebanese Muslim village,* Cambridge, Mass.: Harvard University Press

Gordon, David C. (1983) *Lebanon: The fragmented nation,* London: Croom Helm

Haley, P. Edward, and Lewis W. Snider (eds.) (1979), *Lebanon in crisis: Participants and issues,* Syracuse, NY: Syracuse University Press

Harik, Ilya (1968), *Politics and change in a traditional society, Lebanon 1711–1845,* Princeton, NJ: Princeton University Press

Hitti, Philip K. (1957), *Lebanon in history,* London: Macmillan

Hourani, Albert (1946), *Syria and Lebanon: A political essay,* London: Oxford University Press

Hourani, Albert (1981), *The emergence of the modern Middle East,* London: Macmillan

Hudson, Michael (1968), *The precarious republic: Political modernization in Lebanon,* New York: Random House

Iskandar, Marwan, and Elias Baroudi (eds.) (1982), *The Lebanese economy in 1981–2,* Beirut: Middle East Economic Consultants

Joumblatt, Kamal (1982), *I speak for Lebanon,* London: Zed Press

Kerr, Malcolm H. (1959), *Lebanon in the last years of feudalism, 1840–1868* Beirut: American University of Beirut

Khalaf, Samir (1979), *Persistence and change in 19th century Lebanon: A sociological essay,* Beirut: American University of Beirut

Khalidi, Walid (1979), *Conflict and violence in Lebanon: Confrontation in the Middle East,* Cambridge, Mass.: Harvard Centre for International Affairs

Khuri, Fuad I. (1975), *From village to suburb: Order and change in Greater Beirut,* Chicago and London: University of Chicago Press

The Lebanese Constitution: A reference (1960), Beirut: American University of Beirut

Longrigg, Stephen H. (1958), *Syria and Lebanon under French Mandate,* London: Oxford University Press

Makarem, Sami N. (1974), *The Druze faith,* Delmar, NY: Caravan Books

Murphy, Robert (1964) *Diplomat among warriors,* Garden City, NY: Doubleday and Company

Owen, Roger (ed.) (1976), *Essays on the crisis in Lebanon,* London: Ithaca Press

Polk, William R. (1963), *The opening of south Lebanon, 1788–1840,* Cambridge, Mass.: Harvard University Press

Qubain, Fahim I. (1961) *Crisis in Lebanon,* Washington, DC: Middle East Institute

Rabin, Yitzhak (1979), *The Rabin Memoirs,* Boston and Toronto: Little, Brown and Company

Rabinovich, Itamar (1984), *The war for Lebanon 1970–1983,* Ithaca, NY, and London: Cornell University Press

Randal, Jonathan C. (1983), *Going all the way: Christian warlords, Israeli adventures, and the war in Lebanon,* New York: Viking Press

Sadaka, Linda, and Nawaf Salam (1982), *The civil war in Lebanon 1975–1976: A bibliographic guide,* Beirut: American University of Beirut

Salem, Elie, (1973), *Modernization without revolution: Lebanon's experience,*

Bloomington: University of Indiana Press

Salibi, Kamal S. (1959), *Maronite historians of mediaeval Lebanon,* Beirut: American University of Beirut

Salibi, Kamal S. (1965, reprinted 1977), *The modern history of Lebanon,* London: Weidenfeld and Nicolson

Salibi, Kamal S. (1976), *Crossroads to civil war: Lebanon 1958–1976,* Delmar, NY: Caravan Books

Sayigh, Yusif (1962), *Entrepreneurs of Lebanon: The role of the business leader in a developing economy,* Cambridge, Mass.: Harvard University Press

Schiff, Zeev, and Ehud Ya'ari (1984), *Israel's Lebanon war,* New York: Simon and Schuster

Spagnolo, John P. (1977), *France and Ottoman Lebanon 1861–1914,* London: Ithaca Press

Suleiman, Michael (1967), *Political parties in Lebanon: The challenge of a fragmented political culture,* Ithaca, NY: Cornell University Press

Sykes, John (1968), *The mountain Arabs: A window on the Middle East,* London: Hutchinson

Ta'rikh hizb al-kita'ib al-lubnaniyya, al-juz' al-awwal, 1936–1940 ('The history of the Lebanese Ketaeb Party, First Part, 1936–1940'), in Arabic, (1979), Beirut: Dar al-«Amal lil-Nashr

Tibawi, A. L. (1969), *A modern history of Greater Syria, including Lebanon and Palestine,* London: Macmillan

Zuwiyya-Yamak, Labib (1966), *The Syrian Social Nationalist Party: An ideological analysis,* Cambridge, Mass.: Harvard University Press

Articles and studies

Barakat, Halim, 'Social and political integration in Lebanon: A case of social mosaic', *Middle East Journal* (summer 1973), pp. 301–18

Cobban, Helena, 'Lebanon's Chinese puzzle', *Foreign Policy,* no. 53 (winter 1983–4), pp. 34–48

Cobban, Helena, 'Southern Lebanon: Living on a battlefield', *Christian Science Monitor* (7 November 1979), pp. 12–13

Chamie, Joseph, 'Religious groups in Lebanon: A descriptive investigation', *International Journal of Middle East Studies,* 2 (1980), pp. 175–87

Chipaux, Françoise, et Lucien George, 'Moderate Shi'ite leader says Amin Gemayyel must go', *Le Monde/Manchester Guardian Weekly* (26 February 1984), p. 11

Crow, Ralph, 'Religious sectarianism in the Lebanese political system', *Journal of Politics,* 24 (August 1963), pp. 489–520

Entelis, John P., 'The politics of partition: Christian perspectives on Lebanon's nationalist identity', *International Insight* (May–June 1981), pp. 11–15

Farsoun, Samih, 'Family structure and society in modern Lebanon', in

Louise E. Sweet (ed.) (1970), *Peoples and cultures of the Middle East, Volume II: Life in cities, towns and countryside,* New York: Natural History Press, pp. 257–307

Hudson, Michael C., 'The Lebanese crisis: The limits of consociational democracy', *Journal of Palestine Studies* (spring–summer 1976), pp. 109–22

Hudson, Michael C., 'The precarious republic revisited: Reflections on the collapse of pluralist Lebanon', Georgetown University Center for Contemporary Arab Studies (February 1977)

Kempe, Frederick, 'As fighting goes on, Lebanon's Shiites press their quest for power', *Wall Street Journal* (12 December 1983)

Khalaf, Samir, 'Primordial ties and politics in Lebanon', *Middle East Studies,* **4** (April 1968), pp. 243–69

Khalidi, Tarif, 'Shaykh Ahmad «Arif al-Zayn and *al*-«Irfan', in Marwan R. Buheiry (ed) (1981), *Intellectual life in the Arab East, 1890–1939,* Beirut: American University of Beirut, pp. 110–24

Khuri, Fuad I., 'The changing class structure in Lebanon', *Middle East Journal* (winter 1969), pp. 29–44

Nasr, Selim, 'Conflit libanais et restructuration de l'espace urbain de Beyrouth', in J. Mettral (ed.) (1984) *Politiques urbaines au Machreq et au Magreb,* Lyons, France: Presses universitaires de Lyons

Nasr, Selim, 'Mobilisation communautaire, symbolique religieuse et violence dans le mouvement de l'Imam Sadr (Liban 1970–1975)' in O. Carre (ed.) (1984), *Radicalismes islamiques d'aujourd'hui,* Paris: Maisonneuve et Larosse

Norton, Augustus R., 'Political violence and Shi'a factionalism in Lebanon', *Middle East Insight* (Washington, DC) **3** no. 2 (August–October 1983), pp. 9–16

Norton, Augustus R., 'Making enemies in south Lebanon: Harakat Amal, the IDF, and south Lebanon', ibid., **3** no. 3 (January–February 1984), pp. 13–20

Ottoway, David B., 'Baalbek seen as staging area for terrorism', *Washington Post* (9 January 1984), pp. 1, 21

Picard, Elizabeth, 'Role et évolution du Front libanais dans la guerre civile' ('The role and evolution of the Lebanese Front during the civil war'), *Magreb-Machrek: Monde Arabe,* La documentation française (October–November–December 1980), pp. 16-39

Quandt, William B., 'Reagan's Lebanon policy: trial and error', *The Middle East Journal,* **38** no. 2 (spring 1984), pp. 237–54

Salame, Ghassan, 'Liban: Une année pour rien' ('Lebanon: A year for nothing'), *Politique Etrangère,* no. 3 (autumn 1983)

Salibi, Kamal, 'Lebanon under Fuad Chehab 1958 –64', *Middle East Studies,* **2** (1966), pp. 211–26

Sarkissian, Bishop Karekin, 'The Armenian church in contemporary times', in A. J. Arberry (ed.) (1969), *Religion in the Middle East*, Cambridge: Cambridge University Press

Schiff, Ze'ev, 'Dealing with Syria', *Foreign Policy*, no. 55 (summer 1984), pp. 92–112

Weymouth, Lally, 'What the Shias want in bloody Lebanon', *Los Angeles Times* (13 November 1983), part IV, p. 2

Acknowledgements

The author and publishers would like to thank the following copyright holders for their kind permission to reproduce the illustrations in this volume:

Penny Williams Yaqub pp. 34 and 76; MEPHA p. 60; John van Hasselt, MEPHA p. 150; Mahmoud Kahil pp. 180 and 208.

Index

f. = following page
ff. = following two pages
passim = intermittent references